# Mastering Proxmox
## *Second Edition*

Master the skills you need to build a rock-solid
virtualization environment with the all new Proxmox 4

**Wasim Ahmed**

BIRMINGHAM - MUMBAI

# Mastering Proxmox

*Second Edition*

First published: July 2014

Second edition: May 2016

Production reference: 1230516

Published by Packt Publishing Ltd.
Livery Place
35 Livery Street
Birmingham B3 2PB, UK.

ISBN 978-1-78588-824-3

www.packtpub.com

# Credits

**Author**
Wasim Ahmed

**Reviewer**
Rocco Alfonzetti

**Commissioning Editor**
Kartikey Pandey

**Acquisition Editor**
Rahul Nair

**Content Development Editor**
Samantha Gonsalves

**Technical Editor**
Naveenkumar Jain

**Copy Editor**
Rashmi Sawant

**Project Coordinator**
Sanchita Mandal

**Proofreader**
Safis editing

**Indexer**
Hemangini Bari

**Graphics**
Kirk D'Penha

**Production Coordinator**
Shantanu N. Zagade

**Cover Work**
Shantanu N. Zagade

# About the Author

**Wasim Ahmed**, born in Bangladesh and now a citizen of Canada, is a veteran of the IT world. He came into close contact with computers in 1992 and never looked back. Wasim has much deeper knowledge and understanding of network, virtualization, big data storage, and network security. By profession, Wasim is the CEO of an IT support and cloud service provider company based in Calgary, Alberta. He serves many companies and organizations through his company on a daily basis. Wasim's strength comes from his experience that comes from learning and serving continually. Wasim strives to find the most effective solution at the most competitive price. He has built over 20 enterprise production virtual infrastructures using Proxmox and the Ceph storage system.

Wasim is notoriously known not to simply accept a technology based on its description alone, but puts it through rigorous testing to check its validity. Any new technology that his company provides goes through months of continuous testing before it is accepted. Proxmox made the cut superbly.

He would like to thank the entire staff at Proxmox for their support and dedication to the hypervisor community. Wasim would also like to thank Packt Publishing for their vision of moving forward with such a one of a kind book on Proxmox and their support throughout the journey of publishing this book.

# About the Reviewer

**Rocco Alfonzetti** works for PaperClip, Inc. as an e-mail encryption expert, bringing to market PaperClip eM4, a state-of-the-art e-mail encryption solution for individuals and businesses alike. PaperClip's newest innovation is Mojo, which is a ground breaking and innovative Forms recognition technology that is cloud-born and crowdsourced. PaperClip, Inc. has innovated and excelled in the Document Management world for over 20 years.

Rocco's career includes working as a small business computer consultant in the New York City business area for at least 15 years, where his advanced networking, Windows, Linux, and Open Source skills were polished. Rocco also blogs and consults for OpenCIO, an innovative cloud consulting firm, which has focuses on helping small businesses deploy, engineer, and license Proxmox installations, as well as place their workloads in AWS, Azure, and other Cloud solutions.

Rocco runs his own large Proxmox clusters both in development and production, where he runs many complex workloads and Linux systems. He welcomes any notes or communication from readers and maintains a personal e-mail address of `fonzetti@gmail.com`.

Rocco lives in rural Connecticut with his wife and their three young children. When he is not working, Rocco enjoys gardening, raising animals, beekeeping, and cooking. Rocco is also a proud Freemason, volunteering his time to the local community.

# www.PacktPub.com

## eBooks, discount offers, and more

Did you know that Packt offers eBook versions of every book published, with PDF and ePub files available? You can upgrade to the eBook version at www.PacktPub.com and as a print book customer, you are entitled to a discount on the eBook copy. Get in touch with us at customercare@packtpub.com for more details.

At www.PacktPub.com, you can also read a collection of free technical articles, sign up for a range of free newsletters and receive exclusive discounts and offers on Packt books and eBooks.

https://www2.packtpub.com/books/subscription/packtlib

Do you need instant solutions to your IT questions? PacktLib is Packt's online digital book library. Here, you can search, access, and read Packt's entire library of books.

## Why subscribe?

- Fully searchable across every book published by Packt
- Copy and paste, print, and bookmark content
- On demand and accessible via a web browser

This book is dedicated to,

My dear wife, Brigitta, whose love, constant support, and unshakeable faith in me has allowed me to do what I do best, while she took care of the rest.

Also dedicated to my daughter, Viktoria, whose patience with me was both fuel for writing this book and a character-building experience for myself.

# Table of Contents

# Preface

Based on the foundation laid out by the first edition, this book, *Mastering Proxmox, Second Edition*, brings updated information and details of new features about the Proxmox. Since the first edition of this book was published, Proxmox has been through many changes. Through this second edition, I am confident that readers will be able to upgrade their skills while building and managing even better Proxmox clusters.

This book shows the inner workings of Proxmox, including virtual network components, shared storage systems, Proxmox firewall, and high availability.

## What this book covers

*Chapter 1, Understanding Proxmox VE and Advanced Installation*, gives a brief description of what Proxmox VE actually is, its strengths and weaknesses, and advanced features. This chapter will also guide a user to understand advanced installation in the Proxmox cluster.

*Chapter 2, Exploring the Proxmox GUI*, discusses the graphical user interface. The bulk of the Proxmox cluster is managed through GUI.

*Chapter 3, Proxmox under the Hood*, explains the Proxmox directory structure and configuration files. This chapter will also show what mounting options Proxmox uses for its storage system. Configuration files will be analyzed line by line to show their functions.

*Chapter 4, Storage Systems*, explains how Proxmox interacts with the storage system and types of storage system supported. It will also show what types of image format are supported and when to use them in detail. Both local and shared storage systems will be covered.

*Chapter 5, KVM Virtual Machines,* covers how to create and manage any number of KVM virtual machines and their advanced configuration.

*Chapter 6, LXC Virtual Machines,* covers how to create and manage any number of LXC containers and their advanced configuration. LXC has been added to Proxmox version 4 to replace OpenVZ-based VM completely.

*Chapter 7, Network of Virtual Networks,* goes into the details of how networking is handled in Proxmox 4. It explains the different networking components used in Proxmox to build virtual networks.

*Chapter 8, The Proxmox Firewall,* shows built-in firewall options for Proxmox clusters and how to protect a cluster as a whole, or a VM and host nodes individually.

*Chapter 9, Proxmox High Availability,* shows new HA features introduced in Proxmox VE 4 along with a brand new HA simulator. This chapter also shows high availability for storage system to truly have an HA cluster.

*Chapter 10, Backup/Restore VMs,* dives deeper in the backup/restore strategy of Proxmox. It explains in detail the backup and restore feature of Proxmox for disaster planning.

*Chapter 11, Updating and Upgrading Proxmox,* shows how to properly update and upgrade a Proxmox node. It explains how to keep Proxmox up to date.

*Chapter 12, Monitoring a Proxmox Cluster,* shows how to use Zabbix to monitor an entire Proxmox cluster, including sending e-mail notifications during a failure.

*Chapter 13, Proxmox Production-Level Setup,* explains different components in a production-level cluster. We will look at how to put a Proxmox cluster in a production environment with minimum downtime. We will go through TO DOs, production requirements, and enterprise class hardware setup for Proxmox.

*Chapter 14, Proxmox Troubleshooting,* lists real incidents with solutions that may arise in the Proxmox cluster. All information is taken from real-world scenarios based on real issues.

# What you need for this book

Since we will be working with Proxmox clusters throughout the book, it will be extremely helpful to have a working Proxmox cluster of your own. A very basic cluster of two to three nodes will be fine. The steps should be performed as listed in a way that it prepares the system environment to be able to test the codes of the book:

1.  Proxmox VE:

    ◦ Download ISO, then burn a disk from the image.

    ◦ Load CD/DVD into drive and power up the node.

    ◦ Press **Enter** at the prompt boot to begin installation.

    ◦ The entire installation process is graphical with some text boxes to fill in. When prompted, enter a new password, select **country, IP address**, and **netmask, gateway**. IP address, netmask, and gateway should be based on the network the server is being installed on.

    ◦ When prompted, eject the disk and reboot to finish installation.

    ◦ Follow these steps for the other Proxmox node.

    ◦ Use a browser and enter the link in this format to go to the Proxmox GUI, `https://<node_ip_address>:8006`. When prompted, enter the user name, root, and password, the same one created during installation.

    ◦ Click **OK** when prompted with nonsubscription message box.

    ◦ Use Putty software to access Proxmox Node through SSH. Use `<node_ip_address>` as host and port 22.

    ◦ CEPH requires a separate network to operate correctly. Here, we will configure the second network interface card for all Proxmox nodes with a different subnet. Do this on all nodes:

    ```
    # nano /etc/network/interfaces
    auto eth2
    iface eth2 inet static
    address 192.168.20.1
    netmask 255.255.255.0
    ```

    ◦ Use the preceding format for other two nodes and use IP address `192.168.20.2` and `192.168.20.3`, respectively.

    ◦ Install CEPH on all Proxmox nodes by running this command:

    ```
    # pveceph install -version firefly
    ```

    ◦ Create the initial CEPH cluster from one node only:

    ```
    # pveceph init -network 192.168.20.0/24
    ```

    ◦ Create the first CEPH monitor from the first Proxmox node:

    ```
    # pveceph createmon
    ```

        °   Create other two monitors from the Proxmox **GUI** | **CEPH** | **Mon** menu system.

        °   Create OSDs from the Proxmox **GUI** | **CEPH** | **OSD** menu. Select a drive other than the drive used to install Proxmox OS.

2. FreeNAS:

        °   Download the FreeNAS ISO file from their website and prepare a disk with the image file.

        °   Plug in an USB flash drive. Load the CD into the drive and power up the node.

        °   FreeNAS also has graphical installation. Simply, press **Enter** to go through every prompt. FreeNAS does not require any text box information.

        °   Select **Install/upgrade** when prompted.

        °   Select the USB flash drive to install FreeNAS when prompted.

        °   Eject the installation disk and select **Reboot** when prompted at the end of installation process.

        °   If the existing network has a DHCP server available, the FreeNAS node will automatically pick up an IP address. You will find the assigned IP address at the prompt after reboot is completed.

        °   Use a browser and enter the IP address to access FreeNAS web management GUI.

# Who this book is for

This book is for readers who want to build and manage a virtual infrastructure based on Proxmox as hypervisor. Whether the reader is a veteran in the virtualized industry but has never worked with Proxmox, or somebody just starting out a promising career in this industry, this book will serve you well.

# Conventions

In this book, you will find a number of text styles that distinguish between different kinds of information. Here are some examples of these styles and an explanation of their meaning.

Code words in text, database table names, folder names, filenames, file extensions, pathnames, dummy URLs, user input, and Twitter handles are shown as follows: "To change the font color, edit the debian theme file in `/etc/grub.d/05_debian_theme`."

A block of code is set as follows:

```
logging {
   debug: on
   to_logfile : yes
   to_syslog : no
   timestamp : on
}
/var/log/<filename>.log  {
   daily
   rotate 5
   copytruncate
}
```

Any command-line input or output is written as follows:

```
# /etc/pve/nodes/pm4-1/qemu-server/110.conf
```

**New terms** and **important words** are shown in bold. Words that you see on the screen, for example, in menus or dialog boxes, appear in the text like this: "Clicking the **Next** button moves you to the next screen."

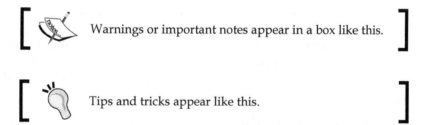

> [ 📝 Warnings or important notes appear in a box like this. ]

> [ 💡 Tips and tricks appear like this. ]

# Reader feedback

Feedback from our readers is always welcome. Let us know what you think about this book — what you liked or disliked. Reader feedback is important for us as it helps us develop titles that you will really get the most out of.

To send us general feedback, simply e-mail feedback@packtpub.com, and mention the book's title in the subject of your message.

If there is a topic that you have expertise in and you are interested in either writing or contributing to a book, see our author guide at www.packtpub.com/authors.

# Customer support

Now that you are the proud owner of a Packt book, we have a number of things to help you to get the most from your purchase.

# Downloading the color images of this book

We also provide you with a PDF file that has color images of the screenshots/diagrams used in this book. The color images will help you better understand the changes in the output. You can download this file from http://www.packtpub.com/sites/default/files/downloads/MasteringProxmoxSecondedition_ColorImages.pdf.

# Errata

Although we have taken every care to ensure the accuracy of our content, mistakes do happen. If you find a mistake in one of our books—maybe a mistake in the text or the code—we would be grateful if you could report this to us. By doing so, you can save other readers from frustration and help us improve subsequent versions of this book. If you find any errata, please report them by visiting http://www.packtpub.com/submit-errata, selecting your book, clicking on the **Errata Submission Form** link, and entering the details of your errata. Once your errata are verified, your submission will be accepted and the errata will be uploaded to our website or added to any list of existing errata under the Errata section of that title.

To view the previously submitted errata, go to https://www.packtpub.com/books/content/support and enter the name of the book in the search field. The required information will appear under the **Errata** section.

# Piracy

Piracy of copyrighted material on the Internet is an ongoing problem across all media. At Packt, we take the protection of our copyright and licenses very seriously. If you come across any illegal copies of our works in any form on the Internet, please provide us with the location address or website name immediately so that we can pursue a remedy.

Please contact us at copyright@packtpub.com with a link to the suspected pirated material.

We appreciate your help in protecting our authors and our ability to bring you valuable content.

## Questions

If you have a problem with any aspect of this book, you can contact us at questions@packtpub.com, and we will do our best to address the problem.

# 1
# Understanding Proxmox VE and Advanced Installation

**Virtualization,** as we all know today, is a decades old technology that was first implemented in mainframes of the 1960s. Virtualization was a way to logically divide the mainframe's resources for different application processing. With the rise in energy costs, running under-utilized server hardware is no longer a luxury. Virtualization enables us to do more with less, thus save energy and money while creating a virtual green data center without geographical boundaries.

A **hypervisor** is a piece of software, hardware, or firmware that creates and manages virtual machines. It is the underlying platform or foundation that allows a virtual world to be built upon. In a way, it is the very building block of all virtualization. A bare metal hypervisor acts as a bridge between physical hardware and the virtual machines by creating an abstraction layer. Because of this unique feature, an entire virtual machine can be moved over a vast distance over the Internet and be made able to function exactly the same. A virtual machine does not see the hardware directly; instead, it sees the layer of the hypervisor, which is the same no matter on what hardware the hypervisor has been installed.

The **Proxmox Virtual Environment** (**VE**) is a cluster-based hypervisor and one of the best kept secrets in the virtualization world. The reason is simple. It allows you to build an enterprise business-class virtual infrastructure at a small business-class price tag without sacrificing stability, performance, and ease of use. Whether it is a massive data center to serve millions of people, or a small educational institution, or a home serving important family members, Proxmox can handle configuration to suit any situation.

If you have picked up this book, no doubt you will be familiar with virtualization and perhaps well versed with other hypervisors, such VMWare, Xen, Hyper-V, and so on. In this chapter and upcoming chapters, we will see the mighty power of Proxmox from the inside out. We will examine scenarios and create a complex virtual environment. We will tackle some heavy day-to-day issues and show resolutions, which might just save the day in a production environment. So, strap yourself in and let's dive into the virtual world with the mighty hypervisor, Proxmox VE.

# Understanding Proxmox features

Before we dive in, it is necessary to understand why one should choose Proxmox over the other main stream hypervisors. Proxmox is not perfect but stands out among other contenders with some hard-to-beat features. The following are some of the features that makes Proxmox a real game changer.

## It is free!

Yes, Proxmox is free! To be more accurate, Proxmox has several subscription levels among which the community edition is completely free. One can simply download Proxmox ISO at no cost and raise a fully functional cluster without missing a single feature and without paying anything. The main difference between the paid and community subscription level is that the paid subscription receives updates, which goes through additional testing and refinement. If you are running a production cluster with a real workload, it is highly recommended that you purchase support and licensing from Proxmox or Proxmox resellers.

## Built-in firewall

Proxmox VE comes with a robust firewall ready to be configured out of the box. This firewall can be configured to protect the entire Proxmox cluster down to a virtual machine. The Per VM firewall option gives you the ability to configure each VM individually by creating individualized firewall rules, a prominent feature in a multi-tenant virtual environment. We will learn about this feature in detail in *Chapter 8*, *The Proxmox Firewall*.

# Open vSwitch

Licensed under the Apache 2.0 license, Open vSwitch is a virtual switch designed to work in a multi-server virtual environment. All hypervisors need a bridge between VMs and the outside network. Open vSwitch enhances features of the standard Linux bridge in an ever-changing virtual environment. Proxmox fully supports Open vSwitch, which allows you to create an intricate virtual environment all the while, reducing virtual network management overhead. For details on Open vSwitch, refer to `http://openvswitch.org/`.

We will learn about Open vSwitch management in Proxmox in *Chapter 7, Network of Virtual Networks*.

# The graphical user interface

Proxmox comes with a fully functional graphical user interface, or GUI, out of the box. The GUI allows an administrator to manage and configure almost all the aspects of a Proxmox cluster. The GUI has been designed keeping simplicity in mind with functions and features separated into menus for easier navigation. The following screenshot shows an example of the Proxmox GUI dashboard:

We will dissect the Proxmox GUI dashboard in *Chapter 2, Exploring the Proxmox GUI*.

# KVM

KVM or Kernel-based virtual machine is a kernel module that is added to Linux for full virtualization to create isolated fully independent virtual machines. KVM VMs are not dependent on the host operating system in any way, but they do require the virtualization feature in BIOS to be enabled. KVM allows a wide variety of operating systems for virtual machines, such as Linux and Windows. Proxmox provides a very stable environment for KVM-based VMs. We will learn how to create KVM VMs and also how to manage them in *Chapter 5, KVM Virtual Machines*.

## Linux containers or LXC

Introduced recently in Proxmox VE 4.0, Linux containers allow multiple Linux instances on the same Linux host. All the containers are dependent on the host Linux operating system and only Linux flavors can be virtualized as containers. There are no containers for the Windows operating system. LXC replace prior OpenVZ containers, which were the primary containers in the virtualization method in the previous Proxmox versions. If you are not familiar with LXC, and for details on LXC, refer to `https://linuxcontainers.org/`.

We will learn how to create LXC containers and manage them in *Chapter 6, LXC Virtual Machines*.

## Storage plugins

Out of the box, Proxmox VE supports a variety of storage systems to store virtual disk images, ISO templates, backups, and so on. All plug-ins are quite stable and work great with Proxmox. Being able to choose different storage systems gives an administrator the flexibility to leverage the existing storage in the network. As of Proxmox VE 4.0, the following storage plugins are supported:

- The local directory mount points
- iSCSI
- LVM Group
- NFS Share
- GlusterFS
- Ceph RBD
- ZFS

We will learn the usage of different storage systems and the types of file they can store in detail in *Chapter 4, Storage Systems*.

# Vibrant culture

Proxmox has a growing community of users who are always helping others to learn Proxmox and troubleshoot various issues. With so many active users around the world and through active participation of Proxmox developers, the community has now become a culture of its own. Feature requests are continuously being worked on, and the existing features are being strengthened on a regular basis. With so many users supporting Proxmox, it is here to stay.

# The basic installation of Proxmox

The installation of a Proxmox node is very straightforward. Simply accept the default options, select localization, and enter the network information to install Proxmox VE. We can summarize the installation process in the following steps:

1.  Download ISO from the official Proxmox site and prepare a disk with the image (`http://proxmox.com/en/downloads`).

2.  Boot the node with the disk and hit *Enter* to start the installation from the installation GUI. We can also install Proxmox from a USB drive.

3.  Progress through the prompts to select options or type in information.

4.  After the installation is complete, access the Proxmox GUI dashboard using the IP address, as follows:

    `https://<proxmox_node_ip:8006`

5.  In some cases, it may be necessary to open the firewall port to allow access to the GUI over port 8006.

# The advanced installation option

Although the basic installation works in all scenarios, there may be times when the advanced installation option may be necessary. Only the advanced installation option provides you the ability to customize the main OS drive.

A common practice for the operating system drive is to use a mirror RAID array using a controller interface. This provides drive redundancy if one of the drives fails. This same level of redundancy can also be achieved using a software-based RAID array, such as ZFS. Proxmox now offers options to select ZFS-based arrays for the operating system drive right at the beginning of the installation. For details on ZFS, if you are not familiar with it, refer to `https://en.wikipedia.org/wiki/ZFS`.

It is a common question to ask why one should choose ZFS software-based RAID over tried and tested hardware-based RAID. The simple answer is flexibility. A hardware-based RAID is locked or fully dependent on the hardware RAID controller interface that created the array, whereas a ZFS software-based RAID is not dependent on any hardware, and the array can easily be ported to different hardware nodes. Should a RAID controller failure occur, the entire array created from that controller is lost unless there is an identical controller interface available for replacement. The ZFS array is only lost when all the drives or maximum tolerable number of drives are lost in the array.

Besides ZFS, we can also select other filesystem types, such as ext3, ext4, or xfs, from the same advanced option. We can also set the custom disk or partition sizes through the advanced option. The following screenshot shows the installation interface with the Target Harddisk selection page:

Click on **Options,** as shown in the preceding screenshot, to open the advanced option for the Hard disk. The following screenshot shows the options window after clicking on the **Options** button:

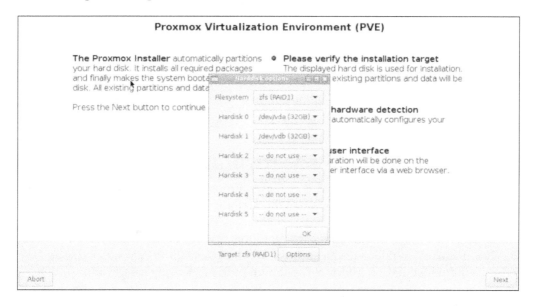

In the preceding screenshot, we selected ZFS RAID1 for mirroring and the two drives, **Harddisk 0** and **Harddisk 1** respectively, to install Proxmox. If we pick one of the filesystems such as ext3, ext4, or xfs instead of ZFS, the **Harddisk options** dialog box will look like the following screenshot, that is, with different set of options:

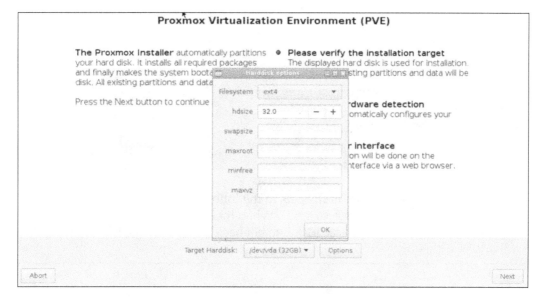

Selecting a filesystem gives us the following advanced options:

- **hdsize**: This is the total drive size to be used by the Proxmox installation.

- **swapsize**: This defines the swap partition size.

- **maxroot**: This defines the maximum size to be used by the root partition.

- **minfree**: This defines the minimum free space that should remain after the Proxmox installation.

- **maxvz**: This defines the maximum size for data partition. This is usually `/var/lib/vz`.

# Debugging the Proxmox installation

Debugging features are part of any good operating system. Proxmox has debugging features that will help you during a failed installation. Some common reasons are unsupported hardware, conflicts between devices, ISO image errors, and so on. Debugging mode logs and displays installation activities in real time. When the standard installation fails, we can start the Proxmox installation in debug mode from the main installation interface, as shown in the following screenshot:

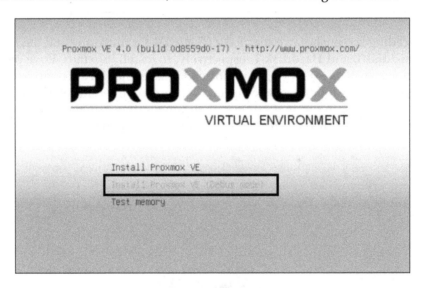

The debug installation mode will drop us in the following prompt. To start the installation, we need to press *Ctrl* + *D*. When there is an error during the installation, we can simply press *Ctrl* + *C* to get back to this console to continue with our investigation:

```
Proxmox startup
mounting proc filesystem
mounting sys filesystem
comandline: BOOT_IMAGE=/boot/linux26 ro ramdisk_size=16777216 rw quiet splash=verbose proxdebug
loading drivers:   i2c_piix4 shpchp pata_acpi 8250_fintek floppy mac_hid input_leds serio_raw psmouse pcspkr
searching for cdrom
testing cdrom /dev/sr0
found proxmox cdrom
Debugging mode (type exit or CTRL-D to continue startup)
/ #
```

From the console, we can check the installation log using the following command:

```
# cat /tmp/install.log
```

From the main installation menu, we can also press *e* to enter edit mode to change the loader information, as shown in the following screenshot:

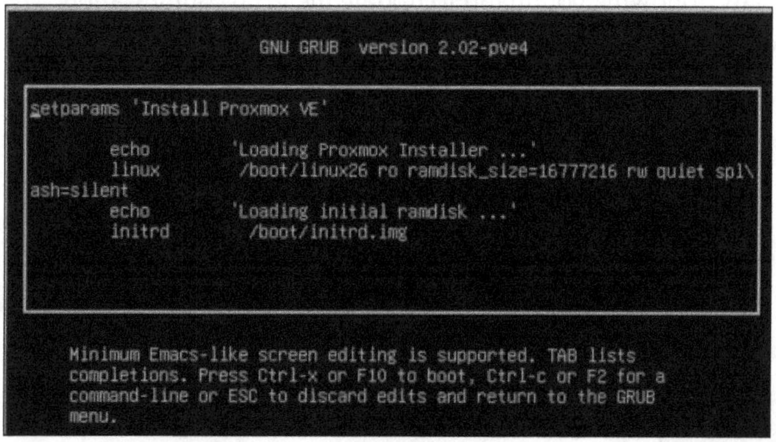

```
                      GNU GRUB   version 2.02-pve4


 setparams 'Install Proxmox VE'

          echo          'Loading Proxmox Installer ...'
          linux         /boot/linux26 ro ramdisk_size=16777216 rw quiet spl\
ash=silent
          echo          'Loading initial ramdisk ...'
          initrd        /boot/initrd.img




     Minimum Emacs-like screen editing is supported. TAB lists
     completions. Press Ctrl-x or F10 to boot, Ctrl-c or F2 for a
     command-line or ESC to discard edits and return to the GRUB
     menu.
```

At times, it may be necessary to edit the loader information when normal booting does not function. This is a common case when Proxmox is unable to show the video output due to UEFI or a non-supported resolution. In such cases, the booting process may hang. One way to continue with booting is to add the nomodeset argument by editing the loader. The loader will look as follows after editing:

```
linux/boot/linux26 ro ramdisk_size=16777216 rw quiet nomodeset
```

# Customizing the Proxmox splash screen

When building a custom Proxmox solution, it may be necessary to change the default blue splash screen to something more appealing in order to identify the company or department the server belongs to. In this section, we will see how easily we can integrate any image as the splash screen background.

The splash screen image must be in the `.tga` format and must have fixed standard sizes, such as 640 x 480, 800 x 600, or 1024 x 768. If you do not have any image software that supports the `.tga` format, you can easily convert an `jpg`, `gif`, or `png` image to the `.tga` format using a free online image converter (`http://image.online-convert.com/convert-to-tga`).

Once the desired image is ready in the `.tga` format, the following steps will integrate the image as the Proxmox splash screen:

1.  Copy the `.tga` image in the Proxmox node in the `/boot/grub` directory.

2.  Edit the grub file in `/etc/default/grub` to add the following code, and click on **save**:

    GRUB_BACKGROUND=/boot/grub/<image_name>.tga

3.  Run the following command to update the grub configuration:

    `# update-grub`

4.  Reboot.

The following screenshot shows an example of how the splash screen may look after we add a custom image to it:

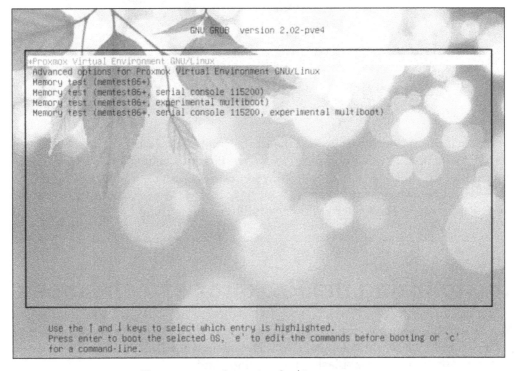

Picture courtesy of `www.techcitynews.com`

We can also change the font color to make it properly visible, depending on the custom image used. To change the font color, edit the debian theme file in /etc/grub.d/05_debian_theme, and find the following line of code:

```
set_background_image "${GRUB_BACKGROUND}" || set_default_theme
```

Edit the line to add the font color, as shown in the following format. In our example, we have changed the font color to black and highlighted the font color to light blue:

```
set_background_image "${GRUB_BACKGROUND}" "black/black" "light-blue/
black" || set_default_theme
```

After making the necessary changes, update grub, and reboot to see the changes.

# Summary

In this chapter, we looked at why Proxmox is a good option as a hypervisor, what advanced installation options are available during an installation, and why we choose software-based RAID for the operating system drive. We also looked at the cost of Proxmox, storage options, and network flexibility using Open vSwitch. We learned the presence of the debugging features and customization options of the Proxmox splash screen.

In next chapter, we will take a closer look at the Proxmox GUI and see how easy it is to centrally manage a Proxmox cluster from a web browser.

# 2
# Exploring the Proxmox GUI

The Proxmox Graphical User Interface, or the Proxmox GUI, allows users to interact with the Proxmox cluster graphically using menus and a visual representation of the cluster status. Even though all of the management can be done from the **command line interface (CLI)**, it can be overwhelming at times, and managing a cluster can become a daunting task. To properly utilize a Proxmox cluster, it is very important to have a clear understanding of the Proxmox GUI.

In this chapter, we are going to explore the different parts of the Proxmox Web GUI, such as how the menu system is organized and its functions. The GUI can be easily accessed from just about any browser though a URL similar to `https://<node_ip>:8006`.

The following screenshot shows an example of the Proxmox GUI for a demo cluster:

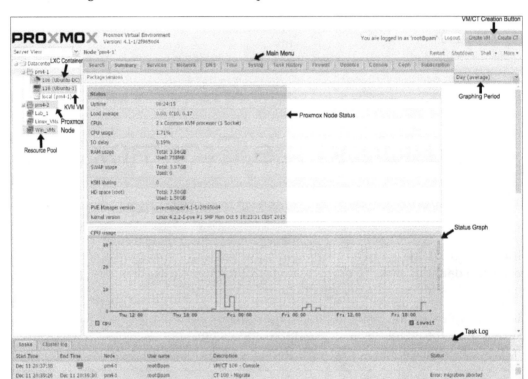

# The GUI menu system

The Proxmox GUI is a single page administration control panel. This means that no matter which feature one is managing, the browser does not open a new page or leave the existing page. Menus on the admin page change depending on which feature is being administered. For example, in the preceding screenshot, the **pm4-1** node is selected, so the main menu only shows node-specific menus. If a virtual machine is selected, the menu looks like the following screenshot:

The following chart is a visual representation of the Proxmox GUI menu system. Some menu options are system settings that need to be set up once during installation and do not need any regular attention, such as DNS, time, and services, and so on. Other menu items require regular visits to ensure a healthy cluster environment, such as **Summary**, **Syslog**, **Backup**, **Permissions**, and so on:

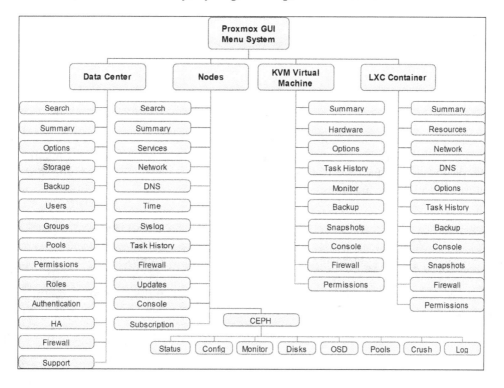

# The Datacenter menu

In the Proxmox GUI, Datacenter is the main level folder of Proxmox Node/VM tree. Each Datacenter can only hold one Proxmox cluster. Any tasks performed through the Datacenter menu affects the cluster as a whole.

## Datacenter | Search

It is very easy to manage a cluster with a small number of virtual machines with an even smaller number of Proxmox and storage nodes. When maintaining a large number of virtual machines and Proxmox nodes, the search feature prevents you from scrolling and manually looking for a particular resource. Scrolling through a list of virtual machines to find a particular one becomes very time-consuming for a busy administrator. This is where the **Search** menu option can come in handy. The following screenshot shows a search result after typing the partial virtual machine name in the search box in our example cluster:

The search box under **Datacenter | Search** shows the results in real time as you type in the box. It can search with any string in the Type or Description columns. It can be the partial name of a VM, VMID, or VM Type (qemu, lxc). Note that wildcards are not supported in search strings.

## Datacenter | Summary

The **Summary** menu in Datacenter shows a list of all the member nodes in the Proxmox cluster. It also shows their IDs, subscription levels, and assigned IP addresses. The following screenshot shows the node list in the **Summary** menu for our cluster:

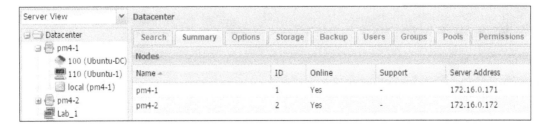

# Datacenter | Options

**Options** in the datacenter menu allows you to set the keyboard layout language, HTTP proxy, default console viewer, and e-mail address format that the Proxmox node sends root e-mails from. Note that the default console viewer only applies to the Proxmox GUI dashboard when you click on the **Console** button without selecting any other viewer from the drop-down menu. The following screenshot shows the **Console** drop-down menu with the available consoles:

# Datacenter | Storage

The **Storage** menu is probably one of the most important menu options in the GUI. This is where the Proxmox Cluster and storage system come together. This is the menu to attach any storage system with Proxmox. As of Proxmox VE 4.1, Proxmox supports the following storage types:

- The Local directory mount point
- LVM/iSCSI
- NFS
- GlusterFS
- Ceph RBD
- ZFS

In *Chapter 4*, *Storage System*, we are going to dive deeper into the Proxmox storage system. The following screenshot shows attached storages in a Proxmox cluster:

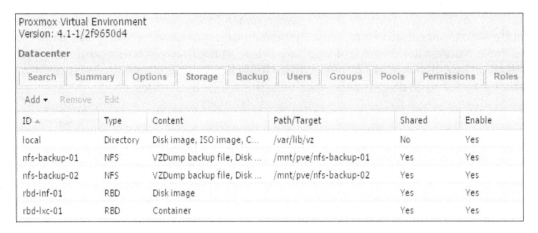

# Datacenter | Backup

Cluster-wide backup schedules are created through this menu. No backup tasks can be directly performed here. A good backup plan is the first line of defense against any disaster that can cause major or minor data loss. In our ultra-modern digital world, data is much more valuable than ever before. Every virtual environment administrator struggles with a backup strategy of their virtual environment.

The fine line between granular files and an entire virtual machine backup is somewhat diminished in a virtual environment. To take the daily struggle of a backup plan out of the equation, Proxmox added an excellent backup system right in the hypervisor itself.

As of Proxmox VE 4.1, we can only schedule backup tasks up to one week. Although the backup feature cannot backup individual files inside a virtual machine, it works well while backing up an entire virtual machine.

Proxmox backups can be scheduled over multiple storage systems, multiple days, and times. The following screenshot shows the backup schedules of a cluster:

In our previous example, there are two backup tasks that are scheduled with two separate backup nodes.

# Datacenter | Users

This menu allows the creation of new users and allows us to assign different permission levels of access to a Proxmox cluster or a virtual machine. Changes in user details, removal of users and change of passwords, and assigning groups are also performed from this menu. The following screenshot shows the user creation window with some example data:

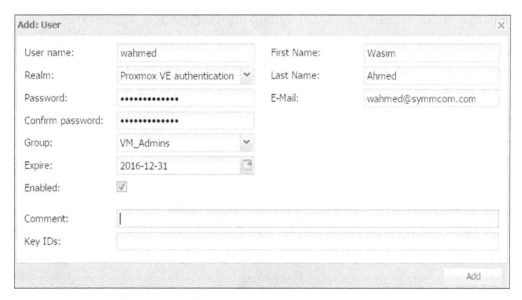

Proxmox user management allows you to set a user's access expiration date. This is very useful when giving a user temporary access, which must be deactivated after a certain time period. This option is good for temporary access, such as contracted employees or vendor access. In our previous example, the user's access is set to expire on December 31, 2016.

# Datacenter | Groups

This menu helps you create, edit, and remove groups. When the same permission is to be granted to multiple users, it is easier to assign those users to a group and then assign the permission level to that group instead of all the users individually. This saves a lot of time and makes user management much simpler. The following screenshot shows a list of three groups in the example cluster:

# Datacenter | Pools

**Pools** in a Proxmox cluster is a way to group together different entities, such as storage, virtual machines, and so on. For example, in a multi-tenant virtual environment, we can assign storage to virtual machines that belong to a client in a separate pool so that it is easy to view resources assigned to that client. The following screenshot shows the pool menu with some examples of pools:

# Datacenter | Permissions

This **Permissions** menu allows you to set cluster-wide access permission levels to a user. The menu also shows you a complete list of all the permissions already assigned to users. The same permissions can be set from the virtual machines and **Storage Specific** permission menu. When setting permissions from the **Datacenter** permission menu, we have to type in the path for the entity we want to set the permission for. For example, the following screenshot shows storage and virtual machines assigned to users:

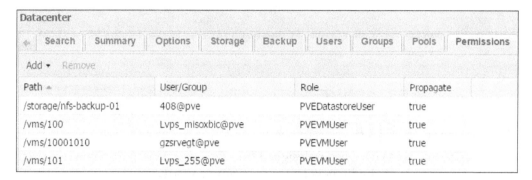

To assign the user permission level for both the KVM and LXC virtual machines, the path format is /vms/<vm/lxc_id>.

To assign the user permission level for storage, the path format is /storage/<storage_name>.

The group permission level can also be set from this permissions menu.

# Datacenter | Roles

This menu only shows predefined **roles** or permission levels that come with Proxmox 4.1. There are no options to edit or add new levels. The menu also shows defined privileges for each roles. These roles can be assigned to users or user groups to set different user permission levels.

# Datacenter | Authentication

By default, Proxmox creates the PAM and PVE authentication realm. Through this menu, we can create a new authentication realm, such as LDAP and Active Directory Server. We can also configure two-factor authentication from this menu. We will take a look at authentication in *Chapter 3, Proxmox under the Hood*. The following screenshot shows the authentication menu with three realms for our example cluster:

# Datacenter | HA

**High Availability (HA)** has been redesigned from Proxmox VE 4.0. It is much simpler to configure and is loaded with new features. In simple words, an HA-enabled virtual machine is automatically moved to a different node during node failure. We will learn how to configure and leverage HA in *Chapter 9, Proxmox High Availability*.

# Datacenter | Firewall

The Proxmox built-in firewall is one of the most prominent features of recent versions. It allows firewall rules down to the virtual machine level while protecting with cluster-wide level rules. A firewall works at both the cluster and virtual machine level, which can be configured to allow or deny connections to and from specific IP addresses. *Chapter 8, The Proxmox Firewall*, has been dedicated to learn about the firewall feature at greater length. The following screenshot shows the firewall menu with two data center rules. The first rule is to allow GUI access on port 8006 from a specific IP only and the second rule is to drop SSH connections to all nodes:

# Datacenter | Support

This menu tab shows support options that are available when there is a paid subscription applied to a node. Without any paid subscription level, the menu displays no support information, as shown in the following screenshot:

When there is a paid subscription enabled node, the information is similar to the following screenshot:

# Node menu

These menu options are specific to each node in the cluster. New menu tabs become available as each individual node is selected from the left-hand side navigation pane.

# Node | Search

This is similar to the **Search** option in the Datacenter-specific menu; this search option limits the scope of your search to the selected node.

# Node | Summary

The **Summary** menu option for a node is a visual representation of the node's health. It shows vital information, such as uptime and resource consumption. The **Summary** menu also shows **CPU Usage**, **Server Load**, **Memory Usage**, and **Network Traffic** in a very easy-to-understand graph. An administrator can get the necessary information of a node just by glancing at the summary. Summary can be viewed on a hourly, daily, weekly, monthly, and yearly basis:

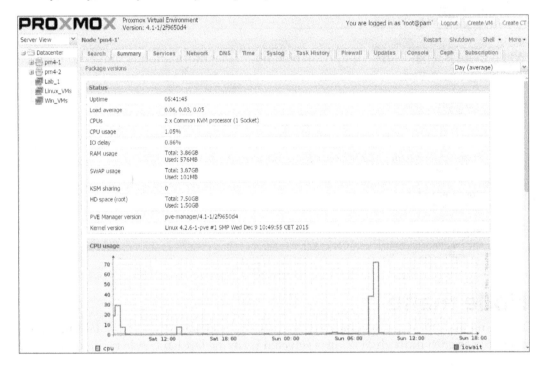

# Node | Services

This menu displays the status of all the vital services in the node. We can also start or stop a specific service from this menu without going through the CLI. During troubleshooting or node maintenance, services may need to start or stop.
The following screenshot shows services running in one of the nodes in our example cluster:

**Node 'pm4-1'**

| Search | Summary | Services | Network | DNS | Time | Syslog | Task History |
|--------|---------|----------|---------|-----|------|--------|--------------|

Start   Stop   Restart

| Name ▴ | Status | Description |
|--------|--------|-------------|
| corosync | running | Corosync Cluster Engine |
| cron | running | Regular background program processing daemon |
| ksmtuned | running | Kernel Samepage Merging (KSM) Tuning Daemon |
| postfix | running | LSB: Postfix Mail Transport Agent |
| pve-cluster | running | The Proxmox VE cluster filesystem |
| pve-firewall | running | Proxmox VE firewall |
| pve-ha-crm | running | PVE Cluster Ressource Manager Daemon |
| pve-ha-lrm | running | PVE Local HA Ressource Manager Daemon |
| pvedaemon | running | PVE API Daemon |
| pvefw-logger | running | Proxmox VE firewall logger |
| pveproxy | running | PVE API Proxy Server |
| pvestatd | running | PVE Status Daemon |
| spiceproxy | running | PVE SPICE Proxy Server |
| sshd | running | OpenBSD Secure Shell server |
| syslog | running | System Logging Service |
| systemd-timesyncd | running | Network Time Synchronization |

# Node | Network

The **Network** menu acts as glue between all virtual machines, nodes, and shared storage systems. Without a proper **Network Interface Card** (**NIC**) or **Virtual NIC** (**vNIC**) and a virtual bridge setup, no communication can take place. A deeper understanding of this menu will allow you to create a very complex web of clusters, nodes, and virtual machines. We will take a closer look at the network components later in this book in *Chapter 7, Network of Virtual Networks*. The following screenshot shows the node network menu with some interfaces already configured:

| Search | Summary | Services | Network | DNS | Time | Syslog | Task History | Firewall | Updates | Console |
|--------|---------|----------|---------|-----|------|--------|--------------|----------|---------|---------|

Create ▾   Revert changes   Edit   Remove

| Name ▴ | Type | Active | Autostart | Ports/Slaves | IP address | Subnet mask | Gateway |
|--------|------|--------|-----------|--------------|------------|-------------|---------|
| bond0 | OVS Bond | No | No | eth0 eth1 | | | |
| eth0 | Network Device | Yes | No | | | | |
| eth1 | Network Device | Yes | No | | | | |
| ib0 | Unknown | Yes | Yes | | | | |
| vlan50 | OVS IntPort | Yes | No | | | | |
| vmbr0 | OVS Bridge | No | Yes | bond0 vlan50 | | | |

The concept of a virtual network depends on the building blocks of the virtual bridge, virtual NIC, and virtual LAN. Network virtualization is the future transformation of physical networks as server virtualization had been for physical servers. The Proxmox virtual network provides a hardware abstraction layer making the virtual network much more flexible and compatible.

# Node | DNS

The **DNS** menu for the node allows you to set the default DNS server address default domain to search to be used by all virtual machines in the node. The **DNS** settings are very important for containers as they will use the nodes for their access to the Internet.

# Node | Time

Through this menu, we can define the time zone and current time where the node is physically located. This is a useful feature when cluster nodes are spread across regions. For a healthy cluster, it is very important for all nodes' times to be in sync with each other.

# Node | Syslog

The **Syslog** option allows an administrator to view the system log in real time. **Syslog** gives feedback as it happens in the node. It also allows you to scroll up to view logs in the past. More importantly, if any error occurs in the node, Syslog gives that information in real time with the time and date stamp. This helps you to pinpoint an issue exactly when it occurred. An example of a **Syslog** menu visit scenario: if the node cannot connect to a storage system, the **Syslog** screen will show you the error that is preventing the connection:

```
Node 'pm4-1'

  Search  Summary  Services  Network  DNS  Time  Syslog  Task History  Firewall  Updates

Dec 13 17:34:52 pm4-1 pmxcfs[913]: [dcdb] notice: data verification successful
Dec 13 17:39:13 pm4-1 pvedaemon[954]: <root@pam> successful auth for user 'root@pam'
Dec 13 17:42:03 pm4-1 systemd-timesyncd[480]: interval/delta/delay/jitter/drift 2048s/+0.001s/0.072s/0.003s/-14ppm
Dec 13 17:54:13 pm4-1 pvedaemon[954]: <root@pam> successful auth for user 'root@pam'
Dec 13 18:09:13 pm4-1 pvedaemon[953]: <root@pam> successful auth for user 'root@pam'
Dec 13 18:11:03 pm4-1 pveproxy[964]: worker exit
Dec 13 18:11:03 pm4-1 pveproxy[961]: worker 964 finished
Dec 13 18:11:03 pm4-1 pveproxy[961]: starting 1 worker(s)
Dec 13 18:11:03 pm4-1 pveproxy[961]: worker 15123 started
Dec 13 18:11:58 pm4-1 pveproxy[963]: worker exit
Dec 13 18:11:58 pm4-1 pveproxy[961]: worker 963 finished
Dec 13 18:11:58 pm4-1 pveproxy[961]: starting 1 worker(s)
Dec 13 18:11:58 pm4-1 pveproxy[961]: worker 15166 started
Dec 13 18:16:11 pm4-1 systemd-timesyncd[480]: interval/delta/delay/jitter/drift 2048s/-0.000s/0.073s/0.001s/-15ppm
Dec 13 18:17:02 pm4-1 CRON[15380]: pam_unix(cron:session): session opened for user root by (uid=0)
Dec 13 18:17:02 pm4-1 CRON[15381]: (root) CMD (  cd / && run-parts --report /etc/cron.hourly)
Dec 13 18:17:02 pm4-1 CRON[15380]: pam_unix(cron:session): session closed for user root
Dec 13 18:24:13 pm4-1 pvedaemon[953]: <root@pam> successful auth for user 'root@pam'
Dec 13 18:34:52 pm4-1 rrdcached[828]: flushing old values
Dec 13 18:34:52 pm4-1 rrdcached[828]: rotating journals
Dec 13 18:34:52 pm4-1 rrdcached[828]: started new journal /var/lib/rrdcached/journal/rrd.journal.1450056892.175517
Dec 13 18:34:52 pm4-1 rrdcached[828]: removing old journal /var/lib/rrdcached/journal/rrd.journal.1450049692.175448
Dec 13 18:34:52 pm4-1 pmxcfs[913]: [dcdb] notice: data verification successful
```

# Node | Task History

The **Task History** menu displays all the user tasks performed in the node. The following screenshot shows the task history of the pm4-1 node in our example cluster:

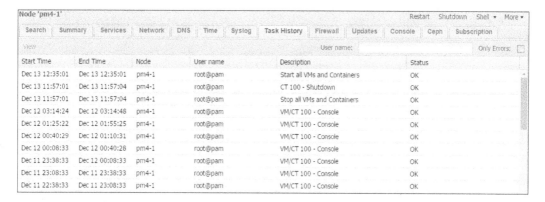

By typing in the user name in the **User name:** textbox, we can filter the history for a specific user. This is very useful in a multi-user cluster where many users manage their own set of virtual machines. We can also view the task with errors only by clicking on the **Only Errors:** checkbox.

# Node | Firewall

The **Firewall** menu for a node allows you to manage rules only specific to virtual machines in that node. We will take a look at the firewall menu in detail in *Chapter 8, The Proxmox Firewall*.

# Node | Updates

The Proxmox node can be updated right from the GUI through the **Updates** tab. Each node checks daily for any available updates and alerts the administrator through an e-mail if there are any new updates. It is important to keep all the nodes up to date by updating regularly. The **Updates** menu enables upgrading by just a few mouse clicks. The following screenshot shows the node's **Update** menu with some pending upgrades available for one of the nodes in our example cluster:

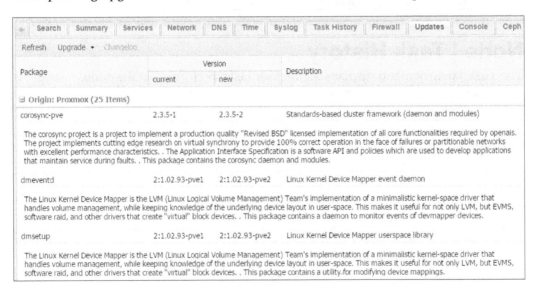

 Always update one node at a time. Some updates require the node to be restarted. If the uptime is important, then migrate all the running virtual machines to a different node before restarting the upgraded node.

# Node | Console

This new feature was introduced in Proxmox VE 4. The **Console** menu allows you to view the node console in the browser itself instead of opening it in a pop-up window. Proxmox uses the no VNC console to display the node. The following screenshot shows the console menu with the console open for the example node:

We can still open the console separately in a browser window using the existing **Shell** button in the GUI, as shown in the following screenshot:

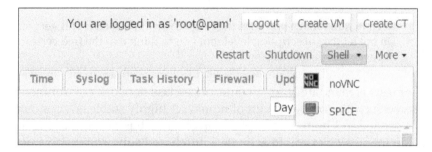

# Node | Ceph

Proxmox seamlessly integrates the **Ceph** RBD storage to store virtual disk images. The superb resiliency of Ceph and its extremely low price makes it a truly enterprise class storage system to rely on. We will learn how to integrate a Ceph cluster and manage it properly to realize its full potential in *Chapter 4, Storage System*. The **Ceph** menu in the Proxmox GUI allows you to view the complete cluster information and manage it.

# Node | Subscription

Proxmox can be downloaded and used for free without any restriction of any features. It is by no means a trialware, shareware, or an n-day evaluation hypervisor. However, Proxmox also has a subscription model, which allows enterprise-class repositories. The free version of Proxmox only comes with standard repositories. The main difference between enterprise and standard repositories is that enterprise repositories go through a higher level of testing to ensure a very stable cluster environment.

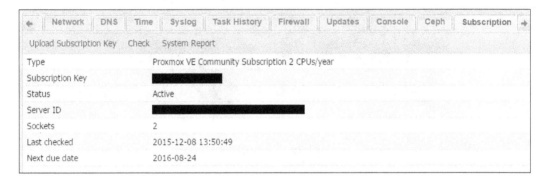

This level of tests is mandatory for an enterprise-class network environment where a small issue can cost a company a lot of money. A highly stable environment is usually not needed in a home-based platform or small business environment. The **Subscription** menu allows you to activate a purchased subscription on a node.

Keep in mind that, even with the free version, Proxmox is still very stable. Do not let the subscription level fool you to think that the free version is not even worth considering.

Proxmox has the very best prices per subscription in the virtualization product industry. The operating cost of a Proxmox cluster is minimal compared to a giant virtual product such as VMWare. Proxmox provides big business virtualization at small business cost. For details of different subscription levels, refer to http://proxmox.com/proxmox-ve/pricing.

# The KVM VM menu

This menu is specific to only KVM-based virtual machines. The menu tab is visible when a KVM virtual machine is selected from the left-hand side navigation pane.

## KVM VM | Summary

This menu tab represents similar information such as the tab accessed by navigating to **Node | Summary**. Valuable information can be gathered that shows the real-time status of a KVM-based virtual machine. One additional feature this menu has is the addition of the Notes textbox. By double-clicking on the **Notes** textbox, it brings up a multiline textbox where an administrator can enter data, such as the department, the usage the VM is intended for, or just about any other information that needs to be on hand. The following screenshot shows the summary of one of the KVM VMs in our example cluster:

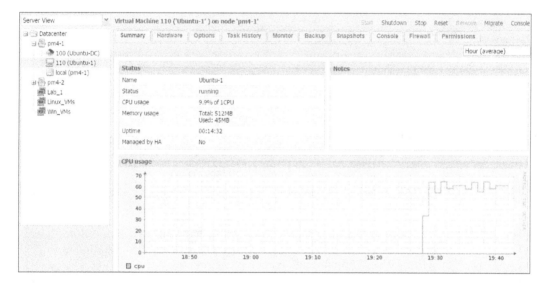

# KVM VM | Hardware

The initially created virtual machine is always never the final configuration. As the functions of VM rise, it becomes necessary to add additional virtual drives or network interfaces. The **Hardware** menu tab under the virtual machine is where the adding and removing of devices happens. Through the **Add** menu, additional CD drives, hard drives, and network interfaces (bridge, vNIC, and so on) can be added to a virtual machine. The following screenshot shows the configured hardware for our example **KVM VM #110**:

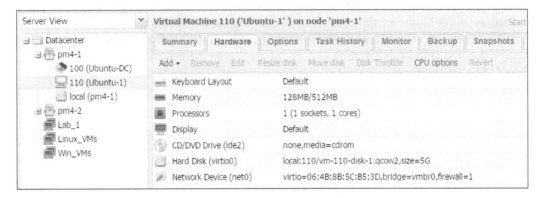

Besides the **Add** menu, other menus, such as **Remove, Edit, Resize Disk**, and **Move Disk** are also available through the **Hardware** menu. All these additional menus except the **Add** menu require a hardware item to be selected. **Resize Disk** and **Move Disk** will be enabled for clicking when a virtual drive is selected. We will cover these in detail in later chapters.

 Move Disk is the safest way to move a virtual hard drive from one storage to another. If the virtual disk is on shared storage, then live migration of the virtual disk is possible, allowing a great amount of time saving.

We will explore the KVM virtual machine configuration in detail in *Chapter 5, KVM Virtual Machines*.

# KVM VM | Options

The **Options** menu under the virtual machine allows further tweaking, such as changing the name, boot order, and so on. Most of the options here can be left to default.

> If you want the virtual machine to auto start as soon as the Proxmox node reboots, set the **Start at boot** option to **Yes**.

The following screenshot shows the **Options** menu for a KVM VM:

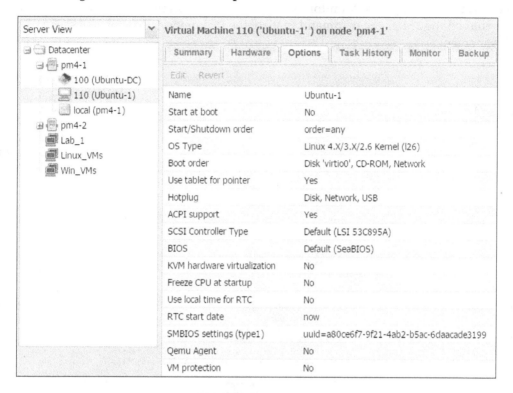

# KVM VM | Task History

The **Task History** menu shows all the tasks performed for that VM only. The functionality is identical to the node-specific task history where it shows all the tasks for all the KVM virtual machines in the node.

# KVM VM | Monitor

The **Monitor** menu in a KVM is an interface used to interact with a running KVM virtual machine directly through the **QEMU Monitor Protocol** (**QMP**). We can initiate monitor commands through the Proxmox monitor interface and see the result on the same page. There is a large number of commands used to perform various tasks through the Monitor menu. For example, in the following screenshot, we entered the `info pci` command to view the PCI devices that the VM sees at this moment:

Monitor is great way to debug a KVM VM-related issue due to the ability to gather a vast amount of debugging data, including the memory core dump, CPU info, and so on. We can also inject configurations, such as balloon memory configuration, additional CPUs, USB devices, and so on through this Monitor menu into a running KVM VM. Type `help` to view a list of all the commands usable with monitor.

# KVM VM | Backup

A **Backup** system is only as good as the ability to restore the **Backup**. Both the backup and restore can be done from a single menu under the virtual machine. It also allows backups, browsing, and manual deletion of any backups. All these are done from a single interface with a few mouse clicks. Due to the importance of a backup strategy in a virtual environment, we will take a look at the Proxmox backup system in detail in *Chapter 10, Backup/Restore VMs*. This menu is usually used to manually perform a backup task for a particular VM. The following screenshot shows the KVM **Backup** menu with all the backup files stored in the backup storage:

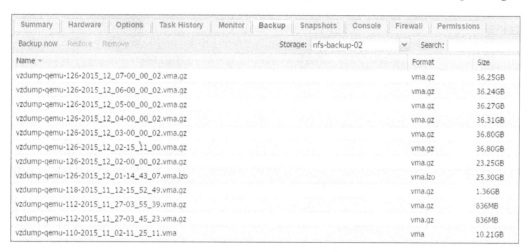

In the preceding screenshot, we can select a particular backup file to delete or to restore. We can also search for a particular backup file of a VM.

# KVM VM | Snapshot

Proxmox Snapshots is a way to roll back a virtual machine to a previous state. Although it provides similar protection to Proxmox Backup, it comes with speed. Proxmox Snapshot is extremely fast when compared to Proxmox Backup, thus allowing a user to take several snapshots a day. The following screenshot shows the **Snapshots** menu with a snapshot taken after a clean installation of the operating system in the virtual machine:

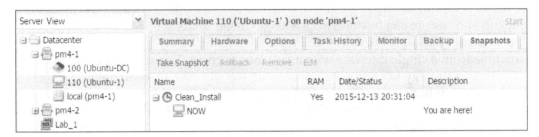

A common scenario where **Snapshots** can be used is when a software developer wants to test the software or available patches need to be applied. They can take a snapshot, execute the program, and if anything goes wrong, then simply roll back to the previous state. It creates a snapshot with the RAM itself, so the virtual machine stays exactly the same as it is running.

 Never fully depend on snapshots only. Snapshots are not a full backup. It is merely a state where the virtual machine is frozen in time. Always do a full backup of virtual machines for maximum protection. Snapshots are never included in the full VM backup. Snapshots are also never automatically deleted. As more and more snapshots are created, they will accumulate over time, consuming storage space.

We will look into the **Snapshots** option as a backup strategy in *Chapter 10, Backup/Restore VMs*.

# KVM VM | Console

Similarly, by navigating to **Datacenter | Console**, the KVM console menu shows the VM in the **noVNC** console within the same browser. To open the VM console in a separate browser, we need to click on a viewer from the Console drop-down menu, as shown in the following screenshot:

From Proxmox VE 4.0, the older Java-based VNC viewer has been removed. When the VM video adapter is not set as **SPICE**, the option to select the **SPICE** console is disabled. **SPICE (Simple Protocol for Independent Computing Environment)** is a protocol that allows you to access a virtual machine or any physical machine remotely. SPICE can be used to access both Windows and Linux-based machines. Unlike **noVNC**, where a browser can be used to access a VM remotely, **SPICE**, however, requires client software locally. Learn more about SPICE at `http://www.spice-space.org/index.html`.

# KVM VM | Firewall

Unlike the **Datacenter | Firewall** feature, which applies to the whole cluster, the KVM **VM | Firewall** applies to the selected VM only. The KVM VM firewall allows you to configure each virtual machine with its own set of firewall rules, thus isolating each VM from the others even further. In a multi-tenant environment where there are many levels of users, this firewall option helps you prevent each VM from accessing another VM. The following screenshot shows the firewall feature for one of our KVM virtual machines, which only allows SSH, HTTPS, and Ping traffic while dropping everything else:

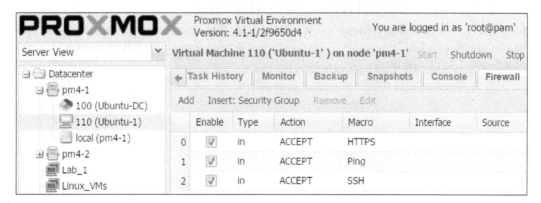

In *Chapter 8*, *The Proxmox Firewall*, we will take a look at the virtual machine firewall in detail.

# KVM VM | Permissions

The **Permissions** menu allows the management of user permissions for a particular virtual machine. It is possible to give multiple users access to the same virtual machine. Just click on **Add** to add users or groups already created by navigating to the **Datacenter | User** menu. The following screenshot shows that our VM has two user permissions:

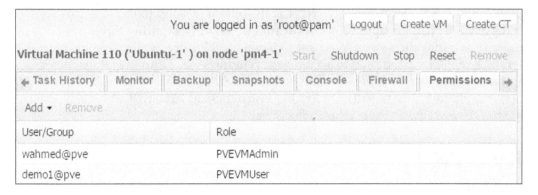

# The LXC Container menu

This menu is specific to only KVM-based virtual machines. The menu tab is visible when a LXC container is selected from the left navigation pane.

# The LXC Container | Summary

Identical to the **Summary** menu under KVM VM, this also shows the stats, notes, and usage graph of a LXC container. The following screenshot shows the **Summary** page of a demo **LXC Container**:

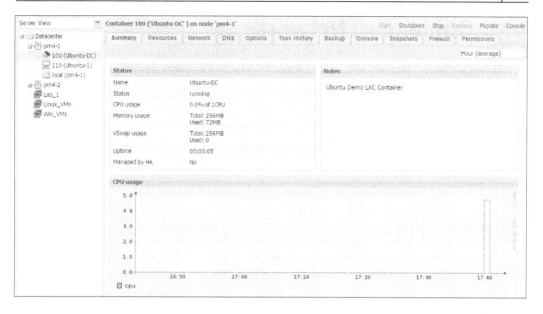

# LXC Container | Resources

Additional resources for LXC containers are adjusted here after a container is created. Changes in the resources get applied to a container in real time. We will look into container resource management in *Chapter 6, LXC Containers*. The following screenshot shows the resources currently allocated for our example container:

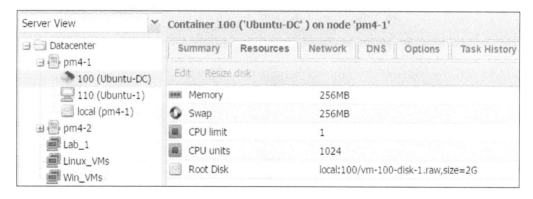

# LXC Container | Network

The **Network** menu for a container shows the currently assigned network interface. We can also make changes to any existing interface. Changes are applied in real time. The following screenshot shows the **network** menu for our example container:

# LXC Container | DNS

Similar to the **DNS** menu under Datacenter, the **DNS** menu for a container is also used to configure the **DNS search domain** and **DNS server address**.

# LXC Container | Options

Similar to the **Options** menu under KVM VM, this menu also provides additional configuration options for containers. Options such as auto start during the node boot, start or shutdown order, and selection of the OS type in the container are available through this **Options** menu. The following screenshot shows the **Options** menu for our example container:

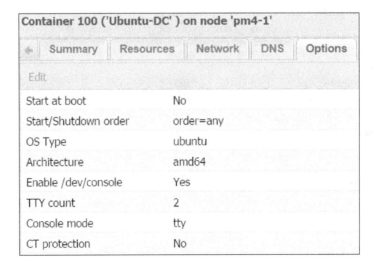

# LXC Container | Task History

The **Task History** menu shows a list of all the tasks performed on the selected container. The following screenshot shows the snippet of the example container's task history:

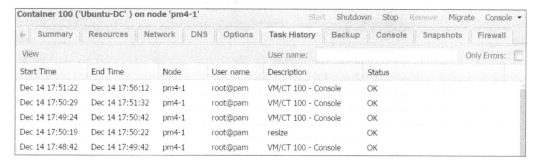

Similar to the **Task History** menu under KVM VM, the container's task history also provides a means to search for tasks performed by specific users or only shows tasks with errors.

# LXC Container | Backup

This menu is identical to the **Backup** menu under KVM VM where we can perform a manual backup of a selected container, remove a backup file, or restore a container from a list of backup files. The details of the backup and restore strategy will be covered in detail in *Chapter 10, Backup/Restore VMs*. The following screenshot shows the **Backup** menu with one backup file listed for an example container:

# LXC Container | Console

This menu opens the **Container** in the **noVNC** console in the same browser window. We can also open the console in a separate window through the **Console** drop-down menu. Unlike KVM virtual machines, the **Console** drop-down menu shows both the **noVNC** and **SPICE** consoles enabled, as shown in the following screenshot:

# LXC Container | Snapshots

Refer to the **Snapshot** menu under KVM VM as they are identical for both the KVM and LXC virtual machines.

# LXC Container | Firewall

Refer to the **Firewall** menu under KVM VM as they are identical for both the KVM and LXC virtual machines.

# LXC Container | Permissions

Refer to the **Permissions** menu under KVM VM as they are identical for both the KVM and LXC virtual machines.

# Pool menu

This menu tab is visible when a **Pool** is selected from the left navigation pane.

# Pool | Summary

The **Summary** menu for the pool only shows the **Comment** description for the **Pool**, as shown in the following screenshot:

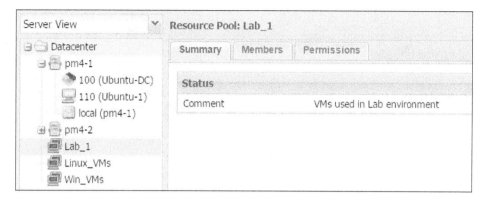

# Pool | Members

This menu shows all the resources currently allocated to the selected **Pool**. For example, in our example pool named `Lab_1`, we have a KVM VM #100, LXC container #100, and local storage allocated, as shown in the following screenshot:

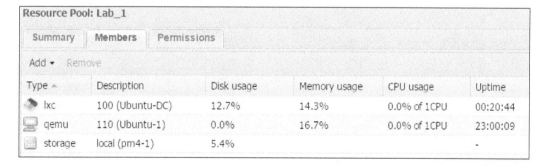

New resources can be added through the **Add** drop-down menu. We can only add virtual machines and storage to a pool. To add a KVM or LXC virtual machine, we will need to know the ID as there is no drop-down list from which you can select a virtual machine. The following screenshot shows the virtual machine's **Add** dialog box:

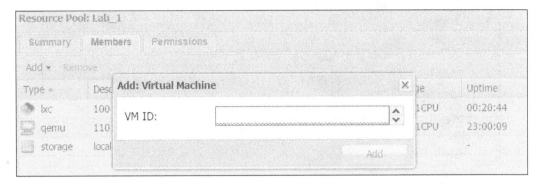

To add **Storage** to a pool, there is a drop-down list with the available storage options attached to a Proxmox cluster, as shown in the following screenshot:

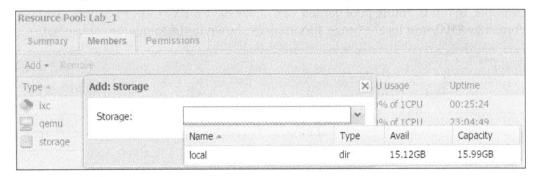

# Pool | Permissions

The **Permissions** menu under **Pool** is the same as the KVM VM and LXC virtual machine permissions. With this permission, we can assign a user to a pool and all the resources under that pool become accessible to that user. This eliminates any need to assign permissions individually by resources. For example, if a user requires access permissions to multiple virtual machines, we can put those virtual machines in a pool and give the user permissions to that pool only. The following screenshot shows that in our example pool named **Lab_1**, the user, **wahmed**, has been given the administrative permission to manage the pool:

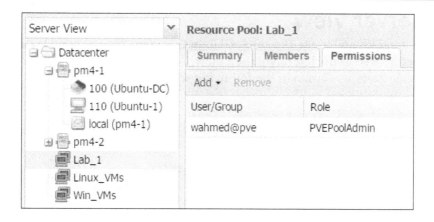

# Cluster view mode

Although not widely used, the Proxmox GUI has the following four cluster view modes:

- The **Server View**
- The **Folder View**
- The **Storage View**
- The **Pool View**

Each view serves a specific purpose and can be used whenever necessary. Knowing what these views are and when to use them can be very helpful in a large cluster. For a small or home-based cluster, anything beyond the **Server View** does not provide much benefit. Depending on which view is selected, the tree structure in the left-hand side navigation pane changes. The following screenshot shows the view's drop-down list in the Proxmox GUI:

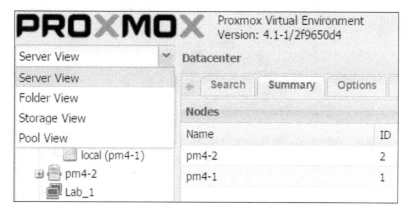

# The Server View

This is the default view in the Proxmox GUI. In this view, Proxmox nodes are roots in the directory tree in the left navigation view. All the resources are presented on a node-by-node basis, as shown in the following screenshot:

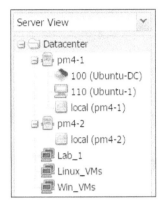

# The Folder View

In this view, each resource is displayed as a folder and put in their respective folder. For example, containers are shown in a LXC container folder, Proxmox nodes are shown in the node list, and so on. The following screenshot shows our example cluster in the **Folder View**:

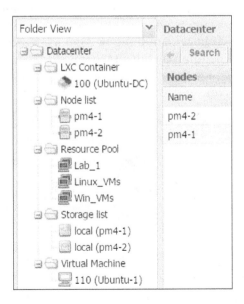

One of the use cases of the folder view is when it is not important to know which node holds a particular resource but it's necessary to view all the resource entities as a whole. In the folder view, it is easier to jump from one folder to another and view resources within. This view also provides the **Search** option within the folder. When a folder is selected, we can see the search option, as shown in the following screenshot:

# Storage view

As the name implies, this view is all about storage attached to a Proxmox cluster. This is similar to the **Server view** except that it does not show any virtual machines in any of the nodes. This is a simpler view specially useful to a storage manager. In a virtual environment where there are many storages attached to a cluster, this view gives the clutter free view of storage per node. The following screenshot shows the **Storage View** of our example cluster:

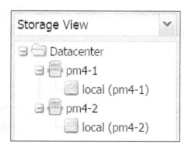

# The Pool View

This view shows all the pools and their allocated resources, such as virtual machines and storages. The view also shows a list of any virtual machines that are not part of any pools. This is a great view in a cluster where pools are used in a great deal to manage the multi-tenant environment. The following screenshot shows the Pool view of our example cluster:

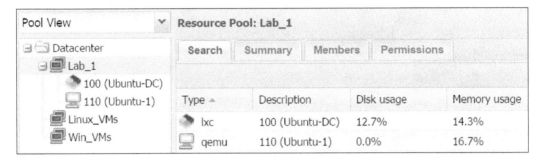

# Summary

In this chapter, we explored the graphical user interface of Proxmox. We learned about how the menu system is divided into different entities and what features are used to manage resources in a Proxmox cluster. We also saw different modes of the viewing option to browse all the resources in a Proxmox cluster.

Being equipped with the knowledge of the Proxmox GUI and its features pave the way for much more advanced topics in the coming chapters. Although Proxmox provides many management options through the CLI, a great deal of time is still spent on the Proxmox GUI for day-to-day cluster management.

In the next chapter, we will see what is under the hood for Proxmox. We will see how the Proxmox directory structure is laid out to store vital configuration files, and what the Proxmox cluster filesystem is, and why it is important.

# 3
# Proxmox under the Hood

In the previous chapter, we have seen what a Proxmox GUI looks like and also looked at its features. In this chapter, we will take a look how configuration files hold a Proxmox virtualization platform together, files to be used for advanced configuration, and how to troubleshoot a Proxmox platform. Proxmox is built on Debian Linux, which is very stable with a large active community. So, it inherited the heavy dependency on configuration of the `.conf` files as the primary means to store various configurations. The Proxmox GUI provides you with the ability to manage a cluster, but does not provide direct access to any configuration files. Any direct changes by advanced users have to be done through a **command-line interface (CLI)**. Commonly used scenarios, such as adding special arguments to configuration files, take place through the CLI. In this chapter, we will cover the following topics:

- The Proxmox cluster filesystem, or pmxcfs
- The Proxmox directory structure
- Configuration files' location and their functions
- Arguments and syntaxes used in configuration files

# The Proxmox cluster filesystem

Proxmox is a cluster-based hypervisor. It is meant to be used with several server nodes. By using multiple nodes in a cluster, we provide redundancy or High Availability to the platform while increasing uptime. A production virtual environment may have several dozen to several hundreds of nodes in a cluster. As an administrator, it may not be a realistic scenario to change configuration files in the cluster one node at a time. Depending on the number of nodes in the cluster, it may take several hours just to change one small argument in a configuration files of all the nodes. To save precious time, Proxmox implemented the clustered filesystem to keep all the configuration files or any other common files shared by all the nodes in the cluster in a synchronous state. Its official name is **Proxmox Cluster file system (pmxcfs)**. pmxcfs is a database-driven filesystem used to store configuration files. Any changes made to any files or copied/deleted files in this filesystem get replicated in real time to all the nodes using Corosync. The Corosync cluster engine is a group communication system used to implement High Availability within an application. You can learn more about corosync by visiting `http://corosync.github.io/corosync/`.

Any file added to this filesystem almost instantly gets replicated to all the nodes in the cluster, thus saving an enormous amount of time for a system administrator.

 The pmxcfs filesystem is a database-driven filesystem used to store the Proxmox cluster configuration files or any other files commonly shared by all the nodes in the Proxmox cluster. To know more about pmxcfs, visit the Proxmox wiki at `http://pve.proxmox.com/wiki/Proxmox_Cluster_file_system_(pmxcfs)`.

The pmxcfs filesystem is mounted at the following path:

```
# /etc/pve
```

All cluster-related files are stored in this folder path.

# Proxmox directory structure

Proxmox comes with a distinct directory structure where all the configuration files and other necessary files are stored. This makes finding those configuration files in times of need very easy. The following table shows the location of the files stored and their functions:

| Filename/location | File function |
|---|---|
| # /etc/pve/datacenter.cfg | Proxmox VE datacenter configuration file. Used to change options such as the default language, keyboard layout, default console, and so on. |
| # /etc/pve/corosync.conf | Cluster main configuration file. Prior to Proxmox VE 4.0, this was known as cluster.conf and can also be used to change the vote of a particular node. |
| # /etc/pve/storage.cfg | PVE storage configuration file. This holds all the information of a local or shared storage system. |
| # /etc/pve/user.cfg | User list and access control configuration for all users and groups in the cluster. |
| # /etc/pve/authkey.pub | Public key used by the ticket system. |
| # /etc/pve/ceph.conf | When a Ceph cluster is integrated with Proxmox, this configuration file is generated for Ceph. |
| # /etc/pve/vzdump.cron | Cluster-wide backup tasks that are not specific to a single node. This file should not be edited manually. All the entries are auto created from the **Backup** menu on the GUI. |
| # /etc/pve/priv/shadow.cfg | Shadow password file for users. |
| # /etc/pve/priv/authkey.key | Private key used by the ticket system. |
| # /etc/pve/priv/ceph.client.admin.keyring | Authentication keyring for a Ceph cluster. This is only created when Ceph is integrated with Proxmox. |
| # /etc/pve/priv/ceph/<storage_id>.keyring | Keyring used to attach the Ceph RBD storage. We will take a look at Ceph in *Chapter 4, Storage Systems*. |
| # /etc/pve/firewall/<vmid>.fw | Firewall rules for all VMs. |
| # /etc/pve/nodes/<name>/pve-ssl.pem | Public SSL key for the web server. Used to access the Proxmox WebGUI. |
| # /etc/pve/nodes/<name>/priv/pve-ssl.key | Private SSL key. |
| # /etc/pve/nodes/<name>/host.fw | Firewall rules for the Proxmox host. |
| # /etc/pve/nodes/<name>/qemu-server/<vmid>.conf | Virtual machine configuration data for KVM VMs. |
| # /etc/pve/nodes/<name>/lxc/<vmid>.conf | Virtual machine configuration data for LXC containers. |
| # /etc/pve/.version | File versions' data to detect file modifications. |

| Filename/location | File function |
|---|---|
| # /etc/pve/.members | Information nodes that are members of the cluster. |
| # /etc/pve/.vmlist | List of all VMs in the cluster. |
| # /etc/pve/.clusterlog | Last 50 entries of the cluster log. |
| # /etc/pve/.rrd | Most recent entries of RRD data. |

Any changes made to these files or any other files inside pmxcfs mounted under the /etc/pve folder will get replicated automatically. For this reason, we will have to take extra care of what we do to these files. For example, if we delete a .conf file from one node by mistake, it will also be deleted from all the other nodes in the Proxmox cluster.

 Creating a regular manual backup of the /etc/pve folder should be a common practice, in case the cluster needs rebuilding after any disaster or accidental file deletion/change.

On a regular day-to-day basis, a system administrator will not need to access these files from the command line since almost all of these are editable from the Proxmox GUI. But knowing the location of these files and what they hold might save the day when the GUI becomes inaccessible for whatever reason.

# Dissecting the configuration files

We now know where all the important files that hold a Proxmox cluster together are placed. We will now look inside some of these files for a better understanding of what they do and what command arguments they use. You can use any Linux editor to view/edit these configuration files. In this book, we will use #nano to view and edit.

During the learning process, it will be a good idea to make a backup of the configuration files before editing them. In case something goes wrong, you will be able to replace it with the original working configuration file. Simply copy the configuration file using the following command:

```
# cp /etc/pve/<config_file> /home/<any_folder>
```

We can also use the SCP command to back up files to another node:

```
# scp /etc/pve/<config_file> <user>@<ip_or_hostname>:/<folder>
```

# The cluster configuration file

The `corosync.conf` configuration file stores parameters needed for a cluster operation. Any empty lines or lines starting with # in this configuration file are completely ignored. The following code is what our `corosync.conf` file currently looks like in our example cluster with two Proxmox nodes. The Proxmox cluster configuration file is located under `/etc/pve/corosync.conf`:

```
logging {
  debug: off
  to_syslog: yes
}

nodelist {
  node {
    nodeid: 2
    quorum_votes: 1
    ring0_addr: pm4-2
  }

  node {
    nodeid: 1
    quorum_votes: 1
    ring0_addr: pm4-1
  }

}

quorum {
  provider: corosync_votequorum
}

totem {
  cluster_name: MasterPmx2ndEd
  config_version: 2
  ip_version: ipv4
  secauth: on
  version: 2
  interface {
    bindnetaddr: 172.16.0.171
    ringnumber: 0
  }

}
```

We are now going to dig into `corosync.conf` to describe the functions of the parameters. This configuration file is automatically created when a new Proxmox cluster is created. There are four segments in this file, which are as follows:

- `logging { }`
- `nodelist { }`
- `quorum { }`
- `totem { }`

## logging { }

This segment contains configuration parameters used for logging. According to the parameters in our example cluster, debugging is off and logs are transferred to `syslog`. If we want to turn debugging on and transfer logs to a `logfile` instead of `syslog`, our parameters will appear as follows. We can also attach a `timestamp` to all the log entries:

```
logging {
   debug: on
   to_logfile : yes
   to_syslog : no
   timestamp : on
}
/var/log/<filename>.log  {
   daily
   rotate 5
   copytruncate
}
```

Note that if we want pass logs to `logfile`, we need an additional `logfile { }` segment along with the `logrotate` and `copytruncate` parameters.

## nodelist { }

As the name implies, this segment is where all the member nodes of a Proxmox cluster are listed. Each node is separated by the `node { }` subsegment. The following are the three main parameters as they appear in our cluster configuration file.

# nodeid

This parameter shows the numeric order of the member nodes as they get added to the cluster. This is optional for IPv4 but mandatory when using IPv6. Each `nodeid` must be unique in the cluster configuration file. If no `nodeid` parameter is used when using IPv4, then the cluster automatically calculates this ID from the 32-bit IPv4 address. With IPv6, this calculation cannot happen since IPv6 is more than 32-bit.

>  WARNING! Never use `nodeid` instead of 0 as it is reserved by `corosync`.

# quorum_votes

This option shows the number of votes that the node must cast to form `quorum`. In a Proxmox cluster, this is no more than one vote per node. Whatever this number is, it should be equal for all nodes. There are simply no reasons to use anything other than 1.

# ring0_addr

This line basically specifies the IP address or the hostname of the node. The actual format of this option is `ringX_addr` where X is the ring number. When multiple network interfaces are used for redundancy purposes, the redundant ring protocol is implemented in corosync. Each of the interfaces is assigned a unique `ringnumber`. This unique `ringnumber` tells the interface to connect to the corresponding ring protocol. For example, in our example cluster, if we use the second interface for redundancy, the `node {     }` segment will appear as follows:

```
node {
  nodeid: 2
  quorum_votes: 1
  ring0_addr: 172.16.0.71
  ring1_addr: 192.168.0.71
}
```

# quorum {  }

This segment tells the cluster which quorum algorithm to use to form `quorum`. As of corosync Version 2.3.5, there is only one provider available, which is `votequorum`. This algorithm ensures that there are no split brain situations and `quorum` is formed only when majority votes are cast. There are no additional options available for this segment.

# totem { }

This segment specifies parameters for totem protocols. Corosync consists of the **Totem Single Ring Protocol (SRP)** and the **Totem Redundant Ring Protocol (RRP)**. This segment also includes a { } subsegment interface to specify the bind address and ring number.

 When only one interface is used for cluster communication, then Totem SRP is implemented. In this protocol, only the ringnumber 0 is used. When multiple interfaces are used for redundancy, then Totem RRP is implemented where more than one ringnumber and interface are used.

The following parameters are created by Proxmox during our example cluster creation:

```
cluster_name: MasterPmx2ndEd
```

This parameter specifies the cluster name that we entered when we created the Proxmox cluster using the following command:

```
# pvecm create <cluster_name>
config_version: 2
```

This parameter specifies the version number of the configuration file after each cluster-wide change, such as adding or removing member nodes. When any changes are being made manually, directly to the file, then it is mandatory to increase the version number manually. The number should only increase incrementally:

```
ip_version: IPv4
```

This parameter specifies the version of IP to be used. By default, IPv4 is used. To use Version 6 of IP, simply use the option, IPv6:

```
secauth: on
```

This parameter tells the cluster to use the SHA1 authentication for encrypting all the transmitting messages. Although this option adds extra overhead for all the transmitting messages, thus reducing the total throughput, it is important to use an encryption to protect the cluster from invaders. By default, this parameter is in Proxmox.

Note that the `secauth` parameter for corosync is deprecated. It is recommended by the corosync maintainers to use `crypto_hash` and `crypto_cipher`. But as of Proxmox 4.1, `secauth` is still used by default. The following is an example of how the recommended setting will appear in the `totem` segment:

```
totem {
  crypto_hash: sha1
  crypto_cipher: aes256
}
```

At the time of writing this book, Proxmox developers have not confirmed whether `crypto_hash` and `crypto_cipher` can be safely used instead of `secauth`:

```
version: 2
```

This parameter specifies the version of the configuration. Currently, the only version for this parameter is 2. This is not the version increment of the configuration file whenever any changes are made.

Besides the parameters mentioned earlier, there are a few other parameters available in the totem segment for various purposes. The following table shows some of these parameters and their functions:

| Parameter | Description |
|---|---|
| `rrp_mode` | Available options: **none, active**, and **passive**.<br><br>This parameter specifies redundant protocol modes. When there is only one interface, corosync automatically chooses none. With multiple interfaces, we can set it to active, which offers a lower latency at the cost of less performance. We can also set the mode to passive, which offers a significant performance boost at the cost of CPU usage. |
| `netmtu` | Available options: 1500 to 8982.<br><br>This specifies the MTU of an interface. It is useful when jumbo frames are used. Linux adds an 18-byte header on the network data packets. So, even though hardware can support 9,000 MTUs, it is wise to set MTUs to 8,982. This way, after Linux adds additional headers, the total number of MTUs does not go beyond 9,000 and hardware will not misbehave. These MTU tips apply to all situations where jumbo frames are intended. |

| Parameter | Description |
|---|---|
| transport | Available options: udp, udpu, and iba. |
| | This specifies the transport protocol. By default, corosync uses UDP. If Infinib and network is used with RDMA, then we can specify iba instead of udp. |

# interface { }

This is a subsegment of the totem segment where the information regarding the network interface is specified. By default, Proxmox only enters the bindnetaddr and ringnumber parameters in this subsegment:

```
bindnetaddr : <ip/network_address>
```

These parameters specify the IP address or network address that Corosync should bind to. This can be any IP address of a node in the cluster. Usually, this is the IP address of the node where the initial Proxmox cluster creation command was executed:

```
ringnumber: 0
```

This parameter specifies a separate ring number for each network interface. A unique ringnumber for each interface allows unique identification of which ring should use which interface. For example, with a single interface where Totem SRP is applied, there is only one ring with ringnumber 0. With dual interfaces and Totem RRP applied, there are two rings with ringnumber 0 and ringnumber 1. Note that the ring number must start from 0.

There are a few other advanced parameters available that are not used by default. The following table shows some of these parameters and their functions:

| Parameter | Description |
|---|---|
| mcastaddr | This specifies a multicast address, which is used by corosync. The address can be IPv4 or IPv6 when IPV6 is used. This parameter is usually not needed if the cluster_name parameter has already been used in the corosync configuration file. But when both are used, mcastaddr will have a higher priority over cluster_name. By default, the Proxmox cluster configuration, mcastaddr, is not used. |

| Parameter | Description |
|---|---|
| mcastport | This specifies the UDP port number for a multicast address. Corosync uses two ports for multicasts: one for receiving and the other for sending. We only need to specify the receiving port since the sending port is automatically calculated using the formula (mcastport – 1). For example, if we specify the receiving port number 5405, then corosync will use 5404 for sending. This is very important to note in a multi-cluster environment on the same network. |

If we put all the totem parameters we have seen so far together, the corosync.conf for our example cluster will appear as follows if the redundant interfaces have been used:

```
totem {
    cluster_name: MasterPmx2ndEd
    config_version: 4
    ip_version: ipv4
    crypto_hash: sha1
    crypto_cipher: aes256
    version: 2
    rrp_mode: passive
    interface {
        bindnetaddr: 172.16.0.71
        ringnumber: 0
        mcastaddr: 224.1.1.1
        mcastport: 5405
    }
    Interface {
        bindnetaddr: 172.16.1.71
        ringnumber: 1
        mcastaddr: 224.1.1.2
        mcastport: 5408
    }
}
```

# Storage configuration file

This is the configuration file where storage to be used with Proxmox is specified. The configuration file is located under `/etc/pve/storage.cfg`. We will take a look at the different storage systems in *Chapter 4, Storage Systems*. The following is the content of the storage configuration file in our example cluster. Currently, we have `local`, `nfs`, `iscsi`, and `lvm` shared storage and ZFS storage attached to the Proxmox cluster:

```
dir: local
    path /var/lib/vz
    content images,iso,vztmpl,rootdir
    maxfiles 0

nfs: ISO-nfs-01
    path /mnt/pve/ISO-nfs-01
    server 192.165.145.11
    export /mnt/pmxnas01
    options vers=3
    content iso,vztmpl
    maxfiles 1

iscsi: nas-iscsi-01
    target iqn.2015-12.org.example.istgt:pmxtgt01
    portal 192.165.145.11
    content none

lvm: nas-lvm-01
    vgname nas-lvm-01
    base nas-iscsi-01:0.0.0.scsi-330000000391132dd
    shared
    content images

nfs: vm-nfs-01
    path /mnt/pve/vm-nfs-01
    server 192.165.145.11
    export /mnt/pmxnas01
    options vers=3
    content images,vztmpl,backup,rootdir
    maxfiles 1
```

```
zfspool: zfs-01
  enable
  pool zfs_pool
  content images, rootdir
```

Almost all the settings in `storage.cfg` can be changed from the Proxmox GUI without using any CLI.

Attached storage abides by the following common format in the `storage.cfg`:

```
storage_type : storage_name
    path </path to folder>
    target <target file name> (for iSCSI)
    portal <server IP address> (for iSCSI)
    vgname <volume group name> (for LVM)
    base <base volume group> (for LVM)
    server <storage server IP address>
    export </shared location on NFS server>
    content <type of files the storage can hold>
    maxfile <maximum number of old backup to keep>
```

# User configuration files

The `user.cfg` file holds all user, group, and access control information in the cluster and is located under `/etc/pve/user.cfg`. It follows the following format to store all user information:

- For user information, the format is as follows:

  ```
  <type>:<user>@realm:enable:expiry:f_name:l_name:email:comment
  ```

- For group information, the format is as follows:

  ```
  <type>:<group_name>:user@realm:comment
  ```

- For pool information, the format is as follows:

  ```
  <type>:<pool_name>:<assigned_resource>:user@realm:comment
  ```

- For access control information, the format is as follows:

  ```
  <type>:<assigned_resource>:user@realm:comment:<assigned_role>
  ```

Based on this format, the following screenshot shows what our `user.cfg` file looks like in our example cluster:

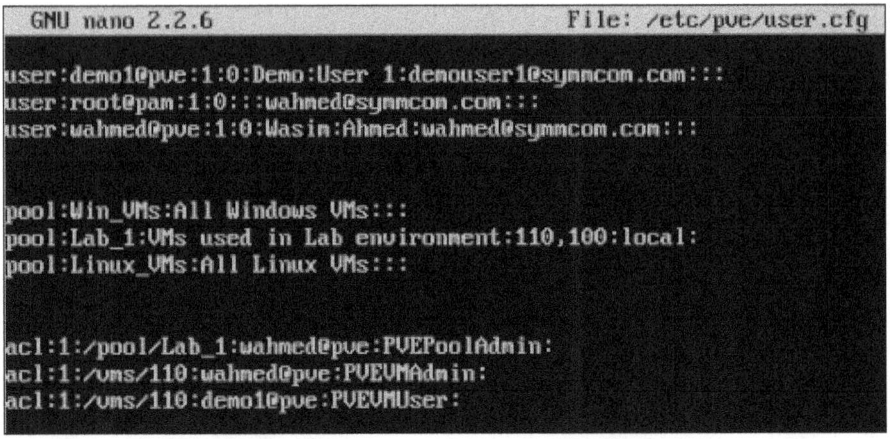

```
  GNU nano 2.2.6                                File: /etc/pve/user.cfg

user:demo1@pve:1:0:Demo:User 1:demouser1@symmcom.com:::
user:root@pam:1:0:::wahmed@symmcom.com:::
user:wahmed@pve:1:0:Wasim:Ahmed:wahmed@symmcom.com:::


pool:Win_VMs:All Windows VMs:::
pool:Lab_1:VMs used in Lab environment:110,100:local:
pool:Linux_VMs:All Linux VMs:::


acl:1:/pool/Lab_1:wahmed@pve:PVEPoolAdmin:
acl:1:/vms/110:wahmed@pve:PVEVMAdmin:
acl:1:/vms/110:demo1@pve:PVEVMUser:
```

Note that the `user.cfg` file does not hold any user password. This information is stored in `/etc/pve/priv/shadow.cfg` in an encrypted form. All the content in this configuration file can be managed through the Proxmox GUI. Whenever we create a new user/group or assign roles, the configuration file gets updated. If the GUI becomes inaccessible, this file can be manually edited.

# The password configuration file

The password configuration file is located under `/etc/pve/priv/shadow.cfg` and stores all the passwords for users in the cluster. The format is rather simple but the function of this file is very crucial. The format to store password information is as follows:

```
<user_name>:<encrypted_password>
```

Notice that the password file is in a `/priv` folder inside `/etc/pve`. Sensitive information, such as passwords, private authorization keys, and known hosts are kept in the `/etc/pve/priv` folder. When a new user is created through the Proxmox GUI, a new entry is added here.

# KVM virtual machine configuration file

The `vmid.conf` file stores configuration information for each virtual machine and is located at `/etc/pve/nodes/<name>/qemu-server/<vmid.conf>`. The directory structure divides all VM configuration files into categories based on nodes. For example, the configuration file for our VM with ID#110 is stored in the following location:

```
# /etc/pve/nodes/pm4-1/qemu-server/110.conf
```

When we migrate a VM from one node to another, Proxmox just moves the configuration file to the destination node. If the VM is powered on during the migration, then the entire memory content of the VM is also migrated to the destination node. For our VM 110, if we migrate it to pm4-2, the second node in the cluster, then the location of the 110.conf file will be as follows:

```
# /etc/pve/nodes/pm4-2/qemu-server/110.conf
```

 If a node with virtual machines in it becomes inaccessible, simply moving the <vm_id>.conf files to a different node will allow accessing all the VMs from a different node. Any files of the folder inside /etc/pve can be seen from any node in the cluster.

We will now take a look at a <vm_id>.conf file itself to see what makes up a virtual machine behind the scenes. This configuration file follows a simple OPTION: value format. The following is the configuration file of our VM #110:

```
balloon: 128
bootdisk: virtio0
cores: 1
ide2: none,media=cdrom
kvm: 0
memory: 512
name: Ubuntu-1
net0: virtio=06:4B:8B:5C:B5:3D,bridge=vmbr0,firewall=1
numa: 0
ostype: l26
parent: Clean_Install
smbios1: uuid=a80ce6f7-9f21-4ab2-b5ac-6daacade3199
sockets: 1
virtio0: local:110/vm-110-disk-1.qcow2,size=5G
```

Almost all the options in this file can be set through the Proxmox GUI under the KVM virtual machine option menu tab. Some option values, such as arguments, have to be added through the CLI. The following table shows some of the possible options. The values can be used as virtual machine configurations:

| Options | Description | Possible values |
| --- | --- | --- |
| acpi: | Enables/disables ACPI for VM. | 1<br><br>0 |
| args: | Allows you to pass arguments to a VM. Features such as sound can be activated using KVM arguments. Refer to section 2.2.6.2 for more details on arguments used in KVM. | See section 2.2.6.2 |
| autostart: | Auto restarts a virtual machine after crash. The default value is 0. | 1<br><br>0 |
| ballon: | Targeted RAM for a VM in MB. | Integer number |
| boot: | Default boot device. | c \| d \| n;<br><br>c=hdd;<br><br>d=cd-rom;<br><br>n=network |
| bootdisk: | Enables booting from a specific disk. | ide \| sata \| scsi \| virtio |
| core: | Number of cores per socket. The default value is 1. | Integer number |
| cpu: | Emulated CPU types. The default value is kvm64. | 486 \| kvm32 \| kvm64 \| qemu32 \| qemu64 \| conroe \| haswell \| nehalem \| opteron_G1/G2/G3/G4/G5 \| penryn \| sandybridge \| westmere \| athlon \| core2duo \| coreduo \| host \| pentium \| pentium2 \| pentium3 \| phenom |
| cpuunits: | This is the CPU weight of the VM. This value is used by the kernel fair scheduler. The larger the value is, the more CPU time a VM will get. Note that this value is relative to the weights of all other running VMs in the cluster. The default value is 1,000. | Integer 0 to 500000 |
| description: | Notes for the VM. | Plain text |
| freeze: | Freezes the CPU at startup. | 1 \| 0 |

| Options | Description | Possible values |
|---|---|---|
| `hostpci(n):` | This option allows a VM direct access to the host hardware. When this option is used, it is not possible to migrate the VM. Caution should be used for this option as it is still in the experimental stage. It is not recommended for the production environment. | HOSTPCIDEVICE<br><br>Syntax for HOSTPCIDEVICE is<br><br>bus: <pci_device_number><br><br>Get the `pci_device_number` from command `#lspci` |
| `hotplug:` | Enables hotplug for disk and network devices. The default value is 0. | 1 \| 0 |
| `ide(n):` | Allows volume to be used as an IDE disk or CD-ROM. N in `ide(n)` is limited to 0-3. | [volume=]image_name],[media=cdrom \| disk], [cyls=c,heads=h, secs=s,[trans=t]], [snapshot=on \| off] , [cache =none \| writethrough \| writeback \| unsafe \| directsync] , [format=f], [backup=yes \| no] , [rerror=ignore \| report \| stop] , [werror=enospc \| ignore \| report \| stop], [aio=native \| threads] |
| `kvm:` | Enables/disables the KVM hardware virtualization. This option disables any hardware acceleration within a VM. A possible usage scenario is when you are setting up a nested virtualized cluster. The default value is 1. | 1 \| 0 |
| `lock:` | Enables locking/unlocking of a VM. | backup \| migrate \| rollback \| snapshot |
| `memory:` | Allocated amount of RAM for the VM. | Integer from 16 to N |
| `migrate_downtime:` | Value in seconds for the maximum tolerated downtime for migration. The default value is 0.1. | Number 0 to N |
| `migrate_speed:` | Value for the maximum speed in MB/s for VM migrations. Set the value to 0 for no limit. The default value is 0. | Integer from 0 to N |
| `name:` | Name of the VM. | Text |
| `net(n):` | Specified network devices.<br><br>**MODEL=XX:XX:XX:XX:XX:XX, [bridge=<dev>],[rate=<mbps>],[tag=<vlanid>]** | MODEL= e1000 \| i82551 \| i82557b \| i82559er \| ne2k_isa \| ne2k_pci \| pcnet \| rtl8139 \| virtio |
| `onboot:` | Enables/disables VM auto start during the host node reboot. | 1 \| 0 |

| Options | Description | Possible values |
|---|---|---|
| `sata(n):` | Allows volume to be used as an SATA disk or CD-ROM. N in sata(n) is limited to 0-5. | [volume=]volume] , [media=cdrom \| disk] , [cyls=c,heads=h,secs=s,[trans=t]], [snapshot=on \| off] ,[cache=none \| writethrough \| writeback \| unsafe \| directsync], [format=f] , [backup=yes \| no] , [rerror=ignore \| report \| stop] , [werror=enospc \| ignore \| report \| stop] , [aio=native \| threads] |
| `scsi(n):` | Allows volume to be used as an SCSI disk or CD-ROM. N in scsi(n) is limited to 0-13. | [volume=]volume] , [media=cdrom \| disk], [cyls=c,heads=h,secs=s[,trans=t]], [snapshot=on \| off] , [cache=none \| writethrough \| writeback \| unsafe \| directsync], [format=f], [backup=yes \| no] , [rerror=ignore \| report \| stop] , [werror=enospc \| ignore \| report \| stop] , [aio=native \| threads] |
| `scsihw:` | SCSI controller type. The default value is lsi. | lsi \| megasas \| virtio-scsi-pci |
| `shares:` | This is the value-allocated amount of RAM for autoballooning. The larger this value is, the more RAM the VM will get. The value 0 disables this option. The default value is 1,000. | Integer from 0 to 50000 |
| `sockets:` | Number of CPU sockets. The default value is 1. | Integer from 1 to N |
| `startdate:` | This option sets the initial date of the real-time clock. | now \| YYYY-MM-DD \| YYYY-MM-DDTHH:MM:SS |
| `startup:` | This option sets the behavior for VM startup and shutdown. Order is a positive integer number, which sets the order in which the VMs will start. Shutdown follows the order value in reverse. The delay of startup and shutdown can be set through up and down in seconds. | [order=+ Int], [up=+ Int] , [down=+ Int] |
| `tablet:` | Enables/disables the USB tablet device in a VM. Without this option. If running lot of console-only VMs on one host, disabling this feature can save context switches. The default value is 1. | 1 \| 0 |

| Options | Description | Possible values |
|---------|-------------|-----------------|
| unused(n): | Unused volumes in a VM. When a virtual drive is deleted from a VM, the volume does not get deleted instantly. Instead, the status changes to unused:<volume_name>. At a later time, if the volume is needed, it can be reattached to the VM by changing the option to ide(n): \| scsi(n): \| sata(n):. | string |
| usb(n): | Enables pass-through direct access to a USB device. N can be set to 0 to 4. When this option is used, it is no longer possible to migrate the VM. | HOSTUSBDEVICE<br><br>Syntax for HOSTUSBDEVICE is<br><br><vendor_id:product_id> Get pci_device_number from command #lsusb -t |
| vga: | VM display type. | cirrus \| std \| vmware \| qxl |
| virtio(n): | Allows volume to be used as a virtio disk. N in virtio(n) is limited to 0-15. | [volume=]volume], [media=cdrom \| disk] , [cyls=c,heads=h,secs=s[,trans=t]], [snapshot=on \| off] , [cache=none \| writethrough \| writeback \| unsafe \| directsync], [format=f] , [backup=yes \| no] , [rerror=ignore \| report \| stop] , [werror=enospc \| ignore \| report \| stop] , [aio=native \| threads] |

# Arguments in the KVM configuration file

Arguments in a virtual machine configuration file are a way to extend the capability of the VM beyond just the default. For example, sound is not enabled for a VM by default. In order to give a VM the ability to play audio/video, an argument has to be passed through the VM configuration file. The following are some examples of arguments that can be used in a Proxmox VM configuration file. Arguments can be added in the following format:

```
args: -<device_arguments_1> -<device_arguments_2> . . . .
ballon: 512
bootdisk: virtio0
cores: 1
ide2: none,media=cdrom
  . . . .
  . . . .
```

Enable a serial device in a VM using the following code:

```
args: -serial /dev/ttyS0
```

Enable sound in a Windows XP VM using the following code:

```
args: -device AC97,addr=0x18
```

Enable sound in a Windows 7 VM using the following code:

```
args -device intel-hda,id=sound5,bus=pci.0,addr=0x18 -device
had-micro,id=sound5-codec0,bus=sound5.0,cad=0 -device had-
duplex,id=sound5-codec1,bus=sound5.0,cad=1
```

Enable UUID in a VM using this line of code:

```
args -uuid f1234a93-20d32-2398-129032ds-2322
```

Enable support for `aio=native` in a VM, as follows:

```
args: -drive file=/dev/VGGRP/VOL,if=virtio,index=1,cache=none,aio=nat
ive
```

# LXC container configuration file

From Proxmox VE 4.0, OpenVZ has been dropped in favor of LXC containers. LXC is derived from OpenVZ for the mainline kernel. One of the main advantages of LXC is that it can used on top of the standard Linux kernel without needing a special kernel, as is the case for OpenVZ.

 When using LXC, keep in mind that live migration of a container is not possible as of Proxmox VE 4.1. The container will need to be powered off to perform offline migration.

The following is the LXC configuration file of the container #100 in our example cluster:

```
#Ubuntu Demo LXC Container
arch: amd64
cpulimit: 1
cpuunits: 1024
hostname: Ubuntu-DC
memory: 284
nameserver: 208.67.222.222 8.8.8.8
net0: bridge=vmbr0,firewall=1,gw=172.16.3.254,hwaddr=3A:30:36:38:66:63,ip=172.16.0.186/20,name=eth0,tag=10,type=veth
ostype: ubuntu
rootfs: local:100/vm-100-disk-1.raw,size=46
searchdomain: symmcom.com
swap: 256
```

LXC container configuration is much simpler than OpenVZ. As with OpenVZ, there are no User Bean Counters in LXCs. It is worth noting here that if your existing cluster is pre-Proxmox 4.0 and has OpenVZ containers running, they cannot be seamlessly upgraded to LXCs during the Proxmox upgrade. All OpenVZ containers must be powered off, commit a full back up, and then restored in the upgraded Proxmox VE 4. We will take a look at the upgrade process in detail in *Chapter 11, Updating and Upgrading Proxmox*.

Like a KVM configuration file, LXC also uses an option: the value format of the configuration in its file. Parameters added by default during the LXC creation in Proxmox are mostly self-explanatory. Most of these parameters for LXC can be changed through the Proxmox GUI. LXC itself has got quite a few configuration parameters, which cannot be controlled through the GUI, but they can be added manually through the CLI, depending on the requirement. A comprehensive list of all the possible configuration parameters for LXC can be found at http://man7. org/linux/man-pages/man5/lxc.container.conf.5.html.

# Version configuration file

The version configuration file shows the version numbers of configuration files in the cluster and is located under /etc/pve/.version. Every time a configuration file is edited, the version number increases in the .version file. The following is the .version file in our cluster at this moment:

```
{
"starttime": 1450035295,
"clinfo": 4,
"vmlist": 21,
"corosync.conf": 2,
"corosync.conf.new": 2,
"storage.cfg": 3,
"user.cfg": 10,
"domains.cfg": 3,
"priv/shadow.cfg": 4,
"datacenter.cfg": 2,
"vzdump.cron": 2,
"ha/crm_commands": 2,
"ha/manager_status": 2,
"ha/resources.cfg": 2,
"ha/groups.cfg": 2,
"ha/fence.cfg": 2,
"status.cfg": 2,
"kvstore": {
"pm4-2": {
"tasklist": 90257}
,
"pm4-1": {
"tasklist": 89511}
}
}
```

There are no manual configurations or editing that are necessary in this file.

# Member nodes

Located under `/etc/pve/.members`, the member node file shows all the member nodes that are part of the Proxmox cluster. It is a great way to see the cluster status when the Proxmox GUI becomes inaccessible for any reason. The following is the `.members` file in our basic cluster:

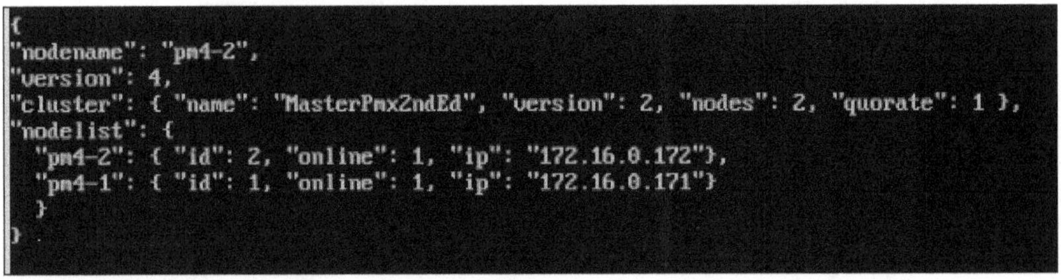

```
{
"nodename": "pm4-2",
"version": 4,
"cluster": { "name": "MasterPmx2ndEd", "version": 2, "nodes": 2, "quorate": 1 },
"nodelist": {
  "pm4-2": { "id": 2, "online": 1, "ip": "172.16.0.172"},
  "pm4-1": { "id": 1, "online": 1, "ip": "172.16.0.171"}
  }
}
```

The previous screenshot shows the current node where the `.members` file is being accessed:

```
"version": 4
```

The `.members` file has its own version numbering system. Like the `.version` file, every time `.members` is changed, the version increases incrementally. For example, when a node is added or removed from the cluster, the version number moves upward:

```
"cluster": { "name": "MasterPmx2ndEd", "version": 2, "nodes": 2,
"quorate": 1 },
```

The previous code shows the cluster information, such as the cluster name, cluster version, number of member nodes, and number of votes (quorate) needed to form a quorum:

```
"pm4-2": { "id": 2, "online": 1, "ip": "172.16.0.172"
```

Nodes mentioned in the node list section provide information that belongs to each node, such as the ID, online/offline status, and IP address.

# Virtual machine list file

Located under /etc/pve/.vmlist, the virtual machine list file stores a list of all the virtual machines within the Proxmox cluster. The .vmlist file uses the following format to store the list:

```
"<vmid>": { "node": "<nodename>", "type": "<vm_type>", "version": <int> }
```

We have two virtual machines and one template in our basic cluster. The following screenshot shows the information stored in the .vmlist file:

```
{
"version": 21,
"ids": {
"100": { "node": "pm4-1", "type": "lxc", "version": 23 },
"110": { "node": "pm4-1", "type": "qemu", "version": 11 }}
}
```

This list allows you another way to view the virtual machines list in the cluster in all the nodes. We can have a hard copy if disaster strikes, making the cluster inaccessible, or we need to rebuild a virtual environment.

# The cluster log file

This is a log file for the cluster itself and is located under /etc/pve/.clusterlog. It mostly maintains a log of the login authentications of users. The following is a snippet of our .clusterlog file:

```
"data": [
{"uid": 322, "time": 1450316440, "pri": 6, "tag": "pvedaemon", "pid": 19540, "node": "pm4-1", "user": "root@pam", "msg": "successful auth for user 'root@$
{"uid": 321, "time": 1450315540, "pri": 6, "tag": "pvedaemon", "pid": 21688, "node": "pm4-1", "user": "root@pam", "msg": "successful auth for user 'root@$
{"uid": 320, "time": 1450314639, "pri": 6, "tag": "pvedaemon", "pid": 19540, "node": "pm4-1", "user": "root@pam", "msg": "successful auth for user 'root@$
{"uid": 319, "time": 1450313739, "pri": 6, "tag": "pvedaemon", "pid": 12837, "node": "pm4-1", "user": "root@pam", "msg": "successful auth for user 'root@$
{"uid": 318, "time": 1450312839, "pri": 6, "tag": "pvedaemon", "pid": 12837, "node": "pm4-1", "user": "root@pam", "msg": "successful auth for user 'root@$
{"uid": 317, "time": 1450311939, "pri": 6, "tag": "pvedaemon", "pid": 12837, "node": "pm4-1", "user": "root@pam", "msg": "successful auth for user 'root@$
{"uid": 316, "time": 1450311039, "pri": 6, "tag": "pvedaemon", "pid": 6182, "node": "pm4-1", "user": "root@pam", "msg": "successful auth for user 'root@p$
{"uid": 315, "time": 1450310138, "pri": 6, "tag": "pvedaemon", "pid": 6182, "node": "pm4-1", "user": "root@pam", "msg": "successful auth for user 'root@p$
{"uid": 314, "time": 1450309238, "pri": 6, "tag": "pvedaemon", "pid": 25841, "node": "pm4-1", "user": "root@pam", "msg": "successful auth for user 'root@$
{"uid": 313, "time": 1450308338, "pri": 6, "tag": "pvedaemon", "pid": 24353, "node": "pm4-1", "user": "root@pam", "msg": "successful auth for user 'root@$
{"uid": 312, "time": 1450307438, "pri": 6, "tag": "pvedaemon", "pid": 25841, "node": "pm4-1", "user": "root@pam", "msg": "successful auth for user 'root@$
```

# Ceph configuration files

Ceph is a kind of a distributed object and file storage system, which fully integrates with Proxmox. Out of the box, Proxmox comes with the Ceph cluster management option through the GUI and a whole array of features to make the integration as seamless as possible. We will dive deep into Ceph in *Chapter 4, Storage Systems*. Ceph can be installed on its own hardware using operating systems, such as Ubuntu, or it can coexist with Proxmox on the same node. Whether it's co-existing or on its own cluster, Proxmox nodes need access to the Ceph configuration file to connect. The configuration file is located in /etc/pve/ceph.conf for the Proxmox+Ceph coexisting node. For noncoexisting Proxmox nodes, the file needs to be stored in /etc/ceph/ceph.conf. In the coexisting node, Proxmox creates a symbolic link of the Ceph configuration file in /etc/ceph/ceph.conf.

Besides the configuration file, Ceph also uses authentication keys, which are stored in the following directories:

```
/etc/pve/priv/ceph.client.admin.keyring
/etc/pve/priv/ceph.mon.keyring
/etc/pve/priv/ceph/<rbd_storage_id>.keyring
```

In order to connect **Ceph RBD (Rados Block Device)** storage, Proxmox requires a separate keyring. The <rbd_storage_id>.keyring is simply a copied and renamed version of ceph.client.admin.keyring. Without this keyring, Proxmox will not be able to connect to Ceph.

# Firewall configuration file

As of Proxmox 4.1, a fully functional firewall is integrated with a Proxmox cluster. It is very powerful and comes with granular customization down to a single virtual machine. Firewall rules can be created separately for a cluster, node, and virtual machine. The following table shows the firewall rules' file locations:

| Cluster wide firewall rules | /etc/pve/firewall/cluster.fw |
| --- | --- |
| Node firewall rules | /etc/pve/nodes/<node_id>/host.fw |
| VM/CT firewall rules | /etc/pve/firewall/cluster.fw |

All the firewall rules can be managed through the Proxmox GUI firewall menu without editing using the command line. We will take a look at the firewall in detail in *Chapter 8, The Proxmox Firewall*.

It is worth mentioning that the Proxmox firewall should be not a substitute for the main gateway firewall where the Internet enters the facility. There should be a dedicated firewall between the WAN and the local network. The Proxmox firewall enhances security by allowing you to prevent inter-virtual machine communication and the fine tuning of the incoming and outgoing network traffic.

# Summary

In this chapter, we looked at the location of the important configuration files needed to run a Proxmox cluster. We also looked inside the configuration files to have a better understanding of the parameters used and other possible values for different parameters. As mentioned earlier, most of these configuration files can be changed via the Proxmox GUI. But when the GUI becomes inaccessible for any reason, knowing where these files are located can save a tremendous amount of time by accessing them through the CLI.

In the next chapter, we will take a look at the various storage systems that can be used with Proxmox and the different types of disk images and their use cases. We will also see how to build an enterprise grade distributed storage system using Ceph and connect it to a Proxmox cluster.

# 4
# Storage Systems

A storage system is a medium to store data for simultaneous access by multiple devices or nodes in a network. As server and desktop virtualizations become the norm, a proper, stable storage system today is much more critical for a virtual environment. In terms of Proxmox, a storage system is where virtual disk images are stored.

Although a Proxmox cluster can fully function with **Direct Attached Storage** (**DAS**) or a local storage system in the same Proxmox node, a shared storage system has many benefits in a production environment, such as increased manageability, seamless storage expansion, and redundancy, just to name a few. In this chapter, we will cover the following topics:

- Local versus shared storage
- Virtual disk image types
- Storage types supported by Proxmox
- Commercial and free shared storage options
- FreeNAS as a low-cost shared storage option
- Ceph as enterprise-grade shared storage

Local or shared, a storage system is a vital component of a Proxmox cluster. A storage system is where all the virtual machines reside. Therefore, a deeper understanding of different storage systems will allow an administrator to properly plan storage requirements for any cluster environment.

# Local storage versus shared storage

Shared storage is not absolutely necessary in a Proxmox cluster environment, but without a doubt, it makes storage management a simpler task. In a small business environment, it may be fine not to have 24/7 uptime and 100% reliability, so a local storage system will suffice. When data grows beyond several terabytes, it may or may not fully justify shared storage. The question is how important is budget, reliability, resiliency, and accessibility. In most enterprise virtual environments with critical data, shared storage is the only logical choice due to the benefits it brings to the whole cluster operation. The following are considered benefits of using shared storage:

- Live migration of a virtual machine
- Seamless expansion of multinode storage space
- Centralized backup
- Multilevel data tiering
- Central storage management

# Live migration of a virtual machine

This is probably one of the important sought after reasons to go for a shared storage system. **Live migration** is when a virtual machine can be moved to a different node without shutting it down first. **Offline migration** is when the virtual machine is powered off prior to migration. The hardware and operating system of Proxmox nodes need updates, patches, and replacements occasionally. Some updates require immediate reboot while some require none at all. The primary function of Proxmox nodes in a cluster is to run virtual machines. When a node needs to be rebooted, all the running VMs must be stopped or migrated to other nodes. Then, migrate them back to the original node after the reboot cycle is complete. In Proxmox, a powered-on VM cannot be migrated using live migration without powering it down first if the VM is on a local disk of the node in question. If a total Proxmox node failure occurs for any reason, all the VMs stored in that node will be completely unavailable until the node is fixed or replaced. This is because VMs cannot be accessed to be moved to a different node until the issue node is powered up.

In most cases, shutting down all the VMs just to reboot the host node is not an option. This causes too much downtime depending on the number of VMs the node handles. In order to migrate locally stored VMs, they must be stopped and then migration should be initiated from the Proxmox GUI. Migration from local storage to another local storage takes a long time, depending on the size of the VM, since Proxmox moves an entire image file using rsync to relocate the VM to another node.

Let's take a look at the following diagram of a cluster with 40 locally stored virtual machines with 10 on each of the four Proxmox nodes:

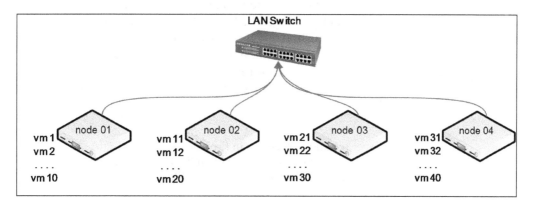

In the preceding overly simplified diagram, there are four Proxmox nodes with 10 virtual machines on each. If node 01 needs to reboot, all 10 virtual machines have to be stopped, the node needs to be rebooted, and then all the virtual machines must be powered up. If node 01 needs to be taken offline for hardware upgrade, then all the virtual machines need to be stopped and manually migrated to different nodes. If node 01 fails completely, then all 10 virtual machines will be inaccessible until node 01 is back on again.

So clearly, a cluster setup with a local storage for virtual machines can cause unwanted downtime when migration is needed. Now, let's take a look at the following diagram where four Proxmox nodes with 40 virtual machines are stored on a shared storage system:

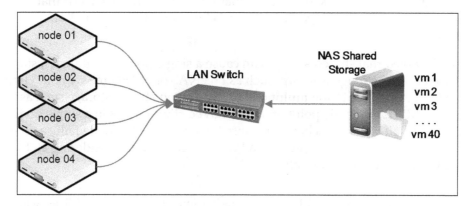

In the preceding diagram, all 40 virtual machines are stored on a shared storage system. The Proxmox node only holds the configuration files for each virtual machine. In this scenario, if node 01 needs to be rebooted due to a security patch or update, all the virtual machines can be simply migrated to another node without powering down a single virtual machine. A virtual machine user will never notice that their machine has actually moved to a different node. If total Proxmox node failure occurs, the virtual machine configuration file can simply be manually moved from /etc/pve/nodes/node01/qemu-server/<vmid>.conf to /etc/pve/nodes/node02/qemu-server/<vmid>.conf.

We can also leverage another feature in Proxmox known as high availability to automate the VM configuration file to move during a node failure. Refer to *Chapter 9, Proxmox High Availability*, to learn about this feature.

Since all the virtual machine configuration files are in a Proxmox-clustered filesystem, they can be accessed from any node. Refer to *Chapter 3, Proxmox under the Hood*, for a Proxmox cluster filesystem or pmxcfs. With virtual machine image files on shared storage, Proxmox migration does not have to move all the image files using rsync from one node to another, which allows much faster virtual machine migration.

Rsync is an open source program and network protocol for Unix-based systems. It provides nonencrypted or encrypted incremental file transfers from one location to another.

When live migrating a VM, keep in mind that the more memory (RAM) that is allocated to the VM, the longer it will take to live migrate a powered-on virtual machine.

It should be noted that shared storage can cause a single point of failure if a single node-based shared storage is set up, such as FreeNAS or NAS4Free without High Availability configured. Using multinode or distributed shared storage such as Ceph, Gluster, or DRBD, the single point of failure can be eliminated. On a single node shared storage, all virtual machines are stored in one node. If a node failure occurs, the storage will become inaccessible by a Proxmox cluster, thus rendering all the running virtual machines unusable.

As of Proxmox VE 4.1, LXC containers cannot be live migrated. They will need to be powered off to commit offline migration. KVM VMs can be live migrated without shutting down the VM.

# Seamless expansion of multinode storage space

Digital data is growing faster than ever before in our modern 24/7 digitally connected world. The growth has been exponential since the introduction of virtualization. Since it is much easier to set up a virtual server at a moment's notice, an administrator can simply clone a virtual server template, and within minutes, a new virtual server is up and running while consuming storage space. If left unchecked, this regular creating and retiring of virtual machines can force a company to grow out of available storage space. A distributed shared storage system is designed keeping this very specific requirement in mind.

In an enterprise environment, storage space should increase on demand without shutting down or interrupting critical nodes or virtual machines. Using a multinode or distributed shared storage system, virtual machines can now go beyond a few node local clusters to scattered multiple nodes spanned across geographical regions. For example, Ceph or Gluster can span across several racks and comprise well over several petabytes of usable storage space. Simply add a new node with a full bay of drives then tell the storage cluster to recognize the new node to increase storage space for the entire cluster. Since shared storage is separated from the virtual machine host nodes, storage can be increased or decreased without disturbing any running virtual machines. Later in this chapter, we will see how we can integrate Ceph into Proxmox.

# Centralized backup

Shared storage makes centralized backup possible by allowing each virtual machine's host nodes to create a backup in one central location. This helps a backup manager or an administrator to implement a solid backup plan and manage the existing backups. Since a Proxmox node failure will not take the shared storage system down, virtual machines can be easily restored to a new node to reduce downtime.

 Always use a separate node for backup purposes. It is not a good practice to store both virtual machines and their backups on the same node.

# Multilevel data tiering

Data tiering is a concept where different files can be stored on different storage pools based on their performance requirements. For example, a virtual file server can provide very fast service if this VM is stored on an SSD storage pool, while a virtual backup server can be stored on a slower HDD storage since backups files are not frequently accessed, and thus, do not require very fast I/O. Tiering can be set up using different shared storage nodes with different performance levels. It can also be set up on the same node by assigning volumes or pools to specific sets of drives.

# Central storage management

By separating shared storage clusters from primary Proxmox clusters, we can manage two clusters without interfering with each other. Since shared storage systems can be set up with separate nodes and physical switches, managing them based on different authorizations and permissions becomes an easier task. NAS, SAN, and other types of shared storage solutions come with their own management programs from where an administrator or operator can check storage cluster health, disk status, free space, and so on. The Ceph storage is configured via CLI, but Proxmox has integrated a great deal of Ceph management options within the Proxmox GUI, which makes Ceph cluster management much easier. Using the API, Proxmox can now collect the Ceph cluster data and display it through the Proxmox GUI, as shown in the following screenshot:

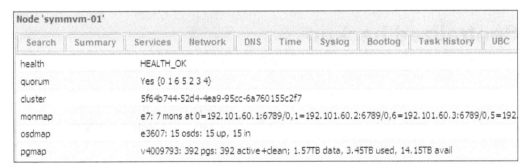

Other NAS solutions such as FreeNAS, OpenMediaVault, and NAS4Free also have a GUI that simplifies management. The following screenshot is an example of the hard drive status from a FreeNAS GUI window:

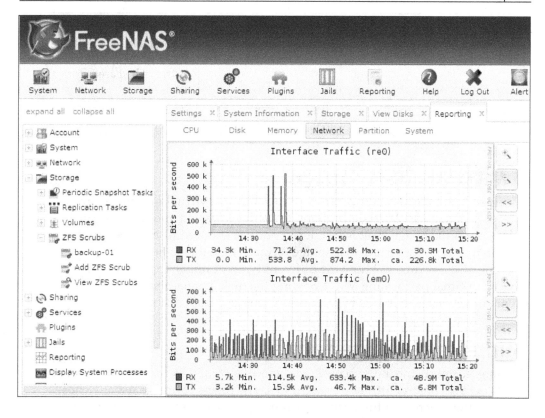

# Local and shared storage comparison

The following table is a comparison of both the local and shared storage for a quick reference:

| | Local storage | Shared storage |
|---|---|---|
| Virtual machine live migration | No | Yes |
| High Availability | No | Yes, when used in multinode shared storage |
| Cost | Lower | Significantly higher |
| I/O performance | Native disk drive speed | Slower than the native disk drive speed |
| Skill requirements | No special storage skills required | Must be skilled on the shared storage option used |

| | Local storage | Shared storage |
|---|---|---|
| Expandability | Limited to available drive bays of a node | Expandable over multiple nodes when a multinode or distributed shared storage is used |
| Maintenance complexity | Virtually maintenance free | Storage nodes or clusters require regular monitoring |

# A virtual disk image

A virtual disk image is a file or group of files where a virtual machine stores its data. In Proxmox, a VM configuration file can be recreated and used to attach a disk image. But if the image itself is lost, it can only be restored from a backup. There are different types of virtual disk image formats available to be used with a virtual machine. It is essential to know the different types of image formats in order to have an optimal performing VM. Knowing the disk images also helps to prevent premature shortage of space by over provisioning virtual disks.

# Supported image formats

Proxmox supports the .raw, .qcow2, and .vmdk virtual disk formats. Each format has its own set of strengths and weaknesses. The image format is usually chosen based on the function of the virtual machine, storage system in use, performance requirement, and available budget. The following screenshot shows the menu where we can choose an image type during a virtual disk creation through the GUI:

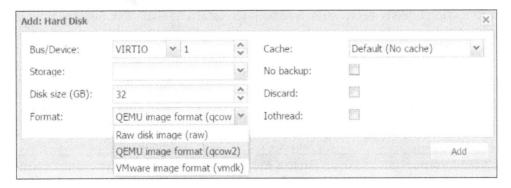

The following table is a brief summary of the different image formats and their possible usage:

| Image Type | Storage Supported | Strength | Weakness |
|---|---|---|---|
| .qcow2 | NFS and directory | Allows dynamic virtual storage image files. | Complex file formats with additional software layers. |
| | | Stable and secure. | High I/O overhead. |
| | | Most features rich among image types. | |
| .raw | LVM, RBD, iSCSI, and directory | No additional software layer. Direct access to image files. | Fixed virtual image only. Cannot be used to store dynamic images. |
| | | Stable, secure, and fastest. | VM takes longer to backup due to the size of image files. |
| .vmdk | NFS and directory | Works exceptionally well with the VMware infrastructure. | Additional software layer, thus slower performance. |
| | | Allows dynamic virtual storage image files. | Not fully tested with Proxmox. |

 Setting up virtual machines with the wrong image format is very forgiving. You can always convert these image types from one format to another. Conversion can be done from both CLI and GUI. Virtual disk image conversion is explained later in this chapter.

# The .qcow2 image type

The .qcow2 type is a very stable VM image format. Proxmox fully supports this file format. A VM disk created using .qcow2 is much smaller since by default it creates thin-provisioned disk images. For example, an Ubuntu VM created with 50 GB storage space may have an image file with a size around 1 GB. As a user stores data in the VM, this image file will grow gradually. The .qcow2 image format allows an administrator to over provision VMs with the .qcow2 disk image file. If not monitored regularly, the shared storage will run out of space to accommodate all the growing virtual image files. Available storage space should be regularly monitored in such an environment. It is a good practice to add additional storage space when the overall storage space consumption reaches around 80%.

Thin provisioning is when the virtual disk image file does not preallocate all the blocks, thus keeping the size of the image file to only what we want. As more data is stored in the virtual machine, the thin-provisioned image file grows until it reaches the maximum size allocated. Thick provisioning, on the other hand, is when the virtual disk image file preallocates all the blocks, thus creating an image file which is exactly of the size set prior to creating the virtual disk image file.

The .qcow2 also has very high I/O overhead due to its additional software layer. Thus, it is a bad choice of image format for a VM such as a database server. Any data being read or written into the image format goes through the qcow2 software layer, which increases the I/O, making it slower. A backup created from a qcow2 image can only be restored to an NFS or local directory.

When budget is the main concern and storage space is very limited, qcow2 is an excellent choice. This image type supports KVM live snapshots to preserve states of virtual machines.

## The .raw image type

The .raw image type is also a very stable and mature VM image format. Its primary strength lies in performance. There is no additional software layer for data to go through. A VM has direct pass-through access to the raw file, which makes it much faster. Also, there is no software component attached to it, so it is much less problem prone. The raw format can only create a fixed-size or thick-provisioned VM image file. For example, an Ubuntu VM created with 50 GB storage space will have a 50 GB image file. This helps an administrator to know exactly how much storage is in use, so there is no chance of an uncontrolled out-of-storage situation.

The .raw type is the preferred file format for all Proxmox VMs. A raw image format VM can be restored to just about any storage type. In a virtual environment, additional virtual disk image files can be added to a virtual machine at any time. So, it is not necessary to initially allocate a larger size .raw virtual disk image file with possible future growth in mind. The VM can start with a smaller .raw image file and add more disk images as needed. For example, a VM with 50 GB data starts with an 80 GB .raw image file. Then, increase the size of the disk image or add more virtual disk images as the need arises. Proxmox allows quite a few additional virtual drives to be added to a VM.

The following table shows the maximum number of allowed disk device per VM by Proxmox:

| Bus/device type | Maximum allowed |
|---|---|
| IDE | 3 |
| SATA | 5 |
| VirtIO | 15 |
| SCSI | 13 |

Since all the .raw disk image files are preallocated, there is no risk of over provisioning beyond the total available storage space. KVM live snapshots are also supported by the .raw image format. There are some shared storages which only support the .raw disk image. Ceph RBD is such a storage. As of Proxmox VE 4.1, we can only store the .raw virtual disk image on the Ceph block device. But the Ceph filesystem or CephFS supports all the virtual disk images. CephFS is one of the three storage types supported on the Ceph platform. Currently, there are no direct storage plugins for CephFS in Proxmox, only for RBD. But we can connect CephFS to Proxmox as an NFS share.

# The .vmdk image type

The .vmdk image format is very common in the VMware infrastructure. The main advantage of Proxmox supporting .vmdk is the ease of VM migration from VMware to a Proxmox cluster. A VM created in VMware with the .vmdk image format can easily be configured to be used in the Proxmox cluster and converted. There are no benefits to keeping a virtual disk image file in the .vmdk format, except during a transitional period, such as converting virtual machines from the VMware infrastructure.

# Managing disk images

A Proxmox virtual image file can be managed from both the WebGUI and CLI.
The WebGUI allows the administrator to use the add, resize (increase only),
move, throttling, and delete options, as shown in the following screenshot:

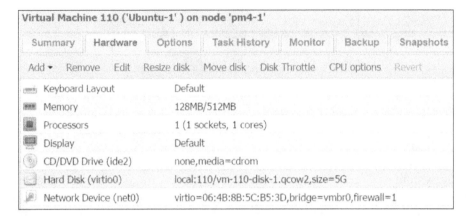

To make any changes to a virtual disk image file, the image must be selected first
from the Hardware tab, as shown in the preceding screenshot. Virtual machine
image files can also be manipulated using the CLI commands. The following table
shows a few examples of the most common commands used to delete, convert, and
resize an image file:

| Command | Function |
| --- | --- |
| `#qemu-img create -f <type> -o <filename> <size>`<br>`#qemu-img create -f raw test.raw 1024M` | Creates an image file |
| `#qemu-img convert <source> -O <type> <destination>`<br>`#qemu-img convert test.vmdk -O qcow2 test.qcow2` | Converts an image file |
| `#qemu-img resize <filename> <+\|-><size>`<br>`#qemu-img resize test.qcow2 +1024M` | Resizes an image file |

# Resizing a virtual disk image

The Resize disk option only supports increasing the size of the virtual disk image
file. It has no shrink function. The Proxmox Resize option only adjusts the size of the
virtual disk image file. After any resizing, the partition must be adjusted from inside
the VM. The safest way to resize partitions is to boot a Linux-based virtual machine
with a partitioning ISO image, such as **gparted** (http://gparted.org/download.
php), and then resize the partitions using the **gparted** graphical interface. It is
also possible to perform an online partition resizing while the virtual machine is
powered on.

Resizing a virtual disk image file involves the following three steps:

1.  Resize the virtual disk image file in Proxmox:
    -   From GUI: Select the virtual disk, and then click on **Resize disk**.
    -   From CLI: Run the following command:

        ```
        # qm resize <vm_id> <virtual_disk> +<size>G
        ```

2.  Resize the partition of the virtual disk image file from inside the VM:
    -   For Windows VM: Resize the disk by going to Computer Management under Administrative Tools
    -   For Linux VM with RAW partition, run the following command:
        ```
        # cfdisk <disk_image>
        ```
    -   For Linux VM with LVM partition, run the following command:
        ```
        # cfdisk </dev/XXX/disk_image>
        ```
    -   For Linux VM with QCOW2 partition, run the following commands:
        ```
        # apt-get install nbd-client
        # qemu-ndb -connect /dev/nbd0     <disk_image>
        # cfdisk /dev/nbd0
        # qemu-nbd -d /dev/nbd0
        ```
    -   Resize the filesystem in the partition of the virtual disk image file:
    -   For a Linux client with LVM:
        ```
        # pvscan     (find PV name)
        # pvresize /dev/xxx   (/dev/xxx found from pvscan)
        # lvscan     (find LVname)
        # lvresize -L+<size>G /dev/xxx/lv_<disk>
        ```
    -   To use 100% free space:
        ```
        # lvresize -l +100%FREE /dev/xxx/lv_<disk>
        # resize2fs /dev/xxx/lv_<disk> (resize filesystem)
        ```

 Steps 2 and 3 are necessary only if online resizing is done without shutting down a VM. If gparted or another bootable partitioning medium is used, then only step 1 is needed before booting the VM with ISO.

# Moving a virtual disk image

Move disk allows the image file to be moved to different storage or converted to a different image type:

In the **Move disk** option menu, just select the **Target Storage** and **Format type**, and then click on **Move disk** to move the image file. Moving can be done live without shutting down the VM.

 The Format type in the Move disk option will be greyed out if the destination storage only supports one image format type. In the preceding screenshot, ssd-ceph-01 is an RBD storage in Ceph Pool. Since RBD only supports the RAW format, the format type has been greyed out automatically.

Clicking on **Delete source** will delete the source image file after the move is complete.

Note that if the virtual machine has any snapshots, Proxmox will not be able to delete the source file automatically. In such cases, the disk image has to be manually deleted after the snapshots are removed. The source image will be listed as Unused disk, as shown in the following screenshot, after the move is done for a disk image with snapshots:

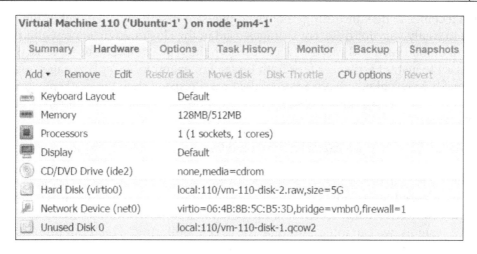

# Throttling a virtual disk image

Proxmox allows throttling or setting a limit on the read/write speed and Input
Output Per Second (IOPS or OP/s) for each virtual disk image. By default, there
are no set limits. Each disk image will try to read and write at the maximum speed
achievable in the storage where the disk image is being stored. For example, if a disk
image is stored on local storage, it will try to perform read and write operations at
about 110 MB/s since that is the theoretical limit of a SATA drive. This performance
will vary for different storage options. In a multi-tenant or large environment, if all
the disk images are not throttled without any limit, this may put pressure on the
network and/or storage bandwidth. By throttling, we can control the bandwidth that
each disk image can utilize. The **Disk Throttle** option is available on the Hardware
tab of a VM. The following screenshot shows the Disk Throttle dialog box with the
option to set limits:

When it comes to disk throttling, there's no one-size-fits-all limit. The set limit is going to vastly vary for different storages used in the cluster environment and the amount of load each VM carries. Depending on the type of storage used, it may be necessary to just set write, read, or both limits. For example, a Ceph storage cluster with an SSD journal may have a much higher write speed than the read speed. So, throttling a VM with a higher read limit while setting a lower write limit may be a viable option.

As mentioned earlier, we can set a limit based on MB/s or OP/s. Setting the mb/s limit is much simpler since we can quantify the read/write speed of a disk drive or network in megabytes easier. For example, a standard SATA drive can achieve a theoretical speed of 115 mb/s while a gigabit network can achieve about 100 mb/s. Knowing the performance in IOPS or op/s requires some extra steps. In some storage systems, we can integrate some forms of monitoring, which can present us the IOPS data in real time. For others, we need to calculate the IOPS data to know the performance matrix of the storage system used. The complete details of the IOPS calculation is beyond the scope of this book. But the following guidelines should serve as a starting point to calculate the op/s of the different storage devices:

To calculate op/s for a single 7200 RPM SATA disk is as follows:

```
IOPS = 1/(avg. latency in seconds + avg. seek time in seconds)
```

Based on the previous formula, we can calculate IOPS of a standard SSD device. To get the average latency and seek time of a device, we can use the Linux tool, ioping. It is not installed in Proxmox by default. So, we can install it using the following command:

```
# apt-get install ioping
```

Ioping is similar to the iperf command but for disk drives. The following command will show the IO latency of our example SSD device:

```
# ioping /dev/sda
```

The following screenshot shows that the result of the ioping for average latency is 1.79 milliseconds or 0.00179 seconds:

```
--- /dev/sdh (block device 111.8 GiB) ioping statistics
5 requests completed in 4.01 s, 558 iops, 2.18 MiB/s
min/avg/max/mdev = 1.52 ms / 1.79 ms / 2.40 ms / 312 us
```

To get the average seek time of a device, we need to run the following ioping command:

```
# ioping -R /dev/sda
```

The following screenshot shows that the result of the `ioping` for the average seek time is 133 microseconds or 0.000133 seconds:

```
--- /dev/sdh (block device 111.8 GiB) ioping statistics ---
21.9 k requests completed in 3.00 s, 7.50 k iops, 29.3 MiB/s
min/avg/max/mdev = 27 us / 133 us / 3.02 ms / 128 us
```

Using the gathered result, we can calculate the IOPS or op/s of the SSD device, as follows:

```
IOPS = 1 / (0.00179 + 0.000133) = 520
```

If we know the maximum IOPS a storage can provide, we can tweak each VM with op/s throttling to prevent IO issues in the cluster. As of Proxmox VE 4.1, we cannot set a cluster-wide throttling limit. Each disk image needs manual throttling separately.

## Caching a virtual disk image

Caching a virtual disk image provides performance and in some instances protection against an ungraceful VM shutdown. Not all caching are safe to use. For optimum VM performance, it is important to be aware of the various caching offered in Proxmox. This option is available under the VM Hardware tab in the disk image creation or edit dialog box. The following screenshot shows the disk image's edit dialog box with the caching drop-down menu for the .raw disk image of our example VM:

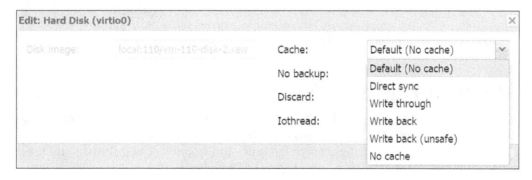

As of Proxmox VE 4.1, the following caching options are available:

| Cache option | Description |
|---|---|
| Direct sync | In this cache option, the Proxmox host does not do any caching, but a VM disk image uses the write through cache. In this cache, writes are only acknowledged when data has been committed to the storage device. Direct sync is recommended for VMs, which does not send flushes when required. This is a safer cache as data is not lost during a power failure but it is also slower. |
| Write through | In this cache option, the Proxmox host page cache is enabled while the VM disk write cache is disabled. This cache provides a good read performance but slow write performance due to write cache being disabled. This is a safer cache as it ensures data integrity. This cache is recommended for local or direct attached storage. |
| Write back | In this cache option, both read and write caching are done by the host. Writes are acknowledged by the VM disk as completed as soon they are committed to the host cache regardless of whether they have been committed to the storage or not. Data loss will occur for VMs in this cache. |
| Write back (unsafe) | This cache is the same as write back except that all the flushes are completely ignored from the guest VM. This is the fastest cache although the most unsafe cache. This cache should never be used in a production cluster. Usually, this cache is used to speed up the OS installation in a VM. After the VM installation, this cache should be disabled and reverted to a different safer cache option. |
| No cache | This is the default caching option in Proxmox. In this option, no caching occurs at the host level, but the guest VM does the write back cache. The VM disk directly receives a write acknowledgment from the storage device in this cache option. Data can be lost in this cache during an abrupt host shutdown due to a power failure. |

# Storage types in Proxmox

Proxmox has excellent plugins for the mainstream storage options. In this section, we are going to see which storage plugins are integrated in Proxmox and also see how to use them to connect to different storage types in Proxmox. The following are the storage types that are natively supported as of Proxmox VE 4.1:

- Directory
- LVM
- NFS
- ZFS
- Ceph RBD
- GlusterFS

# Directory

Directory storage is a mounted folder on the Proxmox local node. It is mainly used as local storage. But we can also mount a remote folder in a different node and use that mount point to create a new **Directory** storage. By default, this location is mounted under /var/lib/vz.

Any VM stored in this Directory storage does not allow live migration. The VM must be stopped before migrating to another node. All virtual disk image file types can be stored in the Directory storage. To create a new storage with a mount point, go to **Datacenter | Storage**, and click on **Add** to select the Directory plugin. The following screenshot shows the Directory storage dialog box where we can add a storage named local-iso, which is mounted in /mnt/iso to store the ISO and container templates:

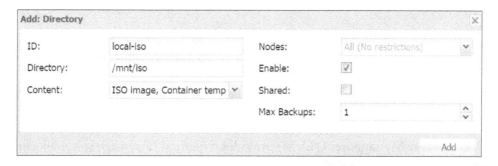

For locally mounted storages, selecting the Shared checkbox is not necessary. This option only pertains to a shared storage system, such as NFS, RBD, and so on.

# iSCSI

iSCSI, which stands for Internet Small Computer System Interface, is based on Internet Protocol, which allows the transmission of SCSI commands over the standard IP-based network. iSCSI devices can be set up locally or over a vast distance to provide storage options. We cannot store virtual disk images directly on the iSCSI device, but we can configure the LVM storage on top of the iSCSI devices, and then store disk images. An attached iSCSI device appears as if it is physically connected even if the device is stored in another remote node. For more details on iSCSI, refer to http://en.wikipedia.org/wiki/ISCSI.

We will assume that you already have an iSCSI device created in a remote node using FreeNAS or any other Linux distribution. To add the device to Proxmox, we are going to use the iSCSI storage plugin, which we can find by navigating to the **Datacenter | Storage | Add** menu. As shown in the following screenshot, we are adding an iSCSI target named test1-iSCSI, which is configured in a remote node, 172.16.0.170:

Note that using LUNs directly is not recommended although the option to enable them is available. It is known to cause an iSCSI device error when accessed directly.

# LVM

**Logical Volume Management (LVM)** provides a method of storage space allocation by using one or more disk partitions or drives as the underlying base storage. The LVM storage requires a base storage to be set up and function properly. We can create a LVM storage with local devices as backing or network backing with iSCSI devices. LVM allows scalable storage space since the base storage can be on the same node or on a different one. The LVM storage only supports the RAW virtual disk image format. We can only store virtual disk images or containers on LVM storage. For more details on LVM, refer to http://en.wikipedia.org/wiki/Logical_Volume_Manager_(Linux).

If the LVM disk array is configured using local direct attach disks in the node, VMs stored on this storage cannot be migrated live without powering down. But by connecting iSCSI devices from a remote node, and then creating the LVM storage on top of the iSCSI volume, we can make the live migration possible since the storage is now considered shared storage. FreeNAS is an excellent option to create the LVM plus iSCSI shared storage at no license cost. It comes with a great graphical user interface and many features, which goes far beyond just LVM or iSCSI. Details on FreeNAS and the download option can be found at http://www.freenas.org/.

To add LVM storage, go to **Datacenter | Storage | Add**, and select the LVM storage plugin. The following screenshot shows the LVM dialog box where we are using the iSCSI device, test1-iscsi, which we added in the previous section to create LVM storage:

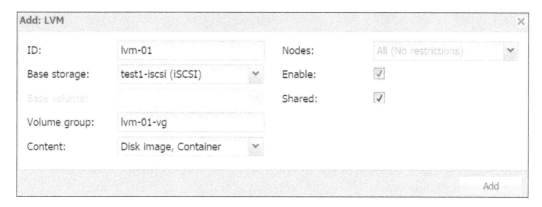

# NFS

Network File System or NFS in short is a well-matured filesystem protocol originally developed by Sun Microsystems in 1984. Currently, Version 4 of the NFS protocol is in effect. But it was not as widely accepted as Version 3 due to a few compatibility issues. But the gap is closing fast between Version 3 and 4. Proxmox, by default, uses Version 3 of the NFS protocol, while administrators can change to Version 4 through the use of options in `storage.cfg`. NFS storage can store the .qcow2, .raw, and .vmdk image formats, providing versatility and flexibility in a clustered environment. NFS is also the easiest to set up and requires the least amount of upfront hardware cost, thus allowing a budget-conscious small business or a home user to get their hands on a stable shared-storage system for the Proxmox cluster.

>  Care should be taken when using NFS Version 4 instead of Version 3 in Proxmox. There are still a few bugs that exist in NFSv4, such as kernel panic during system startup while mounting the NFSv4 share.

The NFS server can be configured on just about any Linux distribution and then connected to a Proxmox cluster. An NFS share is nothing but a mount point on the NFS server, which is read by the Proxmox NFS plugin. We can also use FreeNAS to serve as the NFS server, and thus take advantage of the FreeNAS features and GUI to easily monitor the shared storage. Due to the simplicity of the NFS configuration, this is probably the most widely used storage option in the virtualization world. Almost all the network admins have used the NFS server at least once in their career.

In the following screenshot, we are connecting an NFS storage named **nfs-01** from the remote server, 172.16.0.170:

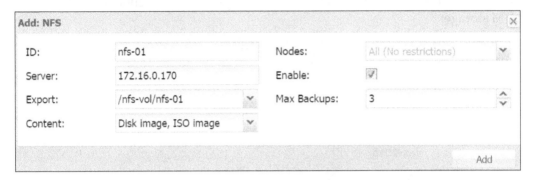

After entering the IP address of the remote server, the Export drop-down menu will scan the remote server for all the NFS shares and display them in the list. In our example, the mount point found by the dialog box is in **/nfs-vol/nfs-01**.

# ZFS

ZFS was originally developed by Sun Microsystems. The ZFS storage is a combination of filesystem and LVM, providing high-capacity storage with important features, such as data protection, data compression, self-healing, and snapshots. ZFS has built-in software defined Raid, which makes the use of a hardware-based Raid unnecessary. A disk array with ZFS Raid can be migrated to a completely different node, and then entirely imported without rebuilding the entire array. We can only store the .raw format virtual disk images on the ZFS storage. For more details on ZFS, refer to `http://en.wikipedia.org/wiki/ZFS`.

As of Proxmox VE 4.1, a ZFS storage plugin is included, which leverages the use of ZFS natively in Proxmox cluster nodes. A ZFS pool supports the following Raid types:

- **RAID-0 pool**: Requires minimum one disk
- **RAID-1 pool**: Requires minimum two disks
- **RAID-10 pool**: Requires minimum four disks
- **RAIDZ-1 pool**: Requires minimum three disks
- **RAIDZ-2 pool**: Requires minimum four disks

ZFS uses pools to define storage. Pools can only be created through a CLI. As of Proxmox VE 4.1, there are no ZFS management options in the GUI. All ZFS creation and management must be done through the CLI. Once the pools are created, they can be attached to Proxmox through the Proxmox GUI. In our example, we are going to create a RAID1 mirrored pool named zfspool1 and connect it to Proxmox. The command used to create the ZFS pool is as follows:

```
# zpool create <pool_name> <raid_type> <dev1_name> <dev2_name> ...
```

So, for our example pool, the command will appear as follows:

```
# zpool create zfspool1 mirror /dev/vdd /dev/vde
```

The following options are available for Raid types:

| Raid type | Option string to use |
|-----------|---------------------|
| RAID0 | No string |
| RAID 1 | Mirror |
| RAIDZ-1 | raidz1 |
| RAIDZ-2 | raidz2 |

To verify that the pool is created, run the following command:

```
# zpool list
```

The following screenshot shows the ZFS pool list as it appears for our example ZFS node:

```
NAME        SIZE  ALLOC   FREE  EXPANDSZ   FRAG   CAP  DEDUP  HEALTH  ALTROOT
zfspool1   9.94G    64K  9.94G         -     0%    0%  1.00x  ONLINE  -
```

We can use the pool directly, or we can create a dataset inside the pool and connect the dataset separately to Proxmox as an individual storage. The advantage of this is to isolate the different types of stored data in each dataset. For example, if we create a dataset to store VM images and another dataset to store backup files, we can turn on the compression for the VM image dataset to compress the disk image files while keeping the compression off backup storing dataset since the backup files are already compressed, thus saving valuable resources. Each ZFS dataset can be configured individually with its own set of configuration options. If we compare a zpool with a directory, the datasets are like subdirectories inside the main directory. The following command is used to create a dataset inside a ZFS pool:

```
#zfs create <zpool_name>/<zfs_dataset_name>
```

Datasets must be mounted in a directory before they can be used. By default, a new `zfs` pool or dataset gets mounted under the root directory. The following command will set a new mount point for a dataset:

```
# zfs set mountpoint=/mnt/zfs-vm zfspool1/zfs-vm
```

To enable compression for the dataset, we can run the following command:

```
# zfs set compression=on zfspool1/zfs-vm
```

The ZFS pool will only function locally from the node where the pool is created. Other nodes in the Proxmox cluster will not be able to share the storage. By mounting a ZFS pool locally and creating the NFS share, it is possible to share the ZFS pool between all the Proxmox nodes. We can mount a zfs dataset in a directory and use that directory to configure the Proxmox node as the NFS server.

The process of mounting and sharing needs to be done through a CLI only. From the Proxmox GUI, we can only attach the NFS share with the underlying ZFS pool. In order to serve the NFS share, we need to install the NFS server in the Proxmox node using the following command:

```
# apt-get install nfs-kernel-server
```

Enter the following line of code in `/etc/exports`:

```
/mnt/zfs/    172.16.0.71/24(rw,nohide,async,no_root_squash)
```

Start the NFS service using the following command:

```
# service nfs-kernel-server start
```

To share the NFS enabled ZFS pool through the Proxmox GUI, we can simply follow the steps laid out for the NFS storage in the previous section. To add a ZFS pool or dataset to the Proxmox cluster through the GUI, we need to log in to the GUI of the node where the ZFS pool is created. In our two node example cluster, we have the ZFS pools in node #1, so we will have to access the GUI for that node. Otherwise, the ZFS pools or datasets cannot be added from different node GUIs. We can find the ZFS storage plugin option by navigating to the **Datacenter** | **Storage** | **Add** menu. Click on the ZFS plugin to open the dialog box. The following screenshot shows the ZFS storage dialog box with the `zfs` pool example and dataset in the drop-down menu:

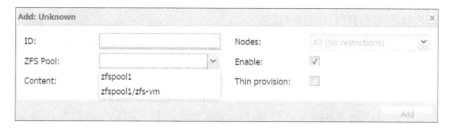

By combining the ZFS pool with an NFS share, we can create shared storage with complete ZFS features, thus creating flexible shared storage to be used with all the Proxmox nodes in the cluster. Using this technique, we can create a backup storage node, which is also manageable through the Proxmox GUI. This way, during a node crisis, we can also migrate VMs to the backup nodes temporarily. The previous steps are applicable to any Linux distribution and not just a Proxmox node. For example, we can set up a ZFS plus NFS server using Ubuntu or CentOS Linux to store virtual disk images or templates. If you are using FreeNAS or a similar storage system, then the steps for ZFS laid out in this section are not required. The entire process of ZFS creation is completed using the FreeNAS GUI.

# Ceph RBD

**Rados Block Device** storage (**RBD**) is provided by the Ceph distributed storage system. It is the most complex storage system, which requires multiple nodes to be set up. By design, Ceph is a distributed storage system and can be spanned over several dozen nodes. The RBD storage can only store raw image formats. To expand a Ceph cluster, simply add a hard drive or a node and let Ceph know about the new addition. Ceph will automatically rebalance data to accommodate the new hard drive or node. Ceph can be scaled to several petabytes or more. Ceph also allows multiple pool creations for different disk drives. For example, we can store database servers' VM images on an SSD-driven pool and backup server images on a slower spinning drive pool. Ceph is the recommended storage system for medium to large cluster environments due to its resiliency against data loss and the simplicity of storage expandability.

As of Proxmox VE Version 4.1, the Ceph server has been integrated into Proxmox to coexist on the same node. The ability to manage Ceph clusters through the Proxmox GUI has also been added. Later in this chapter, we will learn how to create a Ceph cluster and integrate it with Proxmox. Ceph is a truly enterprise storage solution with a learning curve. Once the mechanics of Ceph is understood, it is also one of the easiest to maintain. To know more about Ceph storage, refer to http://ceph.com/docs/master/start/intro/.

# The Ceph components

Before we dive in, let's take a look at some key components that make up a
Ceph cluster.

## A physical node

A physical node is the actual server hardware that holds OSDs, monitors, and MDSs.

## Maps

Maps in Ceph hold information, such as a list of participating nodes in a cluster
and their locations, data paths, and a list of OSDs with certain data chunks. There
are several maps in a Ceph cluster, such as a cluster map, **Object Storage Daemon
(OSD)** map for a list of OSDs, monitor map for known monitor nodes, **Placement
Group (PG)** map for the location of objects or data chunks, and a CRUSH map to
determine how to store and retrieve data by computing the data storage location.

## A cluster map

A cluster map is a map of devices and buckets that comprise a Ceph cluster. Ceph
uses a bucket hierarchy to define nodes or node locations, such as a room, rack, shelf,
host, and so on. For example, let's say there are four disk drives used as four OSDs in
the following bucket hierarchy:

```
Bucket datacenter = dc01
|
Bucket room = 101
|
Bucket rack = 22
|
Bucket host = ceph-node-1
|
Bucket osd = osd.1, osd.2, osd.3, osd.4
```

In the preceding example, we can see that osd.1 to osd.4 are in the node
ceph-node-1, which is in rack number 22, which is in room number 101, which
is in datacenter dc01. If osd.3 fails, and there is an on-site technician, then an
administrator can quickly give the technician the previous bucket hierarchy to
identify the exact disk drive location to replace it. There can be several hundreds
of OSDs in a cluster. A cluster map helps you pinpoint a single host or disk drive
using the bucket hierarchy.

# A CRUSH Map

**Controlled Replication Under Scalable Hashing (CRUSH)** is an algorithm used in Ceph to store and retrieve data by computing data storage locations within the cluster. It does so by providing a per-device weight value to distribute data objects among storage devices. The value is auto assigned based on the actual size of the disk drive being used. For example, a 2 TB disk drive may have an approximate weight of 1.81. The drive will keep writing data until it reaches this weight. By design, CRUSH distributes data evenly among weighted devices to maintain a balanced utilization of storage and device bandwidth resources. A CRUSH map can be customized by a user to fit any cluster environment of any size. For more details on CRUSH maps, refer to `http://ceph.com/docs/master/rados/operations/crush-map/`.

# Monitor

A Ceph Monitor or MON is a cluster monitor deamon node that holds the OSD map, Placement Group (PG) map, CRUSH map, and Monitor map. Monitors can be set up on the same server node with OSDs or on a fully separated machine. For a stable Ceph cluster, setting up separate nodes with Monitors are highly recommended. Since Monitors only keep track of everything that happens within the cluster and not the actual read/write of cluster data, the Monitor node can be very underpowered, and thus less expansive. To achieve a healthy status of the Ceph cluster, a minimum of three monitors are needed to be set up. A healthy status is when every status in the cluster is OK, without any warnings or errors. Note that with the recent integration of Ceph with Proxmox, the same Proxmox node can be used as a Monitor. Starting from Proxmox 3.2, it is possible to set up Ceph monitors on the same Proxmox node, thus eliminating the need to use a separate node for Monitors. Monitors can also be managed from the Proxmox GUI. For details on Ceph Monitors, visit `http://ceph.com/docs/master/man/8/ceph-mon/`.

# OSD

**Object Storage Daemon (OSD)** is the actual storage media or partition within media, such as HDD or SSD that store the actual cluster data. OSDs are responsible for all the data replication, recovery, and rebalancing. Each OSD provides the monitoring information for Ceph Monitors to check for heartbeats. A Ceph cluster requires a minimum of two Object Storage Daemons to be in the `active + clean` state. The Ceph cluster provides feedback for the cluster status at all times. An active + clean state expresses an error or warning-free cluster. Refer to the section Placement Group for other states a Ceph cluster can achieve section. As of Proxmox Version 3.2, OSDs can be managed through the Proxmox GUI..

# OSD Journal

In Ceph, any I/O writes are first written to a Journal before they are transferred to the actual OSD. Journals are simply smaller partitions that accept smaller data at a time while the backend OSDs catch up with the writings. By putting Journals on faster access disk drives, such as SSDs, we can increase a Ceph operation significantly since user data is written to a Journal at a higher speed while the Journal sends short bursts of data to OSDs, giving them time to catch up. Journals for multiple OSDs can be stored in one SSD per node. Or, OSDs can be divided into multiple SSDs. For a small cluster of up to eight OSDs per node, using an SSD improves performance. However, while working with a larger cluster with a higher number of OSDs per node, collocating the Journal with the same OSDs increases performance instead of using SSDs. The combined write speed of all the OSDs together outperforms the speed of one or two SSDs as a Journal.

The important thing to remember about a Journal is that the loss of a Journal partition causes OSD data loss. For this reason, it is highly recommended that you use an enterprise grade SSD device. The Intel DC3700 SSD is well-known to work fine as a Ceph Journal SSD device.

# MDS

**Meta Data Server** (**MDS**) stores meta information for the Ceph filesystem of CephFS. The Ceph block and object storage do not use MDS. So, in a cluster if Block and Object are the only types that are going to be used, it will not be necessary to set up an MDS server. Like Monitors, MDS needs to be set up on a different machine of its own to achieve high performance. As of Proxmox Version 3.2, MDS cannot be managed or created from the Proxmox GUI.

Ceph filesystem is not fully standardized yet and is still in the development phase. It should not be used to store mission critical data. It is mostly stable, but unforeseen bugs may still cause major issues, such as data loss. Note that there have not been many reports of mass data loss due to an unstable CephFS. Two of the virtual machines used to write this book have been running for more than 11 months without any issues.

There should be two MDS nodes in a cluster to provide redundancy because the loss of an MDS node will cause the loss of data on CephFS and will render it inaccessible. Two MDS nodes will act as active-passive when one node failure is taken over by another node and vice versa. To learn about MDS and CephFS, visit `http://ceph.com/docs/master/cephfs/`.

# Placement Group

The main function of Placement Group or PG is to combine several objects into a group, and then map the group to several OSDs. A per-group mechanism is much more efficient than a per-object mechanism since the former uses fewer resources. When data is retrieved, it is far more efficient to call a group than call an individual object in a group. The following diagram shows how PGs are related to OSDs:

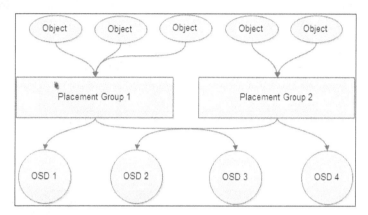

For better efficiency, we recommend a total of 50 to 100 PGs per OSD for all pools. Each PG will consume some resources of the node, such as CPUs and memory. A balance distribution of Placement Group ensures that all the nodes and OSDs in the nodes are not out of memory or that the CPU does not face overload issues. A simple formula to follow while allocating PG for a pool is as follows:

```
Total PGs = (OSD x 100) / Number of Replicas
```

The result of the total PG should be rounded up to the nearest power of two. In a Ceph cluster with 3 nodes (replicas) and 24 OSDs, the total PG count should be as follows:

```
Total PGs = (24 x 100) / 3 = 800
```

If we divide 800 by 24, which is the total number of OSDs, then we get 33.33. This is the number of PGs per replica per OSD. Since we have three replicas, we multiply 33.33 by 4 and get 99.99. This is the total number of PGs per OSD in the previous example. The formula will always calculate the PGs per replica. For a three-replica setup, each PG is written thrice, and thus, we multiplied the PG of 33.33 by 3 to get the total number of PGs per OSD.

Let's take a look at another example to calculate PG. The following setup has 150 OSDs, 3 Ceph nodes, and 2 replicas:

```
Total PGs = (150 x 100) / 2 = 7500
```

If we divide 7,500 by 150, the total number of OSDs that we get is 50. Since we have two replicas, we multiply 50 by 2 and get 100. So, each OSD in this cluster can store 100 PGs. In both the examples, our total PG per OSD was within 50-100 recommended range. Always round up the PG value to remove any decimal point.

To balance the available hardware resources, it is necessary to assign the right number of PGs. The PG number will vary depending on the number of OSDs in a cluster. The following table shows a PG suggestion made by Ceph developers:

| Number of OSDs | Number of PGs |
|---|---|
| Fewer than 5 OSDs | 128 |
| Between 5 – 10 OSDs | 512 |
| Between 10 – 50 OSDs | 1024 |

Selecting the proper number of PGs is crucial since each PG will consume the node resources. Too many PGs for the wrong number of OSDs will actually penalize the resource usage of an OSD node, while very few assigned PGs in a large cluster will put data at risk. A rule of thumb is to start with the lowest number of PGs possible, and then increase them as the number of OSDs increases. For details on Placement Group, visit http://ceph.com/docs/master/rados/operations/placement-groups/.

There's a great PG calculator created by Ceph developers to calculate the recommended number of PGs for various sizes of a Ceph cluster at http://ceph.com/pgcalc/.

## Pools

Pools are like logical partitions where Ceph stores data. When we set a PG or the number of replicas, we actually set them for each pool. When creating a Ceph cluster, three pools are created by default: data, metadata, and RBD. Data and metadata pools are used by the Ceph cluster, while the pool RBD is available to store the actual user data. PGs are set on a per-pool basis. The formula that we discussed earlier in the Placement Group section calculates the PGs required for one pool. So, when creating multiple pools, it is important to modify the formula a bit so that the total PG stays within 50-100 per OSD.

For instance, in the example of 150 OSDs, 3 Ceph nodes, and 2 replicas, our PG was 7,500 for a pool. This gave us 50 PGs per OSD. If we had three pools in that setup and each pool had 7,500 PGs, then the total number of PGs would have been 150 per OSD. In order to balance the PGs across the cluster, we can divide 7,500 by 3 for 3 pools and set a PG of 2,500 for each pool. This gives us 2500/150 OSDs = 16 PGs per pool per OSD or 16 x 3 pools = 48 total PGs per OSD. Since we have two replicas in this setup, the final total PGs per OSD will be 48 x 2 replicas = 96 PGs. This is within the recommended 50-100 range of PGs per OSD.

## The Ceph components summary

If we want to understand the relationship between all the Ceph components we have seen so far, we can think of it this way: each Pool comprises multiple PGs. Each PG comprises multiple OSDs. An OSD map keeps track of the number of OSDs in the cluster and in the nodes they are in. The MON map keeps track of the number of Monitors in a cluster to form a quorum and maintains a master copy of the cluster map. A CRUSH map dictates how much data needs to be written to an OSD and how to write or read it. These are the building blocks of a Ceph cluster.

# Virtual Ceph for training

It is possible to set up an entire Ceph cluster in a virtual environment. But this cluster should only be used for training and learning purposes. If you are learning Ceph for the first time and do not want to invest in the physical hardware, then a virtualized Ceph platform is certainly possible. This will eliminate the need to set up the physical hardware to set up Ceph nodes.

# Ceph cluster

The following diagram is a basic representation of Proxmox and the Ceph cluster. Note that both the clusters are on a separate subnet on separate switches:

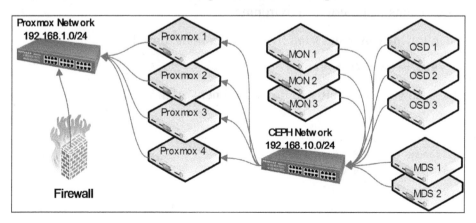

A Ceph cluster should be set up with a separate subnet on a separate switch to keep it isolated from the Proxmox public subnet. The advantage of this practice is to keep Ceph's internal traffic isolated so that it does not interfere with the traffic of the running virtual machines. On a healthy Ceph cluster with the active+clean state, this is not a big issue. However, when Ceph goes into self-healing mode due to an OSD or a node failure, it rebalances itself by moving PGs around, which causes very high bandwidth consumption. On a bad day, separating two clusters ensures that the cluster does not slow down significantly due to the shortage of the network bandwidth.

This also provides added security since the Ceph cluster network is completely hidden from any public access using a separate switch. In our previous example, we have three MONs, two MDSs, and three OSD nodes connected to a dedicated switch used only for the Ceph cluster. The Proxmox cluster connects to the Ceph cluster by creating a storage connection through the Proxmox GUI.

# Ceph on Proxmox

As of Proxmox Version 4.1, it is now possible to install Ceph on the same Proxmox node, thus reducing the number of separate Ceph nodes needed, such as the admin node, Monitor node, or OSD node. Proxmox also provides the GUI features that we can use to view the Ceph cluster and manage OSDs, MONs, pools, and so on. In this section, we will see how to install Ceph on the Proxmox node. As of Version 4.1, MDS server and CRUSH Map management is not possible from the Proxmox GUI.

# Preparing the Proxmox node for Ceph

Since we are installing Ceph on the same Proxmox node, we will set up the network interfaces for a separate network for Ceph traffic only. We will set up three Proxmox nodes: pmxvm01, pmxvm02, and pmxvm03 with Ceph. On all three nodes, we will add the following interfaces section in /c/network/interfaces. You can also use any IP address that suits your network environment.

Run the following command from the Proxmox node, pmxvm01:

```
# nano /etc/network/interfaces
```

Enter the following section to add the second network:

```
auto eth2
iface eth2 inet static
    address 192.168.10.1
    netmask 255.255.255.0
```

Run the following command to make the new interface active:

```
# ifup eth2
```

Follow the previous steps and add additional network interfaces with the IP addresses 192.168.10.2 and 192.168.10.3, consecutively.

# Installing Ceph

Proxmox added a small command-line utility called pveceph to perform various Ceph-related tasks. Currently, pveceph can perform the following tasks through the command line:

| Command | Task Performed |
|---|---|
| pveceph install | Installs Ceph on the Proxmox node. |
| pveceph createmon | Creates Ceph Monitors and must be run from the node to become a Monitor. |
| pveceph createpool <name> | Creates a new pool. It can be used from any node. |
| pveceph destroymon <mon_id> | Removes a Monitor. |
| pveceph destroypool <name> | Removes a Ceph pool. |
| pveceph init --network <x.x.x.0/x> | Creates the initial Ceph configuration file based on the network CIDR used. |
| pveceph start <service> | Starts Ceph daemon services, such as MON, OSD, and MDS. |
| pveceph stop <service> | Stops Ceph daemon services, such as MON, OSD, and MDS. |
| pveceph status | Shows the cluster, Monitor, MDS server, OSD status, and cluster ID. |
| pveceph createosd </dev/X> | Creates OSD daemons. |
| pvecph destroyosd <osdid> | Removes OSD daemons. |
| pveceph purge | Removes Ceph and all Ceph-related data from the node the command is running from. |

Ceph must be installed and at least one Monitor must be created using a command line initially before managing it through the Proxmox GUI. We can perform the following steps to install Ceph on the Proxmox nodes and create the first Monitor (MON):

1. Run the following command to install Ceph on all the Proxmox nodes, which will be part of the Ceph cluster:

   ```
   # pveceph install -version hammer
   ```

Note that the latest version of Ceph at the time of writing this book is codenamed Infernalis. However, the Ceph version, Hammer, has been used for the writing of this book as it is fully supported by Proxmox, as of Proxmox 4.1. Simply change the codename in the command to install the latest Ceph release when they become available in Proxmox.

2. Run the following command to create an initial Ceph configuration file on the first Proxmox node. We only need to run this command once from one node only:

```
# pveceph init --network 192.168.10.0/24
```

3. After running the command, Proxmox will create a Ceph configuration file in /etc/pve/ceph.conf. It also creates a symlink of the configuration file in /etc/ceph/ceph.conf. This way, any custom changes made to the Ceph configuration file get replicated across all Proxmox nodes.

After a successful initial configuration, you will see a warning message, as follows:

```
libust[23466/23466]: Warning: HOME environment variable not set. Disabling LTTng-UST per-user tracing. (in setup_local_apps() at lttng-ust-comm.c:375)
```

This is normal behavior due to a bug in Ceph. In later releases, this warning will be fixed. You will also see this warning during day-to-day Ceph operations.

Run the following command to create the first Ceph Monitor on the same node that we just created in the initial configuration file:

```
# pveceph createmon
```

After performing these steps, we can proceed with the Proxmox GUI to further create MONs, OSDs, or Pools. All the Ceph options can be obtained by navigating to the **Datacenter | Node | Ceph** tab. The following screenshot shows our example Ceph cluster as seen through the Proxmox GUI after the initial configuration:

| Node 'pm4-1' | | | | | | | |
|---|---|---|---|---|---|---|---|
| Search | Summary | Services | Network | DNS | Time | Syslog | Task History |

| | |
|---|---|
| health | HEALTH_ERR 64 pgs stuck inactive; 64 pgs stuck unclean; no osds; |
| quorum | Yes {1 0} |
| cluster | d3df5470-271a-428b-b295-4f82efa96644 |
| monmap | e2: 2 mons at 1=172.16.0.171:6789/0,0=172.16.0.172:6789/0, |
| osdmap | e1: 0 osds: 0 up, 0 in |
| pgmap | v2: 64 pgs: 64 creating; 0 data, 0 used, 0 avail |

It is perfectly normal for the Ceph cluster to show **pgs stuck** inactive and unclean as we have not added any OSDs.

# Creating MONs from Proxmox GUI

To view and create Monitors from the Proxmox GUI, navigate to **Datacenter | pmxvm01 | Ceph | Monitor**. Click on **Create** to open the Monitor creation dialog box. Select a Proxmox node from the drop-down list, as shown in the following screenshot, and then click on the **Create** button to initiate the Monitor creation:

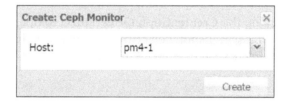

The following screenshot shows the Ceph Monitor interface with two MONs created for our example Ceph cluster:

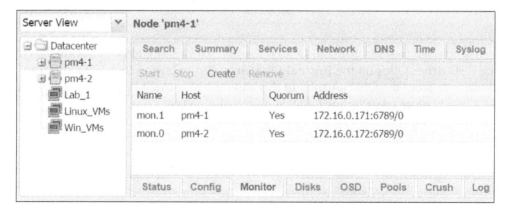

# Creating OSD from Proxmox GUI

To view the installed disk drives in the node and create OSDs from the Proxmox GUI, navigate to **Datacenter** | **pm4-1** | **Ceph** | **Disk**. Select an available disk drive to create an OSD. The following screenshot shows two available disk drives, /dev/vdb and /dev/vdc, to create OSDs in one of the example Proxmox node:

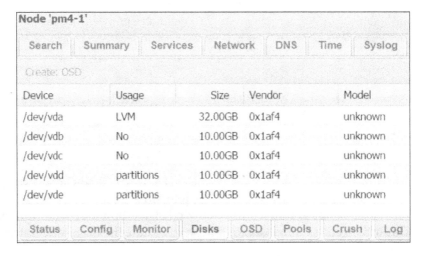

To create an OSD, click on the **Create: Ceph OSD** button to open a dialog box, as shown in the following screenshot. Select an available disk drive from the drop-down list, and then click on the Create button:

There is no need to select **Journal Disk** if the Journal is going to be collocated on the same OSD drive. Click on the **Journal Disk** drop-down button to select a different disk drive to store the OSD journal. In this case, the SSD must be partitioned through the CLI first before creating the OSD using this dialog box.

The following screenshot shows the Ceph Status page after creating two OSDs in one of the nodes:

| Node 'pm4-1' | | | | | | | | |
|---|---|---|---|---|---|---|---|---|
| Search | Summary | Services | Network | DNS | Time | Syslog | Task History | Firewall |
| health | | HEALTH_WARN 64 pgs degraded; 64 pgs stuck unclean; 64 pgs undersized; | | | | | | |
| quorum | | Yes {1 0} | | | | | | |
| cluster | | d3df5470-271a-428b-b295-4f82efa96644 | | | | | | |
| monmap | | e2: 2 mons at 1=172.16.0.171:6789/0,0=172.16.0.172:6789/0, | | | | | | |
| osdmap | | e8: 2 osds: 2 up, 2 in | | | | | | |
| pgmap | | v11: 64 pgs: 64 active+undersized+degraded; 0 data, 66MB used, 9.91GB avail | | | | | | |

Note that even after adding two OSDs in the node, our Ceph cluster is still degraded and unclean. This is because we only created OSDs in one node. By default, Ceph will try to create three replicas and we only have two nodes. So, we are going to add two more OSDs in the second node by following the previous steps and changing the replica size to 2 so that our example cluster can achieve a healthy status. The following command will change the replica of the default Ceph pool rbd from 3 to 2:

```
# ceph osd pool set rbd size 2
```

> Although the Ceph cluster can be managed from the Proxmox GUI, in order to perform advanced tasks, we need to use the CLI. Ceph comes loaded with quite a few commands for various tasks. It is beyond the scope of this book to list all Ceph commands. But a short list of commands used to perform the most common tasks is included later in this chapter.

After we added OSDs to the second node and changed the replica to 2 for the default Ceph pool, our example cluster achieved a healthy status, as shown in the following screenshot:

| Node 'pm4-2' | | | | | | | |
|---|---|---|---|---|---|---|---|
| Search | Summary | Services | Network | DNS | Time | Syslog | Task History |
| health | | HEALTH_OK | | | | | |
| quorum | | Yes {1 0} | | | | | |
| cluster | | d3df5470-271a-428b-b295-4f82efa96644 | | | | | |
| monmap | | e2: 2 mons at 1=172.16.0.171:6789/0,0=172.16.0.172:6789/0, | | | | | |
| osdmap | | e67: 4 osds: 4 up, 4 in | | | | | |
| pgmap | | v138: 64 pgs: 64 active+clean; 0 data, 137MB used, 179.77GB avail | | | | | |

By default, Proxmox created OSDs with the xfs partition. However, sometimes, it is necessary to create OSDs with different partition types due to requirements or performance improvements. As of Proxmox 4.1, we can adjust the partition type during the OSD creation through the GUI. Enter the following command format using the CLI to create OSDs with different partition types:

```
# pveceph createosd -fstype ext4 /dev/sdX
```

## Creating a new Ceph Pool using Proxmox GUI

To create a new pool using the Proxmox GUI, go to **Datacenter** | **<node>** | **Ceph** | **Pools**. The pool interface shows information about existing pools, such as the name, replica number, pg number, and per-pool percentage used. To create a new pool, click on the Create button to open the pool creation dialog box, as shown in the following screenshot. Enter a name for the pool in the Name field, number of replicas in Size, leave Min. Size at 1, and enter the proper pg number based on the pg calculation formula that we have already covered in the earlier section. Click on OK to start the pool's creation:

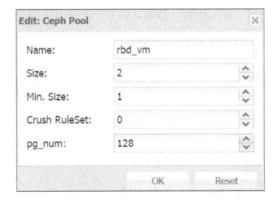

## Connecting RBD to Proxmox

We can connect Ceph storage to the cluster using the Proxmox GUI. However, there is one step that needs to be completed before Proxmox can successfully read the Ceph storage. Ceph uses authentication for its function. Authentication occurs based on keyring which are created at the time of Ceph cluster creation. For each Ceph storage, we need to connect to Proxmox, and we need to copy the main Ceph admin keyring to the Proxmox directory. The keyring that we need to copy is located in:

```
/etc/pve/ceph.client.admin.keyring.
```

This keyring needs to be copied to the following location and in the following format:

```
/etc/pve/ceph/<storage_id>.keyring
```

For example, we are going to create RBD storage named rbd-vm-01. So, we need to copy the keyring, as shown in the following command:

```
# cp /etc/pve/priv/ceph.client.admin.keyring /etc/pve/priv/ceph/rbd-vm-01.keyring
```

We can find the Ceph RBD storage plugin option by navigating to **Datacenter | Storage | Add**. Click on the **RBD** storage plugin to open the dialog box and add the required information, as shown in the following screenshot:

In the preceding screenshot, we are adding RBD storage named **rbd-vm-01** that will store virtual disk images in the Ceph pool named **rbd_vm,** which we created in the earlier section. Enter the IP address of the Ceph MON nodes separated by a semicolon in the **Monitor Host** textbox. There is no need to change the user name as the admin is the default user of the Ceph operation. As of Proxmox VE 4.1, we can now use the Ceph RBD storage to store LXC containers. However, it will only work if we select the **KRBD** option in the dialog box. It is possible to store both the LVM and LXC images on a single KRBD-enabled RBD storage; but for maximum performance and isolation, it is highly recommend that you use two separate Ceph pools for KVM and LXC virtual machine disk images with the KRBD option enabled for the LXC container pool.

The following screenshot shows the RBD storage status from the Proxmox GUI:

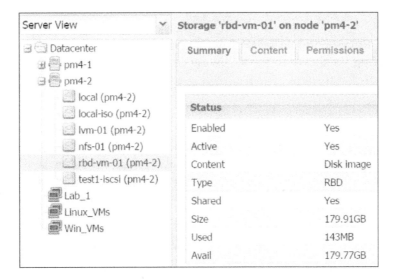

# Ceph command list

The following table shows some of the common Ceph commands used in a cluster:

| | |
|---|---|
| `#ceph -s` | Displays the Ceph cluster status. |
| `#ceph -w` | Displays the Ceph cluster running log. |
| `#ceph health detail` | Displays a detailed error if there are any. |
| `#ceph osd tree` | Displays a list of all OSDs categorized by nodes. |
| `#ceph set osd noout`<br>`#ceph set osd nodown` | Prevents any OSDs from getting marked out and down, so Ceph does not start rebalancing. It is necessary during maintenance when the node requires a reboot due to updates. This commands prevents |
| `#ceph unset osd noout`<br>`#ceph unset osd nodown` | Must be run after the maintenance is over in order to resume normal operation. |
| `#ceph daemon osd.X config show`<br>`  grep <item_name>`<br>`Ex: #ceph daemon osd.2 config`<br>`show  grep threads` | Displays runtime values of Ceph. For example, we can run this command to display all thread-related items in a Ceph cluster. |

| | |
|---|---|
| `#ceph tell osd.* injectargs '<item_name> <value>'`<br>`Ex: #ceph tell osd.* injectargs '—osd-op-threads 8'` | Injects values into items during runtime without restarting any daemons. It is helpful to play around with different values to find optimum numbers. When satisfied, the changes must be entered in `/etc/pve/ceph.conf` or else they will get reset during the node reboot or OSD daemon restart. |
| `#ceph osd lspools` | Lists Pools. |
| `#ceph osd pool create <name> <pg> <pgs>` | Creates a Pool. |
| `#ceph osd pool delete <name> [<name> --yes-i-really-really-mean-it]` | Deletes a Pool. |
| `#ceph osd pool get <name> pg_num` | Gets the number of PGs of a pool. |
| `#ceph osd set pool <pool_name> size <value>` | Changes the replica values of a pool. |

# GlusterFS

GlusterFS is a powerful, distributed filesystem, which can be scaled to several Petabytes under a single mount point. Gluster is a fairly new addition to Proxmox that allows GlusterFS users to take full advantage of the Proxmox cluster. GlusterFS uses the Stripe, Replicate, or Distribute mode to store files. Although the Distribute mode offers the option of scalability, note that in the Stripe mode when a GlusterFS node goes down, all the files in that server become inaccessible. This means that if a particular file is saved by the GlusterFS translator in that server, only that node holds the entire data of that file. Even though all the other nodes are operational, that particular file will no longer be available. GlusterFS can be scaled up to petabytes inside a single mount. The GlusterFS storage can be set up with just two nodes and supports NFS, thus allowing you to store any image file format. To know more about GlusterFS, visit `http://www.gluster.org/community/documentation/index.php/GlusterFS_Concepts`.

We can install Gluster on the same Proxmox node or on a remote node using any Linux distribution to create shared storage. Gluster is a great option for a two node, stable storage system, such as DRBD. The biggest difference is that it can be scaled out to increase the total storage space. For a lower budget virtual environment with redundancy requirements, Gluster can be an excellent option. In a two node Gluster setup, both the nodes sync with each other, and when one node becomes unavailable, the other node simply takes over. The installation of Gluster is rather complex. To learn more about how to set up a GlusterFS cluster, refer to `http://gluster.readthedocs.org/en/latest/Quick-Start-Guide/Quickstart/`.

In this section, we will see how to connect a GlusterFS cluster to Proxmox using the Gluster plugin. We can find the plugin option by navigating to **Datacenter | Storage | Add**. Click on the **GlusterFS** plugin to open the storage creation dialog box, as shown in the following screenshot:

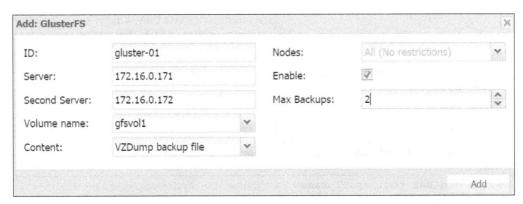

The following table shows the type of information needed and used values for our example to attach GlusterFS:

| Items | Type of values | Example values |
|---|---|---|
| ID | New name of storage. | gluster |
| Server | IP address of the first gluster node. | 172.16.0.171 |
| Second Server | IP address of the second gluster node. | 172.16.0.172 |
| Volume name | Drop-down menu to select available volumes on the Gluster node. | gfsvol11 |
| Content | Selects the type of files to be stored. | VZDump backup file |
| Nodes | Selects nodes that can access the storage. | All |
| Enable | Enables or disables the storage. | Enabled |
| Max Backups | Maximum number of recent backup files can be stored. Older backups will be deleted automatically during the backup process. | 2 |

Since Gluster does not have the built-in software defined RAID option, each Gluster node will require some form of RAIDs for the drive redundancy per node. Like NFS on top of ZFS that we learned earlier in this chapter, we can also put Gluster on top of ZFS and provide drive redundancy that way. Note that this will create some overhead since resources will be consumed by ZFS.

# Noncommercial and commercial storage options

We have discussed which virtual machine image formats and storage types are supported by Proxmox. To better acquaint ourselves for test or practice labs, we are now going to take a look at what noncommercial and commercial options we have out there in order to set up a storage system for the Proxmox-clustered environment. By noncommercial, I mean they are free without any primary features missing and without any trial limits.

These noncommercial options will allow you to set up a fully functional shared storage system with some hard work. Commercial versions usually come with full support from the provider company, and in some cases, the ongoing Service Level Agreement (SLA) contract. The following list is by no means a complete one, but a guideline to guide you in the direction where you need to plan and implement a Proxmox cluster environment. Each of these products can provide everything you need to set up shared storage:

| Noncommercial | | Commercial | |
|---|---|---|---|
| Solaris plus napp-IT | `www.napp-it.org` | Nexenta | `www.nexenta.com` |
| FreeNAS | `www.freenas.org` | FalconStor | `www.falconstor.com` |
| GlusterFS | `www.gluster.org` | EMC2 | `www.emc.com` |
| CEPH | `www.ceph.com` | Yottabyte | `www.yottabyte.com` |
| | | Open-E DSS | `www.open-e.com` |
| | | NetApp | `www.netapp.com` |

A question often asked is *can I set up a Proxmox production cluster environment using only noncommercial solutions?* The short answer is, *YES!*

It is indeed possible to create an entire complex Proxmox cluster using only noncommercial storage solutions. However, you have to be prepared for the unexpected and spend a significant amount of time learning the system. Commercial solutions aside, just studying a system will give an administrator an advantage when unforeseen issues arise. The main difference between these noncommercial and commercial solutions is the company support behind it. Typically, noncommercial solutions only have community-driven support through forums and message boards. Commercial offerings come with technical support with the response time varying from anything between immediate response up to 24 hours.

The trade-off of noncommercial open source solutions is the money that is saved, which usually gets exchanged with the time spent on research and mistakes.

# Summary

In this chapter, we took a look at the storage options that are supported by Proxmox and their advantages and disadvantages. We also saw the types of virtual image files that can be used with Proxmox and when to use them. We learned how to configure different storage options using NFS, ZFS, RBD, and Gluster as storage backends. Storage is an important component for Proxmox clustering because this is where virtual machines are created and they operate from. A properly implemented storage system is very critical to make any cluster a successful one. With proper planning of different storage requirements and choosing the right format and option, a lot of hassle and frustration can be minimized later on.

In the next chapter, we will see how to create and manage KVM-based virtual machines. We will also examine virtual machine configuration files and learn some advanced configuration options.

# 5
# KVM Virtual Machines

So far, we have familiarized ourselves with the Proxmox graphical user interface, configuration files, and directory structure. We have also learned about the different types of storage supported by Proxmox and how to integrate them in the cluster. In this chapter, we are going to take it one step further by looking at **Kernel-based Virtual Machine** (**KVM**) and all that it has to offer. We are going to cover the following topics:

- Exploring KVM
- Creating a KVM
- Configuring a KVM
- Migrating a KVM
- Nested virtual environment
- Proxmox backup/restore system
- Virtual machine snapshots

## Exploring a KVM

As the name implies, a KVM adds the hypervisor ability to a Linux kernel. KVM allows you to create fully isolated virtual machines while not being dependent on the host kernel. The isolation is created by emulating several pieces of hardware, such as CPU, RAM, Sound/Video/Network card, PCI bridges, and Keyboard/Mouse input devices. Since KVM is not dependent on the host kernel, it is able to virtualize a wide range of operating systems, such as Linux, BSD, Windows, OS X, and so on. One of the main differences between KVM and container-based virtual machines is that the allocated resources for KVM is isolated from each other and the host.

Thus, the density of the number of KVM VMs in a node is much lower than containers. KVM are the only choice for non-Linux operating systems and for purpose-built operating systems based on Linux, such as ClearOS, FreeNAS, Zentyal, and so on. For more information on KVM, refer to `https://en.wikipedia.org/wiki/Kernel-based_Virtual_Machine`.

# Creating a KVM

In Proxmox, we can create a KVM VM in the following two ways:

- From scratch
- From a template

# Creating a VM from scratch

This process walks you through the entire virtual machine creation process using a tab-based dialog box. During the process, we have to assign resources and enter the necessary information pertaining to the VM. The following screenshot shows the dialog box after you click on **Create VM** in the Proxmox GUI:

# General tab

The **General** tab of the dialog box is used to mainly assign identification information, such as:

- **Node**: This is a drop-down list to select in which Proxmox node the VM should be created.

- **VM ID**: This is the `textbox` used to enter the numeric ID of the VM. We can also increase or decrease the value of the **VM ID** using the arrows. If we assign an ID that already exists in the cluster, the box will have a red border around it, as shown in the following screenshot:

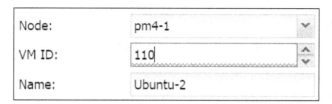

- **Name:** This is the text box used to enter the name of the VM. We can enter any alphanumeric string; only a dash or – is allowed as a special character.

- **Resource Pool**: This is the drop-down list used to select a previously created pool. It is only necessary if we want to assign the VM to a specific pool. For our example VM we are assigning it to pool named **Linux_VMs**.

# OS tab

The **OS** tab is used to select the type of guest operating system that will be installed on the VM. This type of selection allows the VM to be aware of the intended operating system and adjusts the architecture based on the OS selected. In our example VM, we have selected **Linux 4.X/3.X/2.6 Kernel**, as shown in the following screenshot:

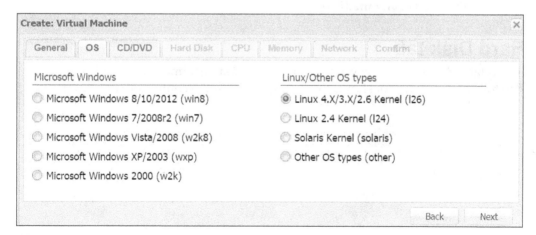

To achieve maximum performance and stability, it is highly recommended that you select the proper OS type.

## CD/DVD tab

Since KVM VMs are fully enclosed and emulate a physical machine, we can only boot the VM or load the operating system using ISO images loaded in the virtual **CD/DVD** drive or through a physical drive attached to the Proxmox host node. In this tab, we can select whether to use a virtual or physical drive or select an ISO image. The following screenshot shows the dialog box for the **CD/DVD** tab:

If we want to create the VM without specifying any disk image, we will need to select the **Do not use any media** option.

## Hard Disk tab

In this tab, we specify the configuration for the first disk image of the VM. The following screenshot shows the dialog box with the configuration for our example VM:

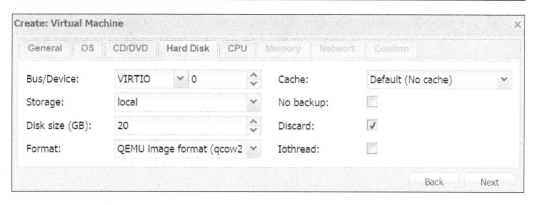

## Bus/Device

There are two drop-down menus available for this option, one to select disk image bus type and the other to select device ID.

 For maximum performance bus VIRTIO is recommended.

For a Windows VM, it is necessary to select IDE since Windows does not have built-in drivers for VIRTIO. In this case we can use the following steps to add VIRTIO capability to a Windows VM:

1. Create the VM with an IDE and install Windows as usual.
2. Add a second disk image with the VIRTIO bus and reboot Windows.
3. Download the latest VIRTIO driver ISO for Windows from the following links then load it through the virtual CD drive:

   `https://fedorapeople.org/groups/virt/virtio-win/direct-downloads/stable-virtio/virtio-win.iso`

   `http://www.linux-kvm.org/page/WindowsGuestDrivers/Download_Drivers`

4. Update the driver for the new hardware found for the VIRTIO disk image.
5. Shutdown the Windows VM and login to the Proxmox dashboard.

6.  From the **Hardware** tab of the VM, select the IDE image and click **Remove**. Note that this does not remove the disk image permanently. The disk image will now show as **Unused**, as shown in the following figure:

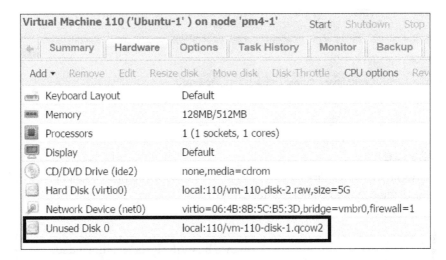

7.  Select **Unused disk** and click on **Edit**. This will open up a dialog box with the option to select **Bus/Device**: type and other configuration option as shown in the following screenshot:

From this dialog box we can select the desired **Bus** type and other configuration options if necessary.

8.  Click **Add** button to add the disk image back to the VM.

    The previous steps are necessary enable to Windows VM to use the VIRTIO disk image. Once the driver is loaded it is not necessary to reload for additional VIRTIO disk images.

## Storage

This is a drop-down menu to select where the disk image should be stored. Along with the name of the storage, the drop down menu also shows the total capacity and the available storage space of attached storage.

## Disk size

This is a text box to define the size of the disk storage in GB. The value can only be numerical. We can also use the up and down arrow of the text box to define the size.

## Format

This is a drop-down menu to select the type of disk image. If we select storage that only supports certain disk types, then this menu option will be greyed out. For example, if we select Ceph RBD storage, then this option will greyed out as (shown in the following figure) since RBD only supports the .raw format:

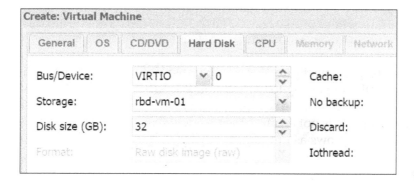

If we select the wrong format of the disk image, or if we decide later to use different format, we can simply use the **Move disk** option in the **Hardware** tab to change the format. This can also be done through the CLI using the following command:

```
#qemu-img convert -O <type> <source_image> <destination_image>
```

If we want to convert a .qcow2 disk image to a .raw image, the command would appear as follows:

```
#qemu-img convert -O raw vm-101-disk-1.qcow2 vm-101-disk-1.raw
```

This command works well for local, NFS, ZFS, and Gluster storage but is not suitable for RBD. To change the disk image format stored on RBD, use the **Move** option in the Proxmox dashboard. Besides the RBD storage disk image, this **Move** option can be used to move any disk image stored on any storage through the GUI without needing to use the CLI at all. This option is also helpful of moving a disk image from one storage to another without powering off the VM. The storage could be from local to shared or vice versa. To move or change the format of a disk image, select the disk image from the **Hardware** tab and click on **Move disk** to open a dialog box, as shown in the following figure:

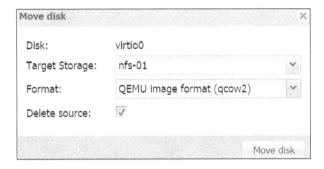

As shown in the previous figure, for our example VM we are moving a disk image to NFS storage while converting to .qcow2 image from .raw image. If we select **Delete source** option it will delete the source file automatically after converting or moving is finished. If the option is not enabled then we will have to manually delete the source file. The source file shows as unused disk image under the **Hardware** tab of the VM.

## Cache

This drop-down menu allows us to select the cache method to use for the disk image. We learned about different cache options in *Chapter 4*, *Storage Systems*, in the *Caching a virtual disk image* section. We can change the cache option at any time, even after the VM is fully created and functioning. After each cache option change, we will need to power cycle the VM to enable the new cache option.

## No backup

If this option is enabled, the virtual disk image will never be included in the backup. By default the option is disabled.

# Discard

Disk images in Proxmox is sparsed regardless the image type. This means that the disk image grows slowly as more data gets stored in it. Over time, data gets created and deleted within the filesystem of the disk image. But with a sparse disk image, even after data is deleted it never reclaims the free space. The VM may report the correct available storage space but Proxmox storage will show higher storage usage. The discard option allows the node to reclaim the free space that is not being consumed by any data. This is equivalent to the TRIM option that was introduced in the SSD drive to do exactly this. Before this option can be used we have to ensure that the VM is using a VIRTIO SCSI controller. We can set the SCSI type under the virtual machine's **Option** tab as shown in the following figure:

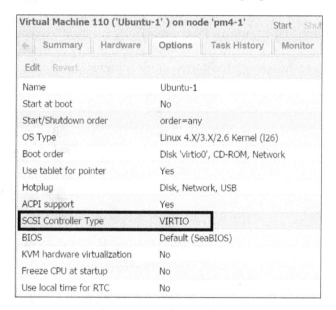

By default, Proxmox configures all VMs with a LSI 53C895A controller. The **Discard** option may not be suitable for all environments, storages, and Oses. Perform enough testing before implementing it in your environment.

In some cases, the **Discard** option may cause a VM to lock up, needing to power cycle. The VM will need to be power cycled if the option is enabled later after powering up the VM.

## Iothread

There are two options for disk images for KVM:

- Io=thread
- Io=native

By default, Proxmox uses ionative for all disk images unless the iothread option is specifically checked for the disk image.

Th iothread option allows each disk image to have its own thread instead of waiting on queue with everything else. Since disk I/O is no longer waiting due to having its own threads it does not hold up other tasks or queues related to the VM, which in turn speeds up the VM's performances, along with the increased disk performance. The iothread option is fairly new in Proxmox. There were a few reported instances where a VM was locked up due to this option, so do plenty of testing before implementing this feature in a production environment.

# CPU tab

This tab allows the configuration of the virtual CPU for the virtual machine. The following figure shows the dialog box with the available CPU options:

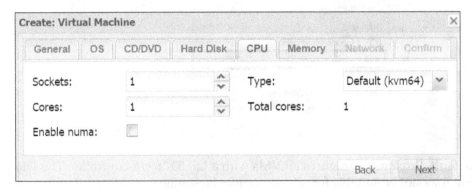

## Sockets

This option is to define number of sockets the VM can use. We can use more than 1 socket for the VM even if the physical node does not have enough sockets. This may only be useful if any application in the VM requires more than 1 socket. But it is not useful at all to increase VM performance in a single socket Proxmox node.

# Cores

This option is to define the number of cores the VM can use. It is a good practice to start a VM with a small number of cores, then increase the number as needed, depending on load. Assigning a large amount of cores in a VM will cause unnecessary stress on the available resources in the node. Usually, VMs can provide good performance with 2 or 4 cores unless it is a high demand VM, such as a remote desktop server or a SQL/Exchange server.

# Enabling NUMA

**Non Uniform Memory Access (NUMA)** is not a new approach to handling memory in a multi-CPU environment, although it is a new addition to Proxmox VE. Basically, with NUMA, memory can be distributed evenly among CPUs, which increases performance since there is no bottleneck due to all CPUs trying to access the same memory bank. In Proxmox, the NUMA option also enables memory and CPU hot plugging. Without this option, hotplug of CPU and memory will not work at all.

Any node with more than one CPU socket is usually NUMA aware. So enabling NUMA for VM in this node will benefit the VM's performance. NUMA will always try to keep the VM to the same CPU package. We can check the NUMA status in the Proxmox cluster using the following command:

```
# numastat
```

This command will show all the nodes in the cluster that are NUMA-aware and their performance statistics.

# Type

This is a drop-down list menu to select the CPU package type. By default, the kvm64 CPU type is selected for all VM.

> For best performance it is best to use the **Host** type. This way the VM will be able to access the CPU directly without an emulation layer. This is the optimal type in an environment where all nodes is identical. For maximum portability of a VM, it is best to choose the kvm or qemu CPU type.

# Memory tab

This tab allows the configuration of the memory allocation of the VM. The following figure shows the dialog box for our example VMs:

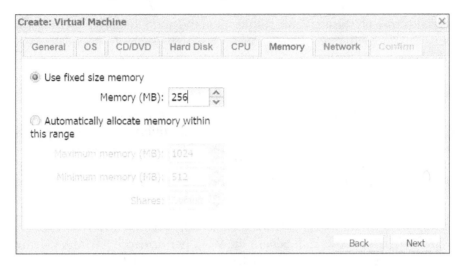

In Proxmox, we can set fixed or dynamic memory for a VM. Automatic range is also known as memory ballooning. For the fixed option, all memory is allocated at the same time. With the dynamic option, memory is allocated based on the VM within the preset range. Automatic memory allocation works well for Linux-based guest VMs, but for a windows VM, memory ballooning consumes higher amount of CPU resource causing the VM to slow down. So for windows VM it is best to use fixed memory whenever possible.

# Network

This tab allows the configuration of the virtual **Network** interface of the VM. The following figure shows the dialog box for the network configuration of our example VM:

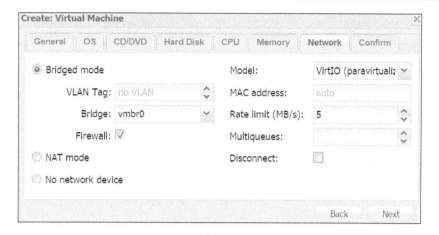

## Bridged mode

This mode allows the VM to connect to the network using a bridge. The VM does not get direct access to the outside network. We can set the VLAN id at the node level, which makes it unnecessary to configure inside the VM. Bridge mode also provides a firewall option for the VM.

## Firewall

To enable Proxmox Firewall for the network interface this option needs to be checked. Without this option no firewall rules will be applied to the interface. We will look Proxmox at Firewall in greater detail in *Chapter 8, The Proxmox Firewall*.

## NAT mode

This mode provides a VM direct access to an outside network. Network traffic does not go through any bridge. If VLAN is used in the network, it must be configured inside the VM. The Proxmox firewall option is not available when using NAT mode.

## No network device

This option will create the VM without any network interface configured.

## Model

This is a drop-down menu to select the virtual network interface type. For maximum network performance, the use of VIRTIO is highly recommended. Windows does not come with a VIRTIO driver, so if this is used for a Windows VM we have to manually load the driver from the ISO we downloaded in the **Hard Disk** tab section in this chapter. We can also use Intel E1000 for Windows VM. From Windows 7 onwards, the driver for Intel is included.

## MAC address

By default, all MAC addresses for virtual network interfaces are automatically assigned. By typing a MAC address in this text box we can specify a particular MAC address the interface. This may be necessary when a specific MAC address is required by an application in the guest VM.

## Rate limit

This is a test box to define the maximum allowable speed of the network interface in megabytes per second. This is a very useful option to limit network per VM basis. Without any value defined, the VM will try to use as much bandwidth as possible.

## Multiqueues

Ordinarily, KVM VMs are single queued, where sending and receiving packets occurs one at a time and not in parallel. Multiqueuing removes this bottleneck by allowing sending and receiving in parallel by leveraging virtual CPU cores for parallel queues. Multiqueuing is especially useful for a VM that is active on numerous clients, for example a web server. In Proxmox **Network** tab for VM creation dialog box we can enter a numeric value to define how many parallel queue the VM should use. This value should not be more than allocated vCPU of the VM. For example, if the VM has virtual core of 4, we can set multiqueue value 4. Multiqueuing increases the network performance of a VM greatly since both sending and receiving can happen in parallel.

 Keep in mind that enabling multiqueuing will also increase CPU usage of the VM since each queue is dependent on each vCPU.

## Disconnect

If this option is enabled, the virtual network interface will be created along with the VM but will not be activated.

# Creating a VM by cloning

When deploying multiple VMs with identical configurations, creating them individually can become a time-consuming process. In such cases we can clone an existing VM or a Template. This way we can create a template using a fully configured VM and simply clone it whenever we need to deploy a new VM. Note that a Template created from a KVM virtual machine is not the same as an **LXC Container Template**, although they are both called **Template**.

In this example, we are going to convert one of the VMs we created in previous section into a template. To convert a VM into a template we need to right-click on the VM to open the context menu, as shown in the following screenshot and click on **Convert to template**:

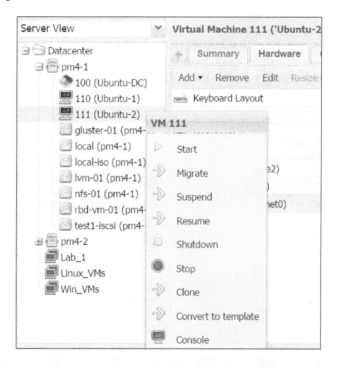

After the VM is converted to a template, the VM itself is no longer useable. But we can, however edit the hardware resources. Another noticeable difference is that the icon in the Proxmox dashboard is unique for KVM templates, as shown in the following screenshot:

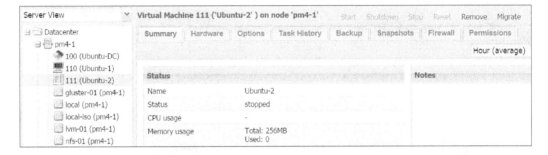

The procedure to clone is same whether it is a VM or a KVM Template. To create a new VM or deploy multiple VMs from the template or a VM, right-click on the template to open the context menu, then click on **Clone**. This will open the cloning dialog box as shown in the following screenshot:

The functions of **Target node**, **VM ID**, **Name**, and **Resource Pool** input boxes are identical to the **General** tab of the KVM VM creation dialog box.

# Mode

There are two cloning modes in Proxmox:

- Full Clone
- Linked Clone

Full Clone creates an identical copy of the VM, including the virtual disk image. This is a truly isolated VM since it is not dependent on the source template or VM in any way. Even if we delete the source template or VM, the newly deployed VM will still function without any issues. Full clone consumes as much storage space as the original VM since the virtual disk is also cloned. Full clones are useful when allocated resources are identical for all deployed VMs but the guest operating system may or may not be different.

Linked Clone creates a duplicate of the original VM minus the original virtual disk image. This creates an additional blank disk image that is referenced to the original virtual disk, and only new data gets placed in the linked clone disk image. All read requests, except for the new data, are automatically redirected to the original disk image. Linked clone is heavily dependent on source template or VM. This clone mode is useful when all cloned VMs will have exactly the same hardware and software configuration, including the guest operating system. Linked Clone consumes much less storage space since the original or base image is never duplicated but only referenced by the new linked clone VM. The disk image of a linked Clone looks like the following screenshot:

As we can see from the previous screenshot the linked disk image is created in a subdirectory directory of the original disk image to store any new data. Since Linked cloned VMs are heavily dependent on the source template, it is very important to ensure the source template or VM is not damaged in any way. A corrupt template will cause all linked clones to fail.

# Creating VMs from templates

In Proxmox we can also clone VM from templates. KVM templates are created by converting a KVM VM. The only difference between a KVM VM and template is that once converted, templates cannot be turned on like a VM. This prevents further changes to the virtual disk image, ensuring each clone is identical to the original VM.

Although we cannot power up the template, we can still make resource changes such as CPU, RAM, and so on, but it is not a recommended practice since any hardware changes may cause issues when a cloned VM is powered on.

To convert a VM into a template, right-click on the VM to open the context menu, then select **Convert to Template** as shown in the following figure:

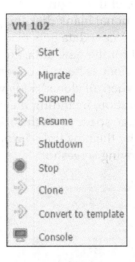

To create a new clone, right-click on the template and select **Clone** to open clone template dialog box as shown in the following figure:

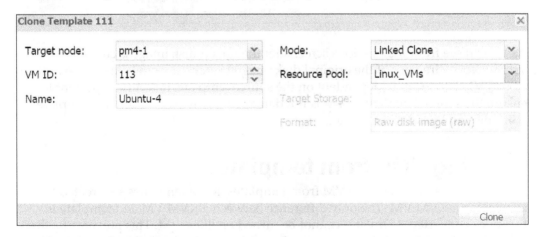

The options in the dialog box are identical to the VM creation process of cloning without a template.

# Advanced configuration options for VM

We will now look at some of the advanced configuration options we can use to extend the capability of KVM virtual machines.

## Configuring a sound device

In this section we are going to see how to add sound support to a VM. Proxmox by default does not add audio hardware to a VM. In order for the VM operating system to start a sound service, some arguments must be added to the VM configuration file through CLI. As of Proxmox VE 4.1 it is not possible to add a sound interface through the GUI. The following steps will add a sound device to a VM:

1. Log in to the **Proxmox** node through SSH or directly in the console.

2. Navigate to the VM configuration directory `/etc/pve/nodes/<node_name>/qemu-server/<vm_id>`.conf.

3. Open the VM configuration file with your favorite text editor and add on of the the following arguments:

   For Windows 10 and later VMs:

   ```
   args: -device intel-had,id=sound5,bus=pci.0,addr=0x18 -device
   hda-micro,id=sound5-codec0,bus=sound5.0,cad=0 -device had-
   duplex,id=sound5-codec1,bus=sound5.0,cad=1
   ```

   For WindowsXP based VM:

   ```
   args: -device AC97,addr=0x18
   ```

4. Save the configuration file and exit the editor.

5. Power cycle the VM to activate the sound device.

## Configuring PCI passthrough

In Proxmox it is possible to passthrough PCI devices directly into a VM. In this section we are going to see how to configure and verify PCI passthrough. Following steps are required to enable and configure pci passthrough in Proxmox:

1. Log in to the **Proxmox** node through SSH or directly in the console.

2. Open the `grub configuration` file using an editor:

   ```
   # nano /etc/default/grub
   ```

3. Change the `GRUB_CMDLINE_LINUX_DEFAULT="quiet"` to on of the following.

   For Intel CPU:

   `GRUB_CMDLINE_LINUX_DEFAULT="quiet intel_iommu=on"`

   For AMD CPU:

   `GRUB_CMDLINE_LINUX_DEFAULT="quiet amd_iommu=on"`

4. Save the changes and exit the editor.

5. Run the following command to update grub:

   ```
   # update-grub
   ```

6. Only if using AMD CPU, add the following line in the configuration file `/etc/modprobe.d/kvm_iommu_map_guest.conf`:

   ```
   options kvm allow_unsafe_assigned_interrupt=1
   ```

7. Reboot the **Proxmox** node.

8. Locate the PCI device address in the form of `xx:xx.x` using the command:

   ```
   # lspci
   ```

9. Enter the following line with the PCI device ID in the VM configuration file:
   `hostpci0: xx:xx.x`.

10. Power cycle the VM.

11. Install the necessary drivers for the PCI device in the VM operating system.

# Configuring GPU Passthrough

In this section we are going to see how to configure a video adapter to be used directly in a VM. PCI Express devices such as Video Adapter card support was added to Proxmox from version 3.3. To enable this passthrough the Proxmox node must have PVE-Kernel 3.10. If you are using Proxmox VE 4.1, you are most likely to have the latest Kernel. We can add PCI express and GPU passthrough to a VM from the CLI by adding arguments to a VM configuration file.

The following steps show how to enable standard non-GPU PCI Express devices, GPU-based devices and GPU devices with embedded audio devices to a VM:

1. Open the VM configuration file in an editor.

2. Locate the PCI Express device ID by following the steps in the previous section using the following command:

   ```
   # lspci
   ```

3. Add the following lines depending on the type of PCI express device being added.

For standard non-GPU PCI Express device:

```
machine: q35
hostpci0: xx:xx.x,pcie=1,driver=vfio
```

For GPU PCI Express video adapters:

```
machine: q35
hostpci0: xx:xx.x,pcie=1,x-vga=on,driver=vfio
```

For GPU PCI Express video adapters with an embedded sound device remove the .x at the end of the PCI device address as follows:

```
machine: q35
hostpci0: xx:xx,pcie=1,x-vga=on,driver=vfio
```

4. Save the configuration file and power cycle the VM.

5. Install the necessary drivers within the VM operating system.

# Configuring Hotplug

In this section we are going to see how to configure the hotplugging option in Proxmox virtual machines. Using the hotplugging feature, we can add and remove devices or resources to VM without restarting or power cycling the VM. As of Proxmox 4.1 we can use the hotplug option for the following resources:

- Disk
- Network interface
- CPU
- Memory
- USB

As of Proxmox 4.1, we can only increase CPU and memory but cannot decrease them. Both the disk and the network interface can be equally hotplugged and unplugged. Following table shows which device types are supported in different operating systems:

| Device | Kernel | Hotplug/Unplug | OS |
|--------|--------|----------------|-----|
| Disk | All | Both | All versions of Linux/Windows |
| NIC | All | Both | All versions of Linux/Windows |
| CPU | >3.10 | Hotplug only for Windows. Both for Linux | All versions of Linux. Windows Server 2008 and above |
| Memory | >3.10 | Hotplug only for Windows. Both for Linux | All versions of Linux. Windows Server 2008 and above |

While the main configuration to enable hotplugging for a Proxmox should be done through the CLI, we can enable a hotplug device through **Proxmox GUI | Option** tab menu, as shown in the following figure:

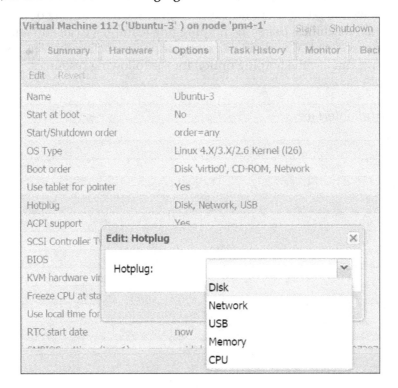

We need to prepare a Linux-based VM first before hotplugging can be used. Two modules must be loaded to enable hotplugging. We can load the modules using the following command:

```
# modprobe acpiphp
# modprobe pci_hotplug
```

To load the modules during boot automatically, we can add them to /etc/modules.

We also need to create a new udev rule file in /lib/udev/rules.d/80-hotplug-cpu-mem.rules file and add the following lines:

```
SUBSYSTEM=="cpu",ACTION=="add",TEST=="online",ATTR{online}=="0",
ATTR=={online}="1"
SUBSYSTEM=="memory",ACTION=="add",TEST=="state", ATTR{state}=="offline
",ATTR=={state}="online"
```

The Proxmox node needs to be power cycled to activate the modules and rules.

The following steps are required to enable hotplugging for a VM through the GUI:

1. Log in to the Proxmox GUI.
2. Select a VM for which hotplugging needs to be enabled; then click on the **Options** tab menu.
3. Select the hotplug line item then click on the **Edit** to open the dialog box as shown in the previous screenshot.
4. Select one or more devices to be hotplugged using the drop-down menu.
5. Click on **Ok** to enable.

To add new resource to a VM, go to **Hardware** tab and click on **Add**. As of Proxmox 4.1 we can only add **Hard Disk** image, **Network Device** and **CD/DVD Drive** through the **Hardware | Add** button as shown in the following figure:

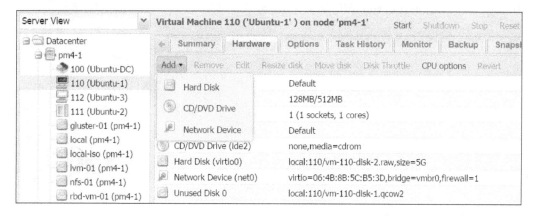

To add or remove a vCPU from the VM, select **Processor** under the **VM | Hardware** tab and click on **Edit** to open the CPU dialog box. We can also add a vCPU by running the following command from the Proxmox node CLI:

```
# qm set <vm_id> -vcpus 2
```

The previous command will add a total of two virtual CPUs to the VM.

The following steps shows how to enable memory hotplug for a VM:

1. If not enabled already, NUMA must be enabled for the vCPU before memory can be hotplugged. Restart the VM after enabling Numa.

2. Define the new allocated memory through the GUI under the **Hardware** tab.

# Migrating a KVM

Proxmox Migration allows a KVM virtual machine to be moved to a Proxmox node in both offline and online or live modes. The most common scenario of VM migration is when a Proxmox node needs a reboot due to a major kernel update or other patches. Other scenarios may include hardware failures, node replacement, software issues, and so on. Without the live migration option, each reboot would be very difficult for an administrator as all the running VMs would have to be stopped first before reboot occurs. This will cause major downtime in a mission-critical virtual environment.

With the live migration option, a running VM can be moved to another node without downtime. During a live migration, the VM does not experience any major slowdown. After the node reboots, simply migrate the VMs back to the original node. Any offline VMs can also be moved with ease.

Proxmox takes a very minimalistic approach to the migration process. Right click on the VM to be migrated to open the context menu, then click on **Migration** to open the dialog box, as shown in the following figure:

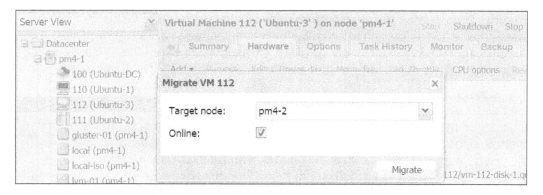

From the dialog simply select the destination node then depending on online or offline migration, click the check box. Then hit the **Migrate** button to get the migration process started. Depending on the size of the virtual drive and allocated memory of the VM, the entire migration process time can vary. Live/Online migration also migrates the virtual memory content of the VM. The bigger the memory, the longer it will take to migrate. In the previous example we are live migrating **VM ID #112** to node **pm4-2**.

# Nested virtual cluster

It is possible to create a virtual cluster using the Proxmox hypervisor on top of an existing Proxmox cluster. Due to the performance drop with a nested hypervisor, the use cases of nested clusters are very limited. It can be used in the following scenarios, but is not limited to these scenarios:

- Practice cluster in a classroom.
- Test cluster to test latest software releases before applying to a real environment.
- Proof of concept cluster to test new configuration ideas.

In this section we are going to see how to enable the nesting feature in Proxmox. Plan ahead if a nested virtual cluster is going to be used on a physical Proxmox cluster. There must be adequate resources, such as CPU and memory available, to support the actual and virtual nested cluster.

In order to have close to native performance of a hypervisor, the virtual machines must have access to some hardware features that leverage virtualization. These features are known as **Hardware Assisted Virtualization Extension**. Visit the following link for detail information on Hardware Assisted Virtualization:

`https://en.wikipedia.org/wiki/Hardware-assisted_virtualization`

The nested hypervisor must have access to these extensions in order to have good enough performance for nested virtual machines. The nested feature seems to work flawlessly with AMD CPUs. Proxmox nodes with Intel CPUs tend to have issues when it comes to nested virtualization. If enabling the hardware assisted extension is not possible, then the KVM hardware virtualization feature must be turned off for a VM before that VM can be used inside a nested environment, as shown in the following figure:

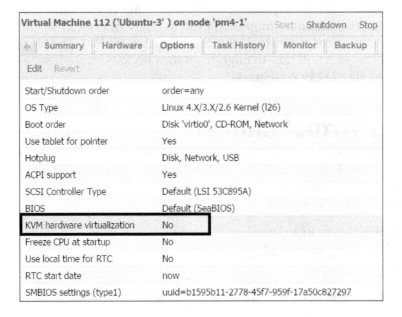

The **KVM hardware virtualization** option is turned on by default for all VMs. If nesting requirements are not met during the node configuration process we can still use a nested virtual machine but only with the KVM virtualization option turned off. If the option is not turned off when trying to start a nested VM, an error message will be displayed, as in the following figure:

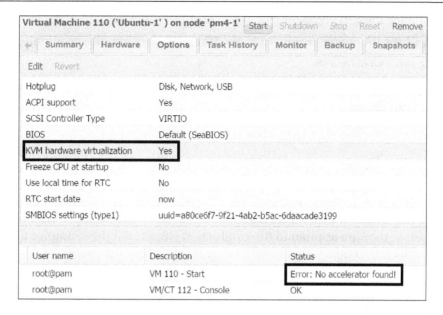

The following steps show how to enable nested features in a Proxmox node and configure:

1. For an Intel CPU, load the module for nesting and enable it using the following commands:

```
# modprobe kvm-intel
# echo "options kvm-intel nested=1" > /etc/modprobe.d/kvm-intel.conf
```

For a Intel CPU load the module for nesting and enable it using the following commands:

```
#modprobe kvm-amd
#echo "options kvm-amd nested=1" > /etc/modprobe.d/kvm-amd.conf
```

2. To load the KVM module automatically during reboot, add the module to /etc/modules.

3. Verify the module is loaded and enabled using the following command:

```
# cat /sys/module/<kvm_intel or kvm_amd>paramters/nested
```

The command should either display Y or 1 if the module is enabled.

4. Change the CPU type for the VM to host through GUI.

5. Add the following argument to the VM configuration file through the CLI:

   `args: -enable-kvm`

6. Power cycle the VM and install Proxmox as a hypervisor, or add a hypervisor of your choice.

A nested virtual cluster should not be used as a production cluster due to its below average performance. A nested virtual machine simply will not be able to achieve full performance even if the underlying hardware is more than adequate. But for learning and testing purposes, this is an ideal option. An entire Proxmox cluster including different storages such as Ceph, Gluster or NFS can be set up for learning purposes. This is also useful for tryingout new features of Proxmox or new updates/patches before they are applied to the production cluster. All the examples used in this book are created on a fully nested Proxmox virtual environment.

# Summary

In this chapter we looked at KVM Virtual Machines, how to create them, clone them, and migrate them when need. We also looked at some advanced configuration such as adding a sound device and enabling `pci/gpu passthrough` for KVM VMs. By leveraging cloning techniques we can scale a virtual cluster effortlessly when deploying identical virtual machines. Optional and non-production setup of a Nested Virtual Environment was also explained.

KVM virtual machine are a best practice for all non-Linux operating systems and also when total resource isolation between VMs is mandatory.

In the next chapter we are going to look at LXC containers in greater detail. We will learn why a Proxmox administrator would choose them over KVM Virtual Machines.

# 6
# LXC Virtual Machines

From Proxmox VE 4.0, the OpenVZ container technology was replaced in favor of an LXC container. In this chapter, we will see the features and benefits of using an LXC container and learn how to create and manage containers in Proxmox. In this chapter, we will cover some of the following topics:

- Exploring an LXC container
- Understanding a container template
- Creating an LXC container
- Managing an LXC container
- Migrating an LXC container
- Accessing an LXC container
- Unprivileged versus privileged containers
- Converting an OpenVZ container to an LXC container

## Exploring an LXC virtual machine

Containers are different forms of virtual machines that are completely dependent on the operating system of the host node. Containers are kernel-based virtualizations that share the host operating system, thereby reducing the overhead that a KVM virtual machine has. Due to the lower overhead, the virtual machine density per node can be tighter and more containers can be hosted than KVM virtual machines. This comes at the price of less virtual machine isolation. Since containers are dependent on the underneath operating system, there can be only Linux-based containers. No Windows operating system can be containerized. Unlike KVM virtual machines, we cannot clone a container or turn a container into a template. Each container is a virtual instance that runs separately.

LXC is just another type of a container technology. OpenVZ is another container technology, which had been in use by Proxmox until Version 4.0. There are two major differences between the LXC and OpenVZ container technology:

- LXC is available on Linux Kernel and doesn't need a separate kernel as in the case of OpenVZ. As of OpenVZ 4.0, it can be run on Linux Kernel 3.0 and later. However, having your own kernel OpenVZ can offer the best performance.

- OpenVZ supports live migration whereas LXC does not.

The following are a few advantages of using LXC containers:

- Extremely fast deployment

- Higher density of virtual machine per node

- Smaller backup files

- Nested LXC containers with almost no overhead

- Ability to directly access data inside the container filesystem from the host node

- Configuration is less complicated due to absence of **User Bean Counter (UBC)**

In Proxmox, LXC containers are identified by a unique icon in the GUI dashboard. The following screenshot shows the icon of a powered off LXC container with **ID#100**:

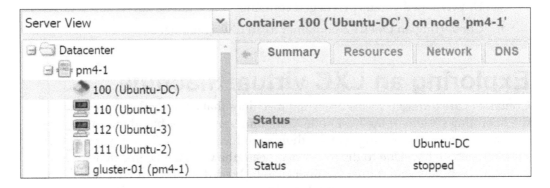

Note here that Proxmox VE 4.0 has been superseded by Version 4.1 in which LXC was first introduced. Some initial issues in Version 4.0 due to LXC containers have been fully addressed in Proxmox VE 4.1. If you are using Proxmox VE 4.0, it is very important to upgrade to Version 4.1 before any attempt is made to use an LXC container.

# Understanding container templates

Unlike KVM virtual machines, which can be installed from ISO images, LXC containers can only be deployed using container templates. These templates can be directly downloaded from the Proxmox repository. To view a list of available templates already downloaded, we need to select an attached storage, which can store container templates, and click on the **Content** tab, as shown in the following screenshot:

In the preceding screenshot, we can see that we have an Ubuntu container template that is already downloaded in our local storage. To view a list of available LXC templates, and to download them from the Proxmox repository, we need to click on the **Templates** menu to open the dialog box, as shown in the following screenshot:

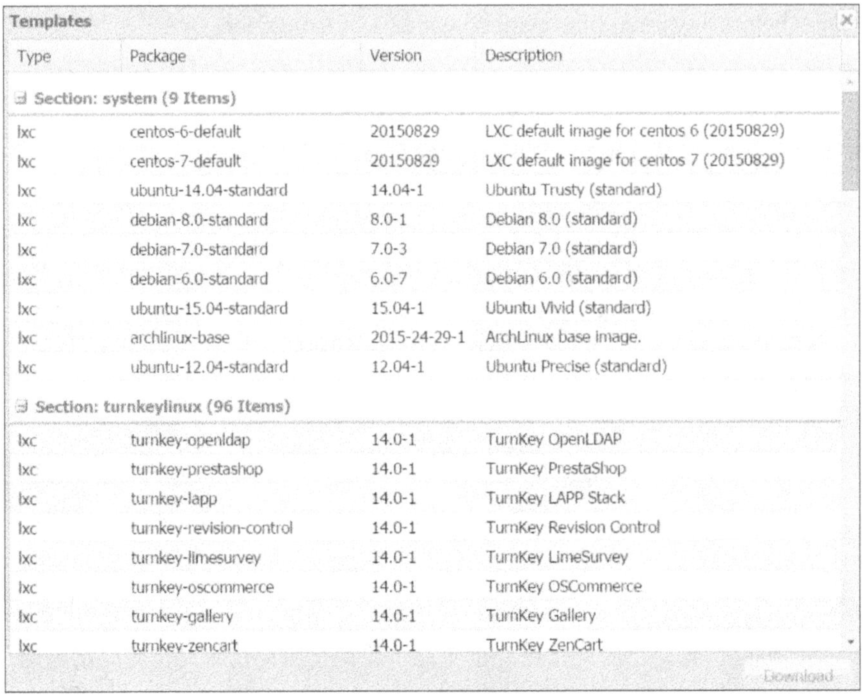

| Type | Package | Version | Description |
|------|---------|---------|-------------|
| **Templates** | | | ✕ |
| *Section: system (9 Items)* | | | |
| lxc | centos-6-default | 20150829 | LXC default image for centos 6 (20150829) |
| lxc | centos-7-default | 20150829 | LXC default image for centos 7 (20150829) |
| lxc | ubuntu-14.04-standard | 14.04-1 | Ubuntu Trusty (standard) |
| lxc | debian-8.0-standard | 8.0-1 | Debian 8.0 (standard) |
| lxc | debian-7.0-standard | 7.0-3 | Debian 7.0 (standard) |
| lxc | debian-6.0-standard | 6.0-7 | Debian 6.0 (standard) |
| lxc | ubuntu-15.04-standard | 15.04-1 | Ubuntu Vivid (standard) |
| lxc | archlinux-base | 2015-24-29-1 | ArchLinux base image. |
| lxc | ubuntu-12.04-standard | 12.04-1 | Ubuntu Precise (standard) |
| *Section: turnkeylinux (96 Items)* | | | |
| lxc | turnkey-openldap | 14.0-1 | TurnKey OpenLDAP |
| lxc | turnkey-prestashop | 14.0-1 | TurnKey PrestaShop |
| lxc | turnkey-lapp | 14.0-1 | TurnKey LAPP Stack |
| lxc | turnkey-revision-control | 14.0-1 | TurnKey Revision Control |
| lxc | turnkey-limesurvey | 14.0-1 | TurnKey LimeSurvey |
| lxc | turnkey-oscommerce | 14.0-1 | TurnKey OSCommerce |
| lxc | turnkey-gallery | 14.0-1 | TurnKey Gallery |
| lxc | turnkey-zencart | 14.0-1 | TurnKey ZenCart |

Download

There are over 100 templates available to be downloaded from this dialog box. If you are not able to see the complete list and it only shows the **Section: system** templates, then run the following command from the CLI to update the template list:

```
# pveam update
```

To download a template, simply select it and click on the **Download** button. The downloaded template will now be available in the storage. The default location to store the containers templates for local storage is as follows:

```
/mnt/pve/<storage>/template/cache
```

The default location to store the containers templates for shared storage is as follows:

```
/var/lib/vz/template/cache
```

# Creating an LXC container

After ensuring that we have the desired template for the container, it is now time to create one. We can click on the **Create CT** button in the top-right corner of the Proxmox GUI to open the container creation dialog box, as shown in the following screenshot:

## General tab

The general tab of the dialog box is used to assign identification information, as outlined below.

## Node

This is a drop-down list used to select in which Proxmox node the container is going to be created. In our example, we will create the container in node **pm4-1**.

## VM ID

This is a textbox used to enter the numeric ID of the container. We can also use the up and down arrows in the box to assign the IDs. If we assign an ID, which already exists in the cluster, the box will show a red border around the textbox. For our example container, we are using ID #**101**.

## Hostname

This is a text box used to enter the hostname of the container. The hostname does not need to be FQDN.

## Resource Pool

This is a drop-down list menu used to select a previously created pool. It is only necessary if we want to assign the container to a specific pool.

# The Template tab

This tab is used to select a template the container is going to be based on. Select **Storage** from the drop-down menu where the template is stored, and then from the **Template** drop-down list, select the template, as shown in the following screenshot:

# The Root Disk tab

This tab is used to define the disk storage space the container can use. The following screenshot shows the dialog box with the configuration for our example container with the Ceph RBD storage selected:

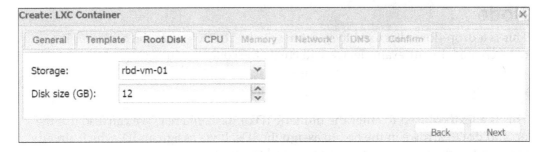

LXC containers can be stored in all storage types without any modification with only one exception for the Ceph RBD storage. **KRBD** must be enabled for the RBD storage in order to store a LXC container. The inclusion of this option now allows leveraging the Ceph distributed storage to be used with the LXC container platform. The following screenshot shows the **KRBD** option from the storage dialog box:

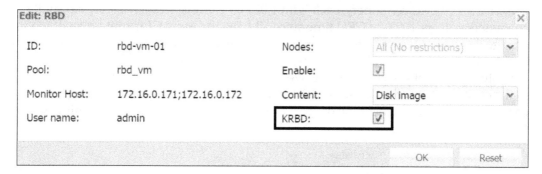

## The CPU tab

This tab allows configuration of a virtual **CPU** for a container. The following screenshot shows the dialog box with the available CPU options:

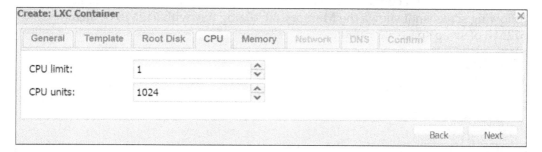

## CPU limits

Unlike KVM virtual machines, we can only allocate CPU cores and not CPU sockets. The CPU limit for a container is how many cores the container can use. For our example container, we have allocated **1** CPU core.

# CPU units

In simple terms, this value is used to define how much CPU time the container can use or the percentage of share it can have. When we take a look at this value on its own, it will make no sense at all. However, when thinking in terms of multiple containers, the correct value will make a lot of sense. For example, think about a cluster with 10 LXC containers, each with 1,024 CPU units. In such a scenario, all the containers will get 100% of CPU time since all have the same CPU unit value. If we change the value to say 512 for two of the containers, they will only get 50% of CPU time while the rest of the eight containers will get 100% CPU time. So, we can see the value itself is of no use as long as we think of it in relation to the other containers in the cluster. **1024** is the default value for the CPU units. If we want any noncritical container to have less CPU time or share, we can simply reduce the CPU unit value for it.

# The Memory tab

This tab is used to define the allocated memory and swap the size for the container. It is a common practice to allocate an equal amount of swap size as the memory. Keep in mind that for LXC containers, this swap allocation actually gets allocated to the host node swap since the container does not have its own kernel running. This size can be adjusted for a container at a later time without restarting the container. The following screenshot shows the **Memory** tab dialog box with **512MB** of memory and **512MB** of swap space allocated:

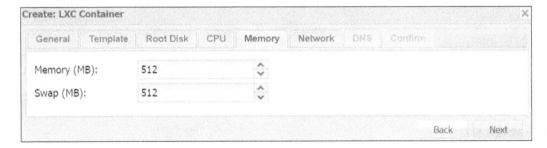

# The Network tab

This tab allows the network configuration of the container. The same dialog box is used to edit or add a new network interface for the container. The following screenshot shows the dialog box for our example container:

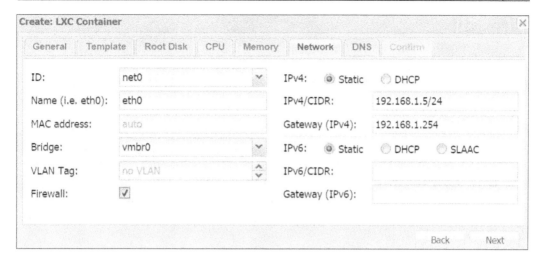

## ID

This is a drop-down list used to select a network interface. We can add a maximum of 10 network interfaces in a LXC container.

## Name

This is a textbox used to define a name for the network interface.

## MAC address

By default, all MAC addresses for virtual network interfaces are automatically assigned. By typing a MAC address in this textbox, we can specify a particular MAC address to the interface. This may be necessary when a specific MAC address is required by an application in the container.

## Bridge

This is a drop-down list used to select a virtual bridge that the interface will be connected to.

## The VLAN Tag

This is used to set VLAN ID to the virtual interface.

# Firewall

To enable the Proxmox firewall for the network interface, this option needs to be checked. Without this option, no firewall rules will be applied to the interface. We will take a look at the Proxmox firewall in detail in *Chapter 8, The Proxmox Firewall*.

## IPv4/IPv6

We can set both IPv4 and IPv6 to the virtual network interface. We can also manually set IP addresses or enable DHCP for an automatic IP assignment. The IP must be entered along with CIDR. Proxmox also supports dynamic IPv6 assignment using stateless configuration, such as SLAAC. To learn about Stateless Auto Configuration or SLAAC, refer to `https://tools.ietf.org/html/rfc4862`.

# The DNS tab

This tab is used to configure the DNS information for the LXC container. Enter the domain name to be used by the container and IP addresse(s) of DNS server(s).

The following screenshot shows the **DNS** domain and **DNS** server information:

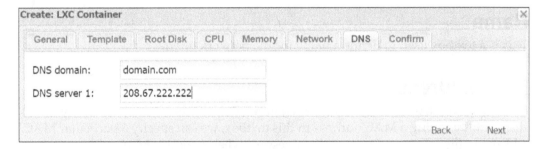

# The Confirm tab

This tab is used to ensure the accuracy of the new container configuration. If any changes need to be made, we can simply click on a tab to go back without losing values already entered or selected. Click on **Finish** to create a container.

The following screenshot shows our new example container powered on and running:

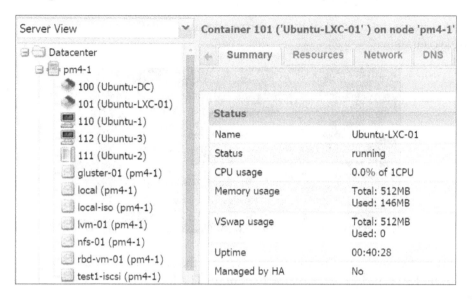

# Managing an LXC container

In Proxmox, each LXC container has two configuration files. One defines the raw resource allocation while the other used by Proxmox is used to define a container. The Proxmox container configuration file can be found at the following location:

```
/etc/pve/local/lxc/<container_id>.conf
```

For our example container ID **#101, the** following are the contents of this configuration file:

```
arch: amd64
cpulimit: 1
cpuunits: 1024
hostname: Ubuntu-LXC-01
memory: 512
nameserver: 208.67.222.222
net0: bridge=vmbr0,gw=172.16.3.254,hwaddr=36:30:65:34:36:37,ip=172.16.0.174/22,name=eth0,tag=101,type=veth
ostype: ubuntu
rootfs: rbd-vm-01:vm-101-disk-1,size=12G
searchdomain: domain.com
swap: 512
```

The raw container configuration file can be found at

`/var/lib/lxc/<container_id>/config.`

The following is the content of the resource allocation configuration file for our example container:

```
lxc.utsname = Ubuntu-LXC-01
lxc.cgroup.memory.limit_in_bytes = 536870912
lxc.cgroup.memory.kmem.limit_in_bytes = 536870912
lxc.cgroup.memory.memsw.limit_in_bytes = 1073741824
lxc.cgroup.cpu.cfs_period_us = 100000
lxc.cgroup.cpu.cfs_quota_us = 100000
lxc.cgroup.cpu.shares = 1024
lxc.rootfs = /var/lib/lxc/101/rootfs
lxc.network.type = veth
lxc.network.veth.pair = veth101i0
lxc.network.hwaddr = 36:30:65:34:36:37
lxc.network.name = eth0
```

There is another directory for the root filesystem that is a mount point for the allocated storage space inside the container. The location of the directory is as follows:

`/var/lib/lxc/<container_id>/rootfs/`

But in Proxmox, this directory is not used to store container data. For local storage, the container virtual disk image is created in:

`/var/lib/vz/images/<container_id>/.`

For shared storage, the container virtual disk image is created in:

`/mnt/pve/<storage>/images/container_id/`

We can adjust allocated resources for a container in real time without power cycling the container. This feature is known as **hotplug** for KVM virtual machines. However, for LXC containers, this feature is built into the container technology without needing any additional modification. There are three ways in which we can adjust allocated resources for a container:

* The Proxmox GUI
* The command line
* Editing a configuration file

# Adjusting resources using the GUI

Using the Proxmox GUI to change the resource allocation is the preferred way to adjust the container resource. Any changes made get committed to the container instantly without the need to power cycle the container. For day-to-day operations, the GUI provides almost all the resource options to be changed with a few clicks. There are three tabbed menus used to change resources for a container:

- Resources: Memory, Swap, CPU limits/units, and disk size
- Network
- DNS

To change a particular resource, we need to select a container from the left-hand side navigation bar, and then we need to select the resource to be changed. For example, if you want to increase the disk size of our container to 18 GB from the previously created 12 GB, we need to click on **Resize disk** to open the dialog box, as shown in the following screenshot, and enter a value to increase the disk size:

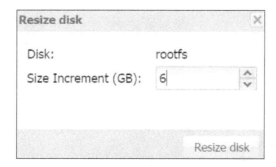

We can verify that the disk space has indeed increased by running the #fdisk command from inside the container. The following screenshot shows the #fdisk command output, which shows the size of the root mount point that is stored in the RBD storage:

```
Filesystem      Size  Used Avail Use% Mounted on
/dev/rbd0        19G  508M   18G   3% /
none            103k  4.1k   99k   4% /dev
cgroup           13k     0   13k   0% /sys/fs/cgroup
tmpfs           193M     0  193M   0% /sys/fs/cgroup/cgmanager
none            404M   54k  404M   1% /run
none            5.3M     0  5.3M   0% /run/lock
none            2.1G     0  2.1G   0% /run/shm
none            105M     0  105M   0% /run/user
root@Ubuntu-LXC-01:/home# 
```

# Adjusting resources using the CLI

LXC comes with a vast number of command-line commands to manage LXC containers. It is not possible to cover all the commands in this book. The good news for Proxmox users is that there are some tools or commands provided by Proxmox to make managing containers an easier task through the CLI. The `pct` command is a script created by Proxmox developers that wraps `lxc` commands. To see the available Proxmox commands for containers, we can run the following command:

```
# pct help
```

We can also get details of all the `pct` command from the Proxmox wiki at https://pve.proxmox.com/wiki/Manual:_pct.

Resource changes made using these commands get committed to the container immediately without the need to restart the container. If the Proxmox GUI becomes inaccessible, we can manage a container entirely using the CLI. The `format` command used to change container resources is as follows:

```
# pct set <ct_id> [options]
```

For example, if we want to change the IP address of the container #101, the command will appear as follows:

```
# pct set 101 -net0 name=eth0,bridge=vmbr0,ip=192.168.1.17/24
```

We can verify that the new network configuration has been applied to the container by checking the network configuration file of the container in `/etc/network/interfaces` as follows:

```
auto lo
iface lo inet loopback

auto eth0
iface eth0 inet static
        address 192.168.1.17
        netmask 255.255.255.0
```

It is very important to note here that the gateway address is now missing from the network configuration. The reason for this is that when we entered the previous command to change the IP address, we did not mention the gateway. The `pct set` command will replace the previous configuration for a resource being changed. If we want to include the gateway address, the entire command will appear as follows:

```
# pct set 101 -net0 name=eth0,bridge=vmbr0,ip=192.168.1.17/24,
gw=192.168.1.254
```

To adjust the allocated memory of the container in real time, we can use the following command:

```
# pct set <ct_id> -memory <int_value>
```

To change the CPU limit of the container, we can use the following command. The value 0 disables any CPU limit:

```
# pct set <ct_id> -cpulimit <0 - 128>
```

The following command changes the hostname of the container:

```
# pct set <ct_id> -hostname <string>
```

To increase the size of the root filesystem of the container, we can use the following command:

```
# pct set <ct_id> -rootfs size=<int_value for GB>
```

At times, due to an incomplete backup, a container may become locked and will be unable to start or stop. The following command will unlock the container from the CLI:

```
# pct set <ct_id> -unlock
```

The following command will show a list of LXC containers in the node:

```
# pct list
```

The following commands will start or stop a LXC container from the CLI:

```
# pct start <ct_id>
# pct stop <ct_id>
```

# Adjusting resources using direct modification

Although modifying a configuration file to change the resources of a container is possible, it is not recommended for day-to-day operations. Any manual modification made to the files does not get passed right away until the container is restarted, thus causing the downtime. However, there are some situations when manually editing the configuration file is necessary. The number of configuration options can then be changed through the GUI, and the pct tools are geared toward standard containers. LXC containers have a large number of configuration options, which cannot be changed through the GUI or pct tools. Only by editing the configuration files and restarting the containers, can these options can be applied. To learn more about the advanced configuration options, refer to:

```
http://manpages.ubuntu.com/manpages/precise/man5/lxc.conf.5.html.
```

# Migrating an LXC container

As of Proxmox VE 4.1, live migration of LXC containers is not possible. The container must be turned off before it can be moved. This is not a limitation of Proxmox but rather a LXC technology itself. If we try to migrate a powered on LXC container live, we will be presented with the following error message in the GUI:

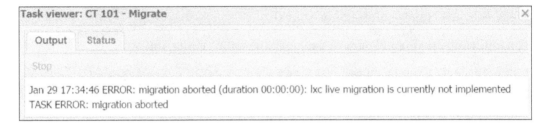

To migrate a powered off container, right-click on **Container** to open the **Context** menu, and then select **Migrate** or click on the **Migrate** button in the top-right corner of the GUI to open the **Migration** dialog box. Select a destination node from the drop-down list then click **Migrate**. After the migration is completed, turn on the container on the destination node. The live migration, however, is at the heavy development stage by LXC, so we should expect it in the mainstream LXC package in the near future. To some of us, the lack of this feature may be a huge deal breaker, especially in a container-dominant environment with many container instances. But unfortunately, Proxmox has moved on to LXC from Version 4.0, dropping OpenVZ completely.

 If you have a container-dominant environment, it may be wise to stay with a prior version of Proxmox VE 4.0 until a stable live migration for a LXC container is made available. There is currently no way to migrate live without powering down an LXC container.

# Accessing an LXC container

There are several ways in which we can access a LXC container:

- The **noVNC** console
- SSH
- Direct shells through the CLI

We can access and view the container directly from the GUI using the noVNC console. It is almost a visual remote access to the instance. The console is identical to a KVM virtual machine. After a long inactivity when we try to access the container using the console, it may appear, as shown in the following screenshot, with just a cursor and no login option:

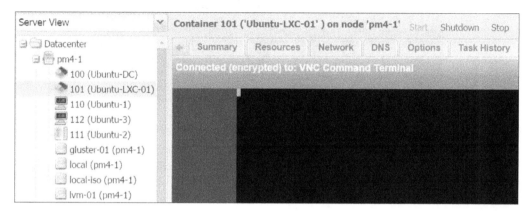

By simply pressing the *Enter* key, we can make the login prompt appear, as shown in the following screenshot:

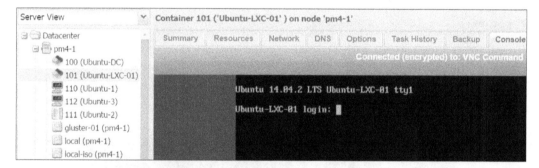

One of the best features of an LXC container is the ability to directly access the container shell through the CLI of the host node. The Proxmox command to access the LXC container shell is as follows:

```
# pct enter <ct_id>
```

This gives us the direct shell prompt of the container, as shown in the following screenshot:

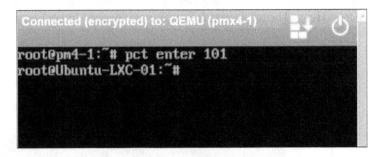

In the previous example, we are accessing the LXC container name, `Ubuntu-LXC-01`, from the Proxmox node, `pm4-1`. Note that no password was asked to be entered into the container from the Proxmox node. Since a container is running as the privileged root, we can perform any tasks inside the container. Once done, we can simply type `exit` to go back to the Proxmox node from the container.

We can also run various commands inside an LXC container without actually entering the container. The following Proxmox `format` command is used to execute commands inside a container:

```
# pct exec <ct_id> -- <command>
```

By following the previous format, if we want to create a directory inside the container and verify that the directory has been created, our command will appear, as shown in the following screenshot:

```
root@pm4-1:~# pct exec 101 mkdir /home/demouser
root@pm4-1:~# pct exec 101 ls /home
demouser  wasim
root@pm4-1:~# _
```

If we try to execute a command with additional arguments using - such as following, we will see a parsing error:

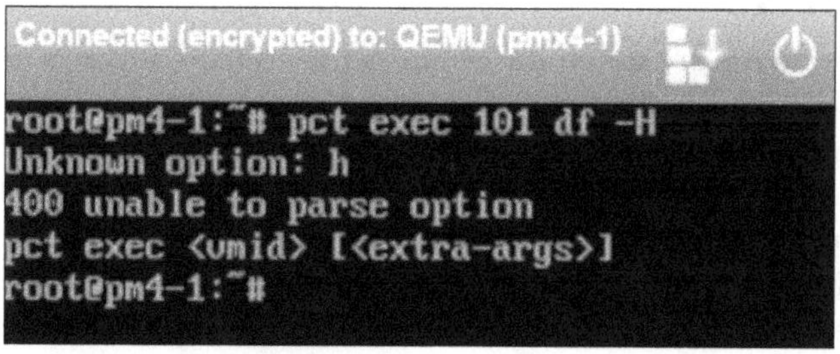

```
Connected (encrypted) to: QEMU (pmx4-1)
root@pm4-1:~# pct exec 101 df -H
Unknown option: h
400 unable to parse option
pct exec <vmid> [<extra-args>]
root@pm4-1:~#
```

In the previous example, we tried to see the storage usages in megabytes inside a container using an additional option argument, -H. In such cases, we have to modify the pct command by adding -- after the container ID, as shown in the following screenshot:

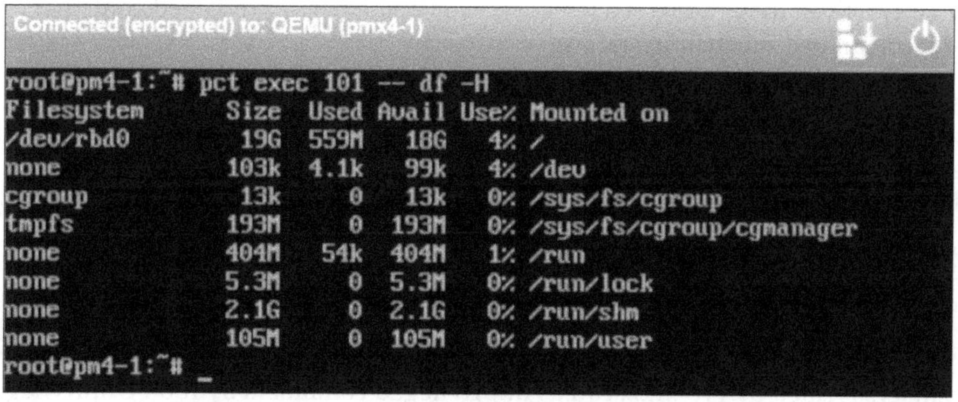

```
Connected (encrypted) to: QEMU (pmx4-1)
root@pm4-1:~# pct exec 101 -- df -H
Filesystem      Size  Used Avail Use% Mounted on
/dev/rbd0       19G   559M  18G    4% /
none            103k  4.1k  99k    4% /dev
cgroup          13k   0     13k    0% /sys/fs/cgroup
tmpfs           193M  0     193M   0% /sys/fs/cgroup/cgmanager
none            404M  54k   404M   1% /run
none            5.3M  0     5.3M   0% /run/lock
none            2.1G  0     2.1G   0% /run/shm
none            105M  0     105M   0% /run/user
root@pm4-1:~# _
```

In the preceding screenshot, we can see that the command to check the storage space has been executed successfully inside the container.

# Unprivileged versus privileged containers

Unprivileged containers are when the container is created and run as a user as opposed to the root. This is the safest way to use a container, because if the container security gets compromised and the intruder breaks out of the container, they will find themselves as a nobody user with extremely limited privileges. Unprivileged containers do not need to be owned by the user since they are run in user namespaces. This is a kernel feature that allows the mapping of a UID of a physical host into a namespace inside where a user with a UID 0 can exist. Unprivileged containers can also be run as root. By assigning a specific UID and GID to root, we can create unprivileged containers throughout the system and run them as root.

Privileged containers are when they are created and run by the root user only. These containers are not secure because all the processes are still run as root. All containers created through the Proxmox GUI or pct tools are privileged containers. Even though this is a lesser secured container, a privileged container is still considered much more secure.

We can create an unprivileged container if we really want to on a Proxmox node alongside the standard Proxmox LXC container, but it will not be managed through the GUI or Proxmox commands nor will they be visible in the GUI. We will not be able to take advantage of the Proxmox cluster features, such as backups, snapshots, migration, and so on. This somewhat defeats the purpose of having a hypervisor. We can use any mainstream Linux distribution on a node, install LXC packages, and then create unprivileged containers without using Proxmox at all.

However, with some modifications, we can configure a Proxmox node so that all the containers created by Proxmox run as unprivileged containers by root. Unprivileged root containers are balanced between fully unprivileged and privileged containers.

## Creating an unprivileged container as root

To create unprivileged containers as root, we first need to find the values of root in /etc/subuid and /etc/subgid. In our example node, the default values are as follows, respectively:

```
root : 100000 : 65536
root : 100000 : 65536
```

We now have to edit /etc/lxc/default.conf, and add the following two lines of code using the root values that we gathered in the previous step:

```
lxc.id_map = u 0 100000 65536
lxc.id_map = g 0 100000 65536
```

From this point on any LXC container created in a Proxmox node will be unprivileged by root. To learn more about unprivileged or privileged LXC containers, refer to:

https://linuxcontainers.org/lxc/getting-started/.

# Checking container processes

We can check to see whether the container processes are running as unprivileged or privileged in the host node. First, we need to see the list of processes running inside the container using the following command:

```
root@pm4-1:~# pct exec 101 -- ps -ef
UID        PID  PPID  C STIME TTY          TIME CMD
root         1     0  0 Jan29 ?        00:00:11 /sbin/init
root       367     1  0 Jan29 ?        00:00:06 upstart-udev-bridge --daemon
message+   426     1  0 Jan29 ?        00:00:02 dbus-daemon --system --fork
root       510     1  0 Jan29 ?        00:00:26 /lib/systemd/systemd-udevd --daemon
syslog     616     1  0 Jan29 ?        00:00:00 rsyslogd
root       722     1  0 Jan29 ?        00:00:01 upstart-file-bridge --daemon
root       723     1  0 Jan29 ?        00:00:02 upstart-socket-bridge --daemon
root       878     1  0 Jan29 ?        00:00:00 cron
root       895     1  0 Jan29 ?        00:00:10 /usr/sbin/irqbalance
root      1304     1  0 Jan29 ?        00:00:00 /usr/lib/postfix/master
postfix   1313  1304  0 Jan29 ?        00:00:00 qmgr -l -t unix -u
root      1377     1  0 Jan29 lxc/console 00:00:00 /sbin/getty -8 38400 console
root      1384     1  0 Jan29 lxc/tty2 00:00:00 /sbin/getty -8 38400 tty2
root      2953     1  0 Jan29 ?        00:00:00 /usr/sbin/sshd -D
postfix  11904  1304  0 01:28 ?        00:00:00 pickup -l -t unix -u -c
root     11916     1  0 01:30 lxc/tty1 00:00:00 /sbin/getty -8 38400 tty1
root     12374     0  0 02:38 ?        00:00:00 ps -ef
root@pm4-1:~#
```

Next, we need to know the process IDs for the running containers using the following command:

```
root@pm4-1:~# lxc-info -Ssip --name 101
State:          RUNNING
PID:            18663
IP:             192.168.1.17
CPU use:        134.92 seconds
Memory use:     156.02 MiB
KMem use:       9.43 MiB
Link:           veth101i0
 TX bytes:      1.70 KiB
 RX bytes:      310.18 MiB
 Total bytes:   310.18 MiB
root@pm4-1:~#
```

In the preceding screenshot, we can see that the process ID for the running container #101 is 18663. Now, we can run the following command to see all the processes running in the host node for the container:

```
root@pm4-1:~# ps -ef | grep 18663
root       11891 18663  0 Jan28 ?        00:00:00 /usr/sbin/sshd -D
root       18663 18606  0 Jan28 ?        00:00:11 /sbin/init
root       18933 18663  0 18:30 pts/0    00:00:00 /sbin/getty -8 38400 tty1
root       19042 18663  0 Jan28 ?        00:00:06 upstart-udev-bridge --daemon
statd      19103 18663  0 Jan28 ?        00:00:02 dbus-daemon --system --fork
root       19190 18663  0 Jan28 ?        00:00:27 /lib/systemd/systemd-udevd --daemon
systemd+   19351 18663  0 Jan28 ?        00:00:00 rsyslogd
root       19459 18663  0 Jan28 ?        00:00:01 upstart-file-bridge --daemon
root       19460 18663  0 Jan28 ?        00:00:02 upstart-socket-bridge --daemon
root       19616 18663  0 Jan28 ?        00:00:00 cron
root       19633 18663  0 Jan28 ?        00:00:11 /usr/sbin/irqbalance
root       20057 18663  0 Jan28 ?        00:00:00 /usr/lib/postfix/master
root       20134 18663  0 Jan28 pts/0    00:00:00 /sbin/getty -8 38400 console
root       20141 18663  0 Jan28 pts/1    00:00:00 /sbin/getty -8 38400 tty2
root       27904 26415  0 19:45 tty1     00:00:00 grep 18663
root@pm4-1:~#
```

In the preceding output, we can see all the container processes running as root in the host node. Since we can see the username root clearly, the container is running in privileged mode. If this was to be an unprivileged root container, then instead of a username, we would have seen 100000 since this is the UID of the root. If this was a nonroot unprivileged container, then we will see a different uid for this particular one in the first column of the previous output.

 If the total security or virtual machine full isolation is the primary concern for an environment, it is best to use a KVM virtual machine, because KVM is a fully independent virtual machine without any dependency on the host operating system or sharing resources.

# Converting OpenVZ to LXC

This section is for container users who are planning to move to Proxmox VE 4.0 or a later version. Since OpenVZ has been completely replaced in Proxmox VE 4.0 and later versions, all OpenVZ containers must be converted to LXCs in order to make them usable. The full conversion can be performed through the Proxmox GUI. The simple process of this conversion can be summarized as follows:

1. Write down the OpenVZ container network information

2. Power off the OpenVZ container, and then perform a full backup

3. Restore the OpenVZ container on Proxmox 4.0 or later

4. Reconfigure the network based on information collected in step 1

 Do not upgrade to Proxmox VE 4.0 or later before making a full backup of the existing OpenVZ containers. Otherwise, these containers will not start in Proxmox 4.0 or later.

The reason why it is important to write down the network configuration in step 1 is that when OpenVZ containers are restored in Proxmox 4.0 or later, the network interfaces are stripped off and need to be reattached and reconfigured.

We can also do the conversion using the CLI without the Proxmox GUI. After collecting the network information of the OpenVZ containers, we can power off the containers and commit a full backup using the following command:

```
# vzctl stop <ct_id> && vzdump <ct_id> -storage <storage_id>
```

Restore the container in Proxmox 4.0 or later using the following command:

```
# pct restore <ct_id> <storage>/dump/<backup_file>.tar
```

# Summary

In this chapter, we learned about LXC containers, how to create and manage them, and the difference between unprivileged and privileged containers. We also learned how to convert OpenVZ containers to LXC containers and use them in Proxmox VE 4.0 or later version. Despite not having the live migration ability, an LXC container is still a better choice of containerization than OpenVZ and works very well in a Proxmox environment.

In the next chapter, we will see some advanced features of network components in a Proxmox cluster. We will learn the benefits of a virtual network, what is OpenvSwitch, and why we should use it heavily in a virtual environment.

# 7
# Network of Virtual Networks

In this chapter, we are going to take an in-depth look at how we can create a virtualized network within a virtual environment. We will learn what the network building blocks are that make up the Proxmox hypervisor and how it manages both internal and external network connectivity. We will examine several network diagrams to see how Proxmox can be utilized to create an entire colony of virtual machines connected with virtual networks. We will also take a look at the Open vSwitch implementation in Proxmox along with the network configuration file, network bonding, VLAN, and so on. We can create dozens of virtual machines at will, but without a planned network model, we will fail to run an efficient virtual environment. If we compare virtual machines with bricks as the building blocks, then it is the network that acts as the mortar to create from a basic hut to a cathedral.

In this chapter, we will cover the following topics:

- The definition of a virtual network
- The networking components of Proxmox, such as bridge, vNIC, VLAN, bonding, and so on
- The Proxmox network configuration file
- Open vSwitch implementation
- Adding network components to a VM
- Sample virtual networks
- Multitenant virtual environments

# Exploring a virtual network

A virtual network is a software-defined network where all links and components may or may not have direct interaction with physical hardware. In most cases, direct interaction with physical hardware is made by the hypervisor or host controller. All links between virtual machines, virtual switches, virtual bridges, and virtual network interfaces are made completely virtually. The following are the two types of network virtualization:

- **External network virtualization**: This consists of several local networks operating as one virtual network. Physical LANs can be in the same location or spread over multiple locations. Usually, external virtualization is a cloud network service-based model that multiple companies can use to connect their multisite virtual environment for a service fee. External network virtualization can be easily achieved by combining several internal virtual networks into a single virtualized network using a WAN or the Internet using a technology, such as VPN.

- **Internal network virtualization**: This usually happens locally within a hypervisor between virtual machines. Do not confuse this with the local area network. Here, internal network virtualization is referring to the network connectivity between VMs, bridges, vNICs, and so on, which do not necessarily have to utilize the external LAN. This provides company IT staff with total control over virtual network operation. Network issues can be diagnosed faster; customization of expansion or contraction can happen without delay. Internal virtualization heavily uses virtual components, such as virtual bridges and vNIC, to form a virtual network.

For in-depth information on external and internal network virtualizations, refer to http://en.wikipedia.org/wiki/ Network_virtualization. Specially follow the *References* and *Further reading* book list at the bottom of the Wiki page.

In this book, we will mainly take a look at the internal network virtualization in the Proxmox hypervisor. We will also take a look at some network diagrams of internal and external virtual network combinations later in the book in *Chapter 13, Proxmox Production-Level Setup*.

# A physical network versus a virtual network

We will now see the difference between a physical network and a virtual network. The following diagram represents a physical network without a virtualization platform:

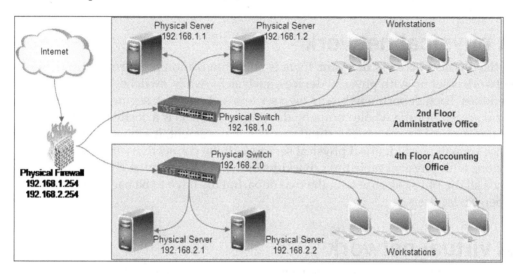

The following diagram represents virtualization as the main infrastructure:

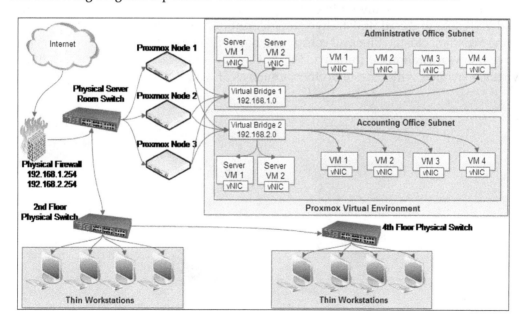

Before we dive into virtual network building blocks, we need to understand how networks are set up in the preceding diagrams. Both the diagrams represent the same office setup where the main administrative department is on the second floor, and the accounting department is on the fourth floor of the building. It is apparent from the diagrams that a physical network is less complex than a virtual network, but by leveraging virtualization, we can cut costs, increase efficiency, reduce hardware maintenance complexity, and increase portability.

# A physical network

In the physical network diagram, there is no virtualization platform set up. The network is set up with physical devices, such as firewalls, switches, servers, and full desktops. Each department has its own servers and network segments. A centralized management for the whole company does not exist. This is a costly solution due to all the physical hardware. If redundancy is a requirement, it will incur twice the cost since we will need identical physical servers. All the connectivity in this network is done with physical cable links. Backups in this setup are quite challenging since all the physical servers in the two departments have to be backed up on a per-device basis.

# A virtual network

The virtual network diagram represents how Proxmox can handle a setup with multiple departments. All the connections between servers and user's virtual machines happen virtually without a physical network device. Using virtual bridges and vNICs, both the administrative and accounting departments can coexist on the same Proxmox cluster. Since all computing happens in the hypervisor, end users can have thin workstations to minimize the cost significantly. Users can connect to their virtual machines with remote protocols, such as SPICE, VNC, or RDP.

Thin workstations are very underpowered, cheap, and basic computers for the end user, providing just the essentials to connect to dedicated server resources. Since all processing happens in a virtual environment, thin workstations do not need to be very powerful. The main purpose of a thin workstation is to allow the user to connect peripherals, such as the monitor, keyboard, mouse, and network cable. A thin workstation can be purchased for under $200.

In this setup, all servers and user machines are virtualized. If there is a need for a new server, it is just a matter of creating a virtual server with vNIC with a few clicks. Since Proxmox as a hypervisor was built from a group with redundant capabilities. In such a scenario, all virtual machines can simply be migrated to another available Proxmox node, and everything is up and running in minutes. Both the departments are separated by two virtual bridges.

Through the use of the Proxmox GUI, all management can be done from one location, including backup and restore. Virtual servers can be migrated over network links, which can be spread over large or small physical distances. Although a virtual network setup is much more robust and feature-rich, it has a much lower budgetary requirement. New departments can be added by creating new virtual bridges for separate subnets and using virtual LANS or VLANS on existing physical network switches.

# Networking components in Proxmox

We will now take a look at the networking components of Proxmox, which will allow virtual machines to communicate with or be segmented from other internal machines as well as the Internet.

# Virtual Network Interface Card (vNIC)

**Virtual Network Interface Card** (**vNIC**) is a software-defined representation of a **Media Access Control** (**MAC**) interface of physical network interfaces. It is basically a virtual network card for a virtual machine. Multiple vNICs can share a physical network interface of a host node. In a way, networking starts with vNIC when a virtual machine sends data to reach other virtual machines or networking devices within a virtual environment or physical environment. In the following diagram, the virtual machine has two virtual network interfaces assigned with an Intel e1000 driver. Both of them are configured with the bridge vmbr601:

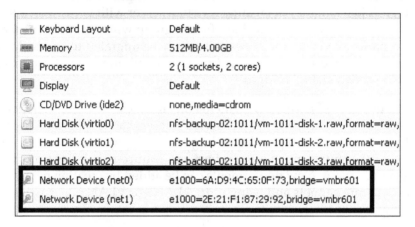

Intel e1000 is a Linux kernel driver used to virtualize Intel architecture-based virtual network interfaces. This is the default vNIC for new virtual machines in Proxmox since it is supported by all major operating systems, such as Linux, Windows, and Mac OS X, without needing additional drivers. Proxmox has four models of virtual network interfaces: Intel e1000, VirtIO, Realtek RTL8139, and VMware vmxnet3. Out of these four models, VirtIO provides the maximum network performance for a VM. All Linux-based operating systems come equipped with VirtIO drivers. For Windows, the VirtIO interface driver can be downloaded from http://www.linux-kvm.org/page/WindowsGuestDrivers/Download_Drivers.

For Mac OS, the VirtIO interface driver can be downloaded from https://github.com/pmj/virtio-net-osx.

Chapter 7

# Adding vNIC

To add a new virtual network interface for a VM, we can open the network device dialog using the **Add** button from the **Hardware** tab of the VM. The dialog box is similar to the network dialog box that we learned in *Chapter 5, KVM Virtual Machines,* in the *Creating KVM virtual machines* section.

If the **Hotplug** option for the network interface is enabled for the VM, we can add or remove the network interface without powering down the VM. The following screenshot shows the **Hotplug** option for KVM VMs:

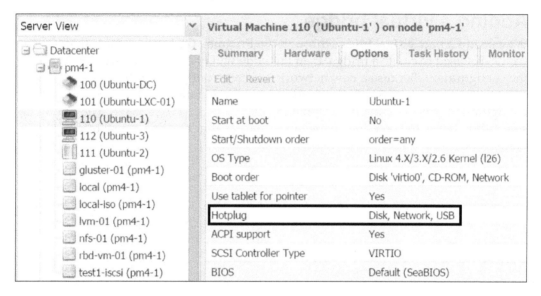

# A virtual bridge

Just as a real-world bridge connects two sides of a river, a virtual bridge connects a Proxmox virtual network to a physical network. A virtual bridge is like a physical network switch where all virtual machines connect to and can be configured using the **Spanning Tree Protocol** (**STP**). A virtual bridge is a great way to create separate subnets. All VMs in the same subnet can connect to their respective bridges. Proxmox creates one virtual bridge by default during the installation process. Each Proxmox node can support up to 4,094 bridges. When the same bridge configuration is entered on all nodes, the bridge can be used from any nodes in the cluster, thus making live migration possible without network connectivity interruption. The default naming format of a bridge is **vmbrX**, where X represents an integral number between 0 and 4,094.

Proxmox will allow a bridge to be created and not connected to a physical NIC. This allows an isolated environment, which has no access to the physical or any other network on the LAN. Using Open vSwitch, however, we can configure one bridge with multiple VLANs, such as a real physical switch. We will take a look at the Open vSwitch implementation later in this chapter.

We can change a virtual bridge of a VM in real time without needing to power cycle it. For example, if a VM is configured with a virtual bridge, vmbr0, and we want to change the bridge to vmbr10 later, we can do so without turning off the VM.

## Adding a virtual bridge

We can add a new virtual bridge through the Proxmox GUI or CLI. Note that if the GUI is used to create a bridge, then the node will need to be restarted to apply the configuration. Because a new network interface configuration through the GUI gets written in /etc/network/interfaces.new, and only by rebooting, the new configuration gets permanently written in /etc/network/interface. The following screenshot shows the pending change information after creating a new bridge named vmbr2:

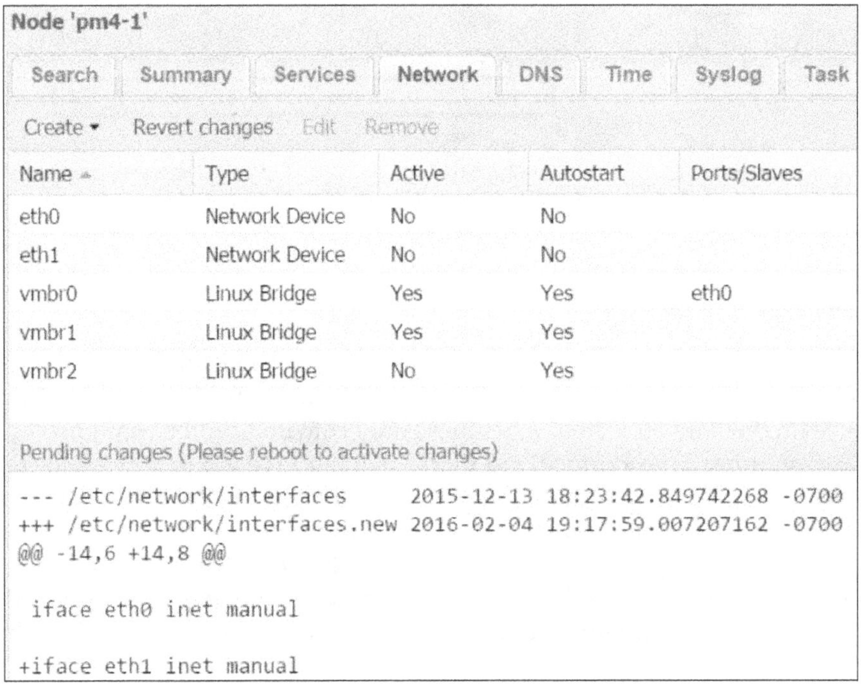

Node 'pm4-1'

| Search | Summary | Services | Network | DNS | Time | Syslog | Task |
|--------|---------|----------|---------|-----|------|--------|------|

Create ▾    Revert changes    Edit    Remove

| Name ⌃ | Type | Active | Autostart | Ports/Slaves |
|--------|------|--------|-----------|--------------|
| eth0 | Network Device | No | No | |
| eth1 | Network Device | No | No | |
| vmbr0 | Linux Bridge | Yes | Yes | eth0 |
| vmbr1 | Linux Bridge | Yes | Yes | |
| vmbr2 | Linux Bridge | No | Yes | |

Pending changes (Please reboot to activate changes)

```
--- /etc/network/interfaces      2015-12-13 18:23:42.849742268 -0700
+++ /etc/network/interfaces.new 2016-02-04 19:17:59.007207162 -0700
@@ -14,6 +14,8 @@

 iface eth0 inet manual

+iface eth1 inet manual
```

To revert the changes before a reboot is committed, we can simply click on the **Revert changes** button.

To create a new bridge through the GUI, we need to click on **Create** under **Network,** and then we need to select the Linux **Bridge option** to open the bridge creation dialog box, as shown in the following screenshot:

| Create: Linux Bridge | | | | ✕ |
|---|---|---|---|---|
| Name: | vmbr2 | Autostart: | ☑ | |
| IP address: | 192.168.0.171 | Vlan Aware: | ☑ | |
| Subnet mask: | 255.255.255.0 | Bridge ports: | eth1 | |
| Gateway: | | | | |
| IPv6 address: | | | | |
| Prefix length: | | | | |
| Gateway: | | | | |
| | | | | Create |

In the preceding screenshot, for our example, we are creating a bridge named vmbr2. The purpose of the **Bridge ports** textbox is to type in the physical network interface of the host to which this bridge will be connected to.

[  It is important to note here that we can only configure one virtual bridge per physical network interface. ]

In our example, there is a bridge, vmbr0, which is already configured to use the interface, eth0. We cannot use the same physical interface to create the new bridge. Thus, in our example, we have used the interface, eth1, as a bridge port. Also, we can only configure a gateway for only one bridge per node. Since the bridge vmbr0 is already configured with a gateway, we have to leave the gateway textbox blank for the new bridge.

The VLAN-aware checkbox is a new addition that allows Proxmox to act as a trunk in a switch that will pipe multiple VLANs over one connection. Although it is not important to enable it, it is, however, a new way of handling VLANs on the bridge. For example, if we need to implement 10 VLANS, we will need to create 10 virtual bridges in the traditional Linux bridge way. However, using the VLAN-aware option, we can create one bridge and just add the VLAN ID to it, thus saving an enormous amount of typing multiple bridge configurations. The following table shows a basic example of configuration between traditional and VLAN-aware virtual bridges:

| Traditional mode | VLAN-aware mode |
|---|---|
| auto vlan0 | auto vmbr0 |
| iface vlan0 inet manual | iface vmbr0 inet manual |
|   vlan_raw_device eth0 |   bridge_vlan_aware yes |
| auto vmbr0 |   bridge_ports eth0 |
| iface vmbr0 inet manual |   bridge_vids 1-10 |
|   bridge_ports vlan0 |   bridge_pvid 1 |
|   bridge_stp off |   bridge_stp off |
|   bridge_fd 0 |   bridge_fd 0 |
| .......... | |
| .......... | |
| auto vlan10 | |
| iface vlan10 inet manual | |
|   vlan_raw_device eth0 | |
| auto vmbr10 | |
| iface vmbr10 inet manual | |
|   bridge_ports vlan10 | |
|   bridge_stp off | |
|   bridge_fd 0 | |

In the preceding table, we can see that there are a lot of bridge instances in the traditional Linux way. However, using the VLAN-aware option, we can reduce the entire configuration to just a few lines.

Here, note that for the traditional Linux bridge, we have used additional lines of configuration to create a VLAN port first, and then we pass that port as a bridge port for the bridge. The configuration option is `vlan_raw_device <physical_port>`. Although there is more than one way to create the VLAN-backed bridge, this is the preferred way of configuration.

The advantage of using the traditional `linux` method is that each VLAN gets its own virtual bridge, thus isolating the network traffic further. For instance, when reconfiguring a bridge of a particular VLAN ID, only that bridge and all the VMs connected to that bridge are affected. For the VLAN aware mode, when there is a misconfiguration, it can interrupt the network connectivity for all the VMs connected to the bridge. The VLAN aware mode provides similar functionalities to Open vSwitch but without the extra package. We will learn about Open vSwitch later in this chapter.

When using the VLAN-aware enabled bridge, we have to tag each virtual interface with the VLAN ID, as shown in the following screenshot:

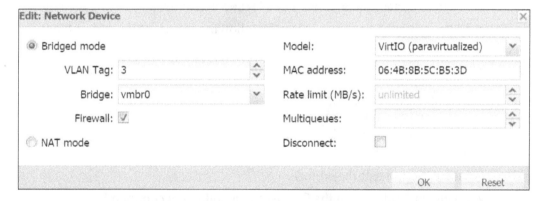

When using traditional mode without the VLAN aware option, we have to select the VLAN tagged bridge itself for the virtual network interface, as shown in the following screenshot:

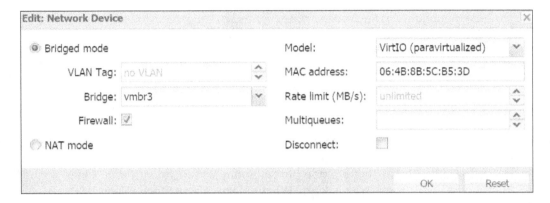

Perform the following steps to create a virtual bridge in Proxmox through the CLI:

1. Log in to the Proxmox node through the console.

2. Open the interface file # `nano /etc/network/interfaces` using an editor.

3. Add the configuration lines using the following format at the end of the file:

```
auto <bridge_name>
iface <bridge_name> inet static
       address <ip_info>
    netmask
       bridge_ports <interface>
       bridge_stp off
       bridge_fd 0
```

4. Save the file and exit the editor.

5. Activate the bridge from the CLI using the following command:

```
# ifup <bridge_name>
```

The new virtual bridge should now be activated and running. If virtual machines are to be migrated to other nodes, then the configuration must be duplicated in all the nodes.

# Extra bridge options

There are two extra bridge options that are usually used with virtual bridge configuration.

# bridge_stp

This option allows multiple bridges to communicate with each other for network discovery and loop avoidance. This is useful to eliminate data cycles to provide optimal packet routing because with **STP** on, bridges can talk to each other and figure out how they are connected, and then provide the best routing possible for the data packet transmission. STP also allows fault tolerance since it checks the network topology if a bridge fails. To turn on the STP option, just modify the bridge configuration, as follows:

```
bridge_stp on
```

STP increases the bandwidth efficiency while posing security issues. Do not use STP when a virtual subnet requires isolation from the other virtual subnet in the same cluster, and you do not want the bridges to talk to each other. It is a useful option when working in a virtual environment of the same company where data can flow freely between departments subnets.

STP is turned off by default.

STP does not have any authentication and assumes all network interfaces to be trustworthy. When a bridge enquires about the network topology from another bridge, information is freely shared without any authentication. Thus, a user in the bridge can potentially gather data about the entire network topology and other bridges in the network. This leads to a dangerous situation when bridging between the internal environment and the Internet.

# bridge_fd

**FD** refers to **Forwarding Delay**. The `bridge_fd` option sets the delay for how long before the interface will be ready. During the delay, the bridge tries to discover other bridges and checks whether there are no network loops if STP is on. By default, the forwarding delay is set to 0, as shown in the following code:

```
bridge_fd 0
```

In most cases, the default value of 0 is enough. In a very complex virtual environment with several dozen bridges, increasing this number to 3 or 4 might help. Without this delay, the bridge will start transmitting data packets regardless of whether the other destination bridge is available or not. Increasing the delay time allows the source bridge to check all the bridges and not transmit any data if the destination bridge is down, thus preventing unnecessary network bandwidth consumption.

There are many more `bridge_` options to be used in a network configuration file, such as `bridge_hello`, `bridge_maxage`, `bridge_bridgeprio`, and so on. Bridge options are Linux-specific and beyond the scope of this book. For in-depth information on bridges, visit `http://www.linuxfoundation.org/collaborate/workgroups/networking/bridge`.

# Virtual LAN

**Virtual Local Area Network** or **VLAN** is a logical local area network within a physical local area network. It can be compared with partitions within a physical disk storage. A physical network interface can be partitioned to transport data for multiple separate subnets. This partition is achieved using VLAN ID. For details on VLANs or IEEE 802.1q standard, refer to `http://en.wikipedia.org/wiki/IEEE_802.1Q`.

Once VLAN data leaves the virtual environment, a physical network switch with the VLAN feature tags each data with an ID and then directs the data to its proper destination. Each subnet should have the same VLAN ID on the virtual environment and on the physical network switch. A VLAN helps reduce the broadcast traffic of multiple domains on the same network. By segmenting a large network into smaller VLANs, broadcasts can be sent only to relevant VLANs without interrupting other data traffic on the network.

A VLAN also provides an added security layer on a multidomain network since a user can no longer just plug in to the network and capture just about any data of any domains on the network. Network segmentation is usually done with a layer 3 device such as a router. However, using a VLAN, significant cost saving can be achieved with the already-existing layer 2 device on the network, such as a managed switch or smart switch. There are seven layers defined by the **Open Systems Interconnection (OSI)** model by which network communication takes place. For in-depth details on OSI, refer to `http://en.wikipedia.org/wiki/OSI_model`.

# Adding a VLAN

VLAN can be set up on both the virtual machines and on bridges. If the VLAN traffic leaves a virtual environment, it is important for each switch and physical network device to be VLAN-aware and tagged properly. Tagging VMs with the VLAN ID is very straightforward through the Proxmox GUI. Just enter the VLAN ID during the addition of a network interface to a VM or edit the already added vNICs. The following screenshot shows a virtual interface for a VM after it was tagged with a VLAN ID:

**Virtual Machine 110 ('Ubuntu-1' ) on node 'pm4-1'**

| Summary | Hardware | Options | Task History | Monitor | Backup | Snapshots |
|---------|----------|---------|--------------|---------|--------|-----------|

Add ▾   Remove   Edit   Resize disk   Move disk   Disk Throttle   CPU options   Revert

| | | |
|---|---|---|
| ▭ | Keyboard Layout | Default |
| ▦ | Memory | 128MB/512MB |
| ▣ | Processors | 1 (1 sockets, 1 cores) |
| ▢ | Display | Default |
| ◉ | CD/DVD Drive (ide2) | none,media=cdrom |
| ▭ | Hard Disk (virtio0) | local:110/vm-110-disk-2.raw,size=5G |
| ▰ | Network Device (net0) | virtio=06:4B:8B:5C:B5:3D,bridge=vmbr0,**tag=2**,firewall=1 |

In the previous example, we have tagged the interface for VLAN ID 2. This tagging works when the bridge has the VLAN aware option enabled, or when Open vSwitch has been implemented. When each virtual bridge is configured with a separate VLAN ID, then instead of assigning a tag ID, we will configure the interface to use the bridge for that VLAN. In the following screenshot, we have configured the network interface to use the bridge vmbr2 instead of tagging:

**Virtual Machine 110 ('Ubuntu-1' ) on node 'pm4-1'**

| Summary | Hardware | Options | Task History | Monitor | Backup | Snapshots |
|---------|----------|---------|--------------|---------|--------|-----------|

Add ▾   Remove   Edit   Resize disk   Move disk   Disk Throttle   CPU options   Revert

| | | |
|---|---|---|
| ▭ | Keyboard Layout | Default |
| ▦ | Memory | 128MB/512MB |
| ▣ | Processors | 1 (1 sockets, 1 cores) |
| ▢ | Display | Default |
| ◉ | CD/DVD Drive (ide2) | none,media=cdrom |
| ▭ | Hard Disk (virtio0) | local:110/vm-110-disk-2.raw,size=5G |
| ▰ | Network Device (net0) | virtio=06:4B:8B:5C:B5:3D,**bridge=vmbr2**,firewall=1 |

We can also configure a VLAN for bonded network interfaces. For this, instead of assigning a physical interface as a VLAN raw device, we need to create a new bonded interface, and then use that for the VLAN raw device, as shown in the following example configuration:

```
auto bond0
iface bond0 inet manual
    slaves eth0 eth1
auto vlan1
ifaec vlan1 inet manual
        vlan-raw-device bond0

auto vmbr1
iface vmbr1 inet manual
        bridge_ports vlan1
        bridge_stp off
        bridge_fd 0
```

In the previous example, we created a bonded interface using the physical ports, eth0 and eth1. Then, we created a VLAN interface vlan1 using the bonded interface as the raw device. The new virtual bridge vmbr1 was created from the vlan1. Notice that nowhere have we used the VLAN tag. Instead, we created the VLAN raw device based on the desired tag. The name of the bridge is not important here, but the name of the VLAN interface is. If we have to create a bridge for VLAN ID 9, then our configuration will look like this:

```
auto vlan9
ifaec vlan9 inet manual
        vlan-raw-device bond0

auto vmbr9
iface vmbr9 inet manual
        bridge_ports vlan9
        bridge_stp off
        bridge_fd 0
```

Besides the tagged virtual bridge and virtual network interface, in order to make the VLAN work, we also have to configure a physical switch. Without a VLAN, the capable switch network traffic will not be able to traverse between nodes or go outside the local network. Traffic will be limited to inside the node only. Each physical switch comes with its own GUI for switch configuration, but the basic idea of the VLAN configuration remains the same for all.

The VLAN configuration is done on a physical switch by configuring trunks or general ports. The option is usually found by navigating to the **Switching | VLAN** menu of the GUI. The following screenshot is an example of the VLAN setting on Netgear GS748T smartswitch:

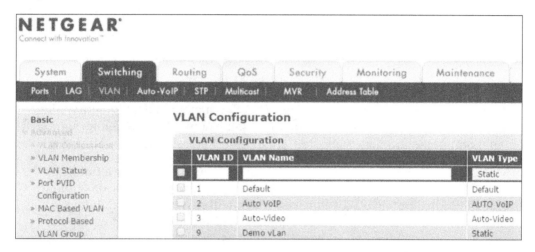

In the previous example, the VLAN Demo VLAN with **ID #9** is set up for the bridge, vmbr9. Next, we have to configure the ports that are part of VLAN 9 under the VLAN Membership menu, as shown in the following screenshot, where we have tagged port 2, 3, 4, and 5 for VLAN 9:

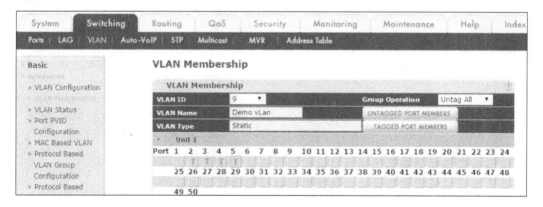

A good practice to identify which VLAN belongs to which bridge is to use the same numeric number for both the interfaces. For example, a bridge, vmbr10, will have the same VLAN ID 10. Without some order in the beginning, bridges and VLANs will quickly get out of control as the network grows over time.

# Network Address Translation/Translator

**Network Address Translation/Translator** (**NAT**) is a methodology of remapping one IP address space into another by modifying the network address information in IP datagram packet headers while they are in transit across a traffic routing device.

NAT secures a device by not directly exposing it to the Internet or to a public network. It also allows more physical devices to be able to communicate without having individual public IPV4 addresses, which will cost money, and there are a limited supply of IP addresses on the Internet. NAT is usually configured in the router or firewall of a network, where the policy is created for local-to-global and global-to-local IP address mapping.

Note that NAT is relevant for IPv4 networks. An IPv6 network diminishes the need to use NAT because IPv6 addressing is always public.

## Adding NAT/masquerading

NAT is a way to hide internal network IP addresses from the external network, such as the Internet. Any outgoing traffic uses the main host IP address instead of using its own local IP address. Add the last three lines of the following post-up and post-down settings to the `/etc/network/interfaces` configuration file. Only, add these lines under the virtual bridge configuration that needs the NAT option:

```
auto vmbr0
iface vmbr0 inet static
address 192.168.145.1
netmask 255.255.255.0
bridge_ports none
bridge_stp off
bridge_fd 0post-up echo 1 > /proc/sys/net/ipv4/ip_forward
post-up iptables -t nat -A POSTROUTING -s '192.168.145.0/24' -o
    eth0 -j MASQUERADE
post-down iptables -t nat -D POSTROUTING -s '192.168.145.0/24' -o
    eth0 -j MASQUERADE
```

It is recommended that all NAT configurations need to be handled by a dedicated physical or virtual firewall. Most of the firewalls have the out-of-the-box NAT option. Also, using virtualized firewalls, we can create truly isolated virtual networks for multiple clients on the same Proxmox cluster. Having a virtual firewall provides the client with control over their own filtering while keeping their network hidden from the other client networks in the cluster.

# Network bonding

**Network bonding** or **Teaming** or **Link aggregation (LAG)** is a concept where multiple interfaces are combined to increase the throughput, set up network redundancy, and balance network load. This concept is heavily used in high-demand environments where downtime and slow network I/O are not acceptable. The Proxmox GUI provides excellent features to create and manage bonding within the cluster node. Bonding modes supported by Proxmox are `balance-rr`, `active-backup`, `balance-xor`, broadcast, **Link Aggregation Control Protocol (LACP)**, or 802.3ad, `balance-tlb`, and `balance-alb`. The following table lists the various bonding modes as well their policies and descriptions:

| Bonding Mode | Policy | Description |
|---|---|---|
| `balance-rr` or `Mode 0` | Round robin | Packet transmission takes places sequentially from the first participating network interface to the last. This provides load balancing and fault tolerance |
| `active-backup` or `Mode 1` | Active backup | Only one participating network interface is active. The next interface becomes active when the previous active interface fails. This only provides fault tolerance. |
| `balance-xor` or `Mode 2` | XOR | This mode selects the same participating interface for each destination MAC address. Transmission takes place based on bonded network interfaces of MAC address XOR'd with the destination MAC address. This provides both load balancing and fault tolerance. |
| `broadcast` or `Mode 3` | Broadcast | Transmission takes place on all participating bonded network interfaces. This provides fault tolerance only. |

| Bonding Mode | Policy | Description |
|---|---|---|
| `802.3ad`<br><br>or<br><br>`Mode 4` | Dynamic link aggregation | All participating network interfaces in the aggregated group share the same speed and duplex settings. All interfaces are utilized according to the 802.3ad specification. A network switch with 802.3ad or the LACP feature is required. This provides fault tolerance. |
| `balance-tlb`<br><br>or<br><br>`Mode 5` | Adaptive transmit load balancing | Outgoing packets are distributed according to the current load on each participated interface. Incoming packets are received on the current interface, and if the same interface fails, then the next available interface takes over. This provides fault tolerance and load balance for only outbound packets. |
| `balance-alb`<br><br>or<br><br>`Mode 6` | Adaptive load balancing | This is the same as `balance-tlb` with the inclusion of load balancing for incoming packets on all interfaces. This provides fault tolerance and load balancing for both incoming and outgoing traffic. |

The following screenshot shows the Proxmox menu system used to create new **Bond**:

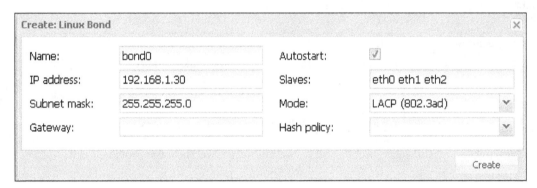

# Adding a bonding interface

We will now see how to add network bonding to our cluster. There are several types of bonding options available. However, only `balance-rr`, `active-backup`, and LACP (802.3ad) are most widely used. The `balance-rr` option provides the round robin method to increase the overall interface bandwidth with failover. The balance-rr option does not require a special network switch. Just about any switch can be used to make this work. The major drawback of balance-rr is the waste of data packets. LACP is known as industry standard bonding.

In this book, we will only take a look at the LACP bonding protocol. However, to give you an idea of what a balance-rr bonding looks like, the following diagram shows the balance-rr bonding between Proxmox nodes and Ceph distributed storage clusters. In this example, the Proxmox public network is on 192.168.10.0/24, while the storage backend is on a private 192.168.201.0/24 subnet. Separate switches are used for the Ceph storage network to increase redundancy. Each Proxmox node has three 1-gigabit NICs. One is used from the main cluster to server virtual machines, and the remaining two are used for balance-rr bonding. This type of bonding is a very economical way to provide network redundancy:

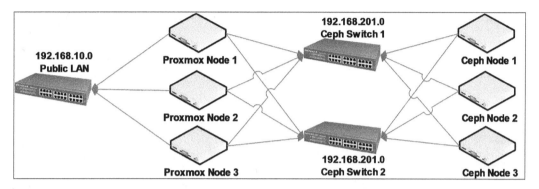

LACP can combine multiple interfaces to increase the total throughput but not the actual connection. For example, an LACP bonding of four 1-gigabit network interfaces will still have a total connection speed of 1 gigabit, but it will be able to respond to more simultaneous requests at closer to 1 gigabit speed.

> To know more about Link aggregation/Bonding/Teaming, refer to
> http://en.wikipedia.org/wiki/Link_Aggregation_Control_
> Protocol#Link_Aggregation_Control_Protocol.

For LACP to work, it is very important to know whether the physical switch supports this feature. A quick visit to a switch manufacturer's website will give us the information if the LACP feature is supported. Some manufacturers will list this feature as 802.3ad.

Like virtual bridges, we can also configure a network bond through the Proxmox GUI or CLI. A bond created through the GUI will only be activated after the node reboots, whereas a bond added through the CLI by editing the network configuration file directly can also be activated through the CLI. We can open the bond interface creation dialog box from the Hardware tab of the node. The following screenshot shows the dialog box for a bonded interface, bond0, in our example Proxmox node:

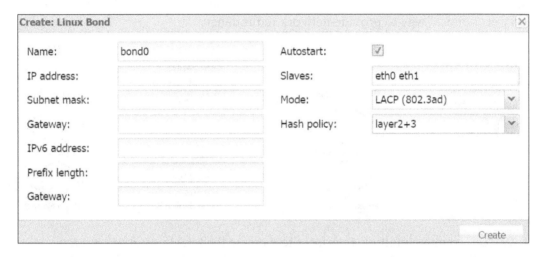

In the previous example, we used physical interfaces, eth0 and eth1, for our bonded interface, **bond0**. We have not used any IP information since this bonded interface will not be directly connected, but we will create VLAN interfaces and virtual bridges based on the bond interface. For bond mode, we are using LACP with the layer 2+3 hash policy. There are three hash policies to choose from the drop-down list:

- Layer 2
- Layer 2+3
- Layer 3+4

To maximize performance and stability of network connectivity, it is important to know the difference between the policies.

## The layer 2 hash policy

If no policy is selected, then Proxmox uses the Layer 2 policy by default. This policy generates the transmission hash based on MAC addresses of the network interface. This policy puts all the network traffic on a single slave interface in the bonded LACP.

# The layer 2+3 hash policy

This policy creates the transmission hash based on the combined MAC and IP addresses. These are also the layer 2 and layer 3 protocols of the network layer. This policy also puts the network traffic to a destination on the same slave interface. However, it provides a more balanced network transmission than just using the layer 2 policy. For best performance and stability, use this policy.

# The layer 3+4 hash policy

This policy creates the transmission hash based on the upper network layer whenever it is available. The combination of layer 3 and 4 allows multiple network traffic or connection spanning over multiple slave interfaces in the bonded LACP. However, one single connection will not span over multiple slave interfaces. For non IP network traffic, this policy uses the layer 2 hash policy. Do keep in mind that the layer 3+4 policy is not fully LACP or 802.3ad compliant.

To create the bonding interface, the following lines need to be added to the configuration file. In our example, we are adding the physical interface ports, eth0 and eth1, to the bonding interface:

```
auto eth1
iface eth1 inet manual
auto eth2
iface eth2 inet manual

# bonding interfaces
auto bond0
iface bond0 inet manual
        slaves eth1 eth2
        bond_miimon 100
        bond_mode 802.3ad
```

We are going to add the following lines of code to create a virtual bridge using the bonded port:

```
auto vmbr1
iface vmbr1 inet static
        address 192.168.10.1
        netmask 255.255.255.0
        bridge_ports bond0
        bridge_stp off
        bridge_fd 0
```

Activate the bridge by rebooting the node or from the CLI by stopping and restarting the bridge. Use the following commands:

```
# ifup bond0
# ifdown vmbr1
# ifup vmbr1
```

After configuring Proxmox nodes with LACP bonding, we now have to set up LACP on a physical switch. Each switch comes with its own documentation on how to configure the LACP link aggregation. In this section, we are going to take a look at the Netgear GS748T smartswitch LACP feature. The option to enable LACP can be found by navigating to **Switching | LAG** in the Neatgear GUI. First, we have to enable LACP for each link group. The following screenshot shows LACP enabled for groups 1 to 3 through the **LAG Configuration** menu:

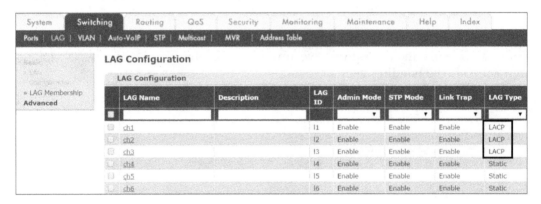

After the link groups are enabled, we will assign switch ports to each group. In our example, we are assigning port 1 and 2 to group 1 named ch1, port 3 and 4 to a group named ch2, and port 5 and 6 to a group named ch3. The following screenshot shows ports enabled for group 1:

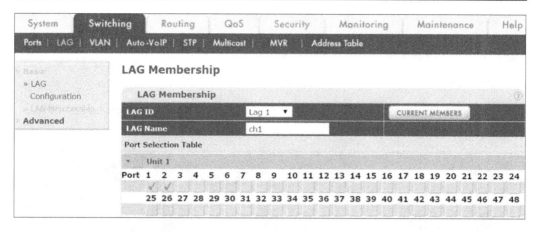

Bonding can also be used with VLAN. Refer to the *Virtual LAN* section in this chapter to learn how to integrate bonding with VLAN.

# Multicast

From Proxmox VE 4.0 and later, multicast is now required for proper cluster communication. In simple words, multicast delivers a single transmission to multiple server nodes in a network simultaneously, whereas unicast sends data packets to a single destination from a single source. The more nodes there are in a cluster the more separate unicast packets needs to be sent by a cluster. Using multicast, this extra amount of traffic is vastly minimized. Due to the increase of packets in the network when using unicast, implementing it in a cluster with five or more nodes should be avoided. In order for multicast to work, the physical switch in the network must be multicast and **IGMP snoop** capable.

**IGMP snooping** is simply a process where the physical switch listens or snoops for an IGMP conversation between the nodes and the switch. This allows the switch to maintain a table or map to determine how and where to direct multicast requests. After enabling the IGMP snoop, it takes a few hours for the switch to establish the table after gathering enough data for all multicast enabled switch ports.

Keep in mind that Open vSwitch currently does not handle multicast. So, for the Open vSwitch environment, the multicast querier router must be configured in the physical switch.

If it is not possible to use multicast at all in a Proxmox environment, then unicast is the only choice. To test whether multicast is functioning in the cluster, we can run the following command in all the Proxmox nodes:

```
# omping <node1_ip> <node2_ip> ……
```

If multicast is fully functioning, the output will show multicast responses, as shown in the following screenshot:

```
root@pm4-2:~# omping -c 10 172.16.0.171 172.16.0.172
172.16.0.171 : waiting for response msg
172.16.0.171 : joined (S,G) = (*, 232.43.211.234), pinging
172.16.0.171 :   unicast, seq=1, size=69 bytes, dist=0, time=0.192ms
172.16.0.171 : multicast, seq=1, size=69 bytes, dist=0, time=0.322ms
172.16.0.171 :   unicast, seq=2, size=69 bytes, dist=0, time=0.235ms
172.16.0.171 : multicast, seq=2, size=69 bytes, dist=0, time=0.278ms
172.16.0.171 :   unicast, seq=3, size=69 bytes, dist=0, time=0.816ms
172.16.0.171 : multicast, seq=3, size=69 bytes, dist=0, time=0.843ms
172.16.0.171 :   unicast, seq=4, size=69 bytes, dist=0, time=0.212ms
172.16.0.171 : multicast, seq=4, size=69 bytes, dist=0, time=0.311ms
172.16.0.171 :   unicast, seq=5, size=69 bytes, dist=0, time=0.364ms
172.16.0.171 : multicast, seq=5, size=69 bytes, dist=0, time=0.378ms
172.16.0.171 :   unicast, seq=6, size=69 bytes, dist=0, time=0.263ms
172.16.0.171 : multicast, seq=6, size=69 bytes, dist=0, time=0.276ms
172.16.0.171 :   unicast, seq=7, size=69 bytes, dist=0, time=0.230ms
172.16.0.171 : multicast, seq=7, size=69 bytes, dist=0, time=0.240ms
172.16.0.171 :   unicast, seq=8, size=69 bytes, dist=0, time=0.242ms
172.16.0.171 : multicast, seq=8, size=69 bytes, dist=0, time=0.304ms
172.16.0.171 :   unicast, seq=9, size=69 bytes, dist=0, time=0.283ms
172.16.0.171 : multicast, seq=9, size=69 bytes, dist=0, time=0.297ms
172.16.0.171 :   unicast, seq=10, size=69 bytes, dist=0, time=0.219ms
172.16.0.171 : multicast, seq=10, size=69 bytes, dist=0, time=0.232ms
172.16.0.171 : given amount of query messages was sent

172.16.0.171 :   unicast, xmt/rcv/%loss = 10/10/0%, min/avg/max/std-dev = 0.192/0.306/0.816/0.186
172.16.0.171 : multicast, xmt/rcv/%loss = 10/10/0%, min/avg/max/std-dev = 0.232/0.348/0.843/0.179
root@pm4-2:~#
```

Unsuccessful multicast responses will show packet loss for the node. The documentation of each physical switch should show if the switch is multicast capable. However, nowadays, almost all smart and managed switches have the multicast feature. It is, however, disabled on all ports and must be enabled for a proper Proxmox cluster communication.

# Configuring multicast on Netgear

In this section, we will see how to configure multicast for Netgear smartswitch GS748T. To configure multicast, navigate to **Switching | Multicast**. First, we are going to enable the IGMP snooping status through the IGMP Snooping Configuration option, as shown in the following screenshot:

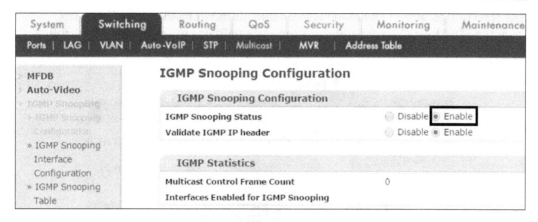

Next, we have to enable admin mode for the interfaces that will be used for IGMP snooping. We can enable them from the `IGMP Snooping Interface Configuration` option. As shown in the following screenshot, in our example switch, we are enabling IGMP snooping for switch ports 1 to 6, which is where Proxmox nodes are connected:

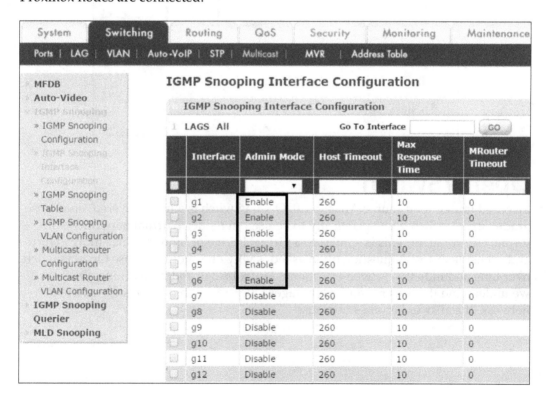

The last configuration to be made is to enable multicast traffic for switch ports from the **Multicast Router Configuration** option. In our example, we are enabling multicast on ports 1 to 6, as shown in the following screenshot:

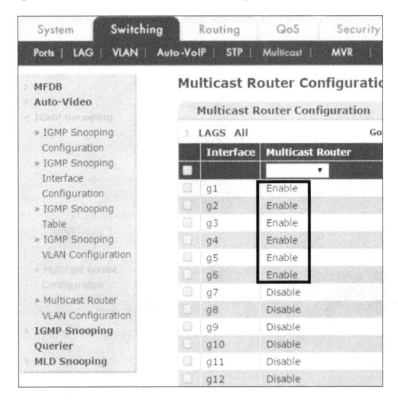

# Open vSwitch

Licensed under open source Apache 2.0, Open vSwitch is a multi-layered, enterprise grade virtual switch born specifically to be used in modern virtual networks of a virtual environment. This is similar to a virtual bridge of Linux but has more ability and robust features. A question often asked is why one should choose Open vSwitch over time and industry-proven traditional Linux bridge and networking. Once we understand the features and advantages Open vSwitch provides for a virtual network, the answer becomes obvious.

# Features of Open vSwitch

The following are some of the features that make Open vSwitch a better option than standard Linux networking:

- **Security**: Open vSwitch provides a high-degree of security by allowing you to set policies per VM virtual interface.

- **LACP and VLAN-aware**: Open vSwitch fully supports the LACP link aggregation and VLAN tagging. We can configure one single Open vSwitch with multiple VLAN tags, thus reducing management overhead of many virtual bridges per VLAN tag.

- **Quality of Service**: QoS or quality of service is fully supported.

- **Network monitoring**: We can get an extreme level of control over network packets passing through Open vSwitch by implementing powerful monitoring using Netflow and sFlow.

- **IPv6**: Open vSwitch fully supports IPv6.

- **Tunneling protocol**: This has full support for multiple tunneling protocols, such as GRE, VXLAN, STT, IPsec, and so on.

- **Proxmox support**: Open vSwitch is fully integrated and supported by Proxmox, making it a viable choice for virtual network configuration.

 For complete details on the Open vSwitch technology, visit the official site at http://Open vSwitch.org/.

It is possible to build the Proxmox cluster entirely with the traditional Linux bridge without using Open vSwitch at all. But for a large environment, Open vSwitch does make great sense since it can lessen tedious virtual network management while providing excellent visibility over network traffic. In a multitenant environment, taking control over what is going on in the network is very important.

Open vSwitch is not installed in Proxmox by default. It must be manually installed and configured. On a clean installed Proxmox node, we have to configure the network as usual, so the node can have Internet connectivity. Then, run the following command to install Open vSwitch:

```
# apt-get install Open vSwitch-switch
```

Even if Open vSwitch is not installed, the Proxmox GUI will still show the menu options for the Open vSwitch bridge and interface under the **Create** tab of the **Network** menu of the node.

An important thing to remember when using Open vSwitch is never to mix traditional Linux components, such as bridge, bond, and VLAN should never mixed with Open vSwitch components. For example, we must not create an Open vSwitch bridge based on the Linux bond and vice versa.

There are three components that we can use with Open vSwitch:

- Open vSwitch bridge
- Open vSwitch bond
- Open vSwitch IntPort

## Adding the Open vSwitch bridge

The Open vSwitch bridge is similar to the Linux bridge except that we can configure one Open vSwitch bridge, such as a physical switch where we can pass several vlans. We do not need to create separate bridges for each vlans, such as Linux bridges. Configuring the Open vSwitch bridge is a little more complicated than the Linux bridge. We need to configure the port first before creating the actual bridge. In our example, we are going to configure the port, eth1, which is what our Open vSwitch bridge, vmbr2, is going to be based on. For this, we need to add the following lines of code to /etc/network/interfaces:

```
allow-vmbr2 eth1
iface eth1 inet manual
  ovs_type OVSPort
  ovs_bridge vmbr2

auto vmbr2
allow-ovs vmbr2
iface vmbr2 inet static
  address 192.168.0.171
  netmask 255.255.255.0
  ovs_type OVSBridge
  ovs_ports eth1
```

Unlike a Linux bridge, where vlans are passed through bridge tagging, in Open vSwitch, we can pass vlans through ports directly. VLAN trunks are configured as additional Open vSwitch options in the configuration, as shown in the following example, where we are passing VLAN 2, 3, and 4:

```
allow-vmbr2 eth1
iface eth1 inet manual
  ovs_type OVSPort
```

```
ovs_bridge vmbr2
ovs_options trunks=2,3,4
```

We can also create the Open vSwitch bridge through the Proxmox GUI. However, we need to keep in mind that any network configuration performed through the GUI is not activated until a node is restarted.

We can open the Open vSwitch bridge creation dialog box from the network tab of a node, as shown in the following screenshot:

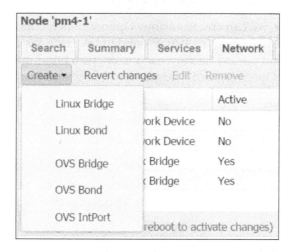

The following screenshot shows the Open vSwitch bridge creation dialog box with the necessary information:

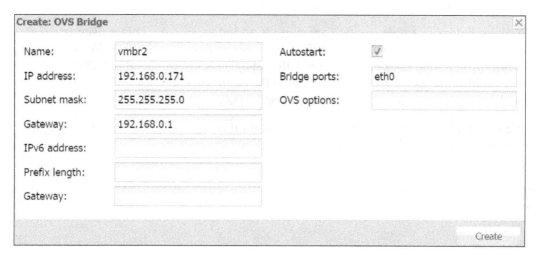

In the OVS options, we can include additional options for the bridge.

 When adding the bridge through the GUI, we do not need to configure the port itself first as we have to do while adding the bridge through the CLI. The GUI automatically defines the port for us.

## Adding the Open vSwitch bond

Like the Linux bridge, we can create various Open vSwitch bond interfaces. In this example, we are going to create the LACP bonded interface for Open vSwitch. The following configuration parameters are used to create a bond interface using the interface to create an Open vSwitch bridge:

```
allow-vmbr2 bond0
iface bond0 inet manual
  ovs_type OVSBond
  ovs_bridge vmbr2
  ovs_bonds eth0 eth1
  pre-up (ifconfig eth0 mtu 8996 && ifconfig eth1 mtu 8996)
  ovs_options bond_mode=balance-tcp lacp=active trunks=2,3,4
  mtu 8996
auto vmbr2
iface vmbr2 inet manual
  ovs_type OVSBridge
  ovs_ports bond0
  mtu 8996
```

In the previous example, a new parameter is added as pre-up. This is used to configure jumbo packets. The default mtu for all the interfaces is 1,500. When configuring jumbo packets, using the value of 8,996 is safer instead of 9,000 since some additional bytes are added on top of the configured mtu for which a data packet may get discarded if mtu goes beyond 9,000.

We can configure the same Open vSwitch bond through the Proxmox GUI using the bond creation dialog box, as shown in the following screenshot:

It is not possible to add the extra parameter, such as configuring the desired `mtu` through the Proxmox GUI. So, before we restart the node, we can add the parameter to `/etc/network/interfaces.new`, so the configuration gets committed in `/etc/network/interfaces` during the node reboot.

# Adding Open vSwitch IntPort

In Open vSwitch, it is possible to give the host or physical node access to a VLAN through the configured Open vSwitch bridge. This is done by creating an Open vSwitch component called IntPort. In simple words, an IntPort splits a VLAN, which we can configure to assign the IP information. This is useful to give the Proxmox node access to VLAN. For example, our example Proxmox node pm4-1 is currently configured to use the Linux bridge, vmbr0. If we want to use Open vSwitch instead, we will have to create Open vSwitch IntPort to give the node access to the Open vSwitch bridge utilizing VLAN. The following parameters need to be added to the network configuration:

```
auto vmbr0
allow-ovs vmbr0
iface vmbr0 inet manual
  ovs_type OVSBridge
  ovs_ports eth0 vlan1

allow-vmbr0 vlan1
iface vlan1 inet static
  ovs_type OVSIntPort
  ovs_bridge vmbr0
  ovs_options tag=50
  ovs_extra set interface ${IFACE} external-ids:iface-id=$(hostname
-s)-${IFACE}-vif
  address 172.16.0.171
  netmask 255.255.255.0
  gateway 172.16.3.254
  mtu 1500
```

Note that in the port configuration, we have added both eth0 and IntPort interface vlan1, as follows:

```
ovs_ports eth0 vlan1
```

 Even though we have specified the Open vSwitch bridge through `ovs_bridge vmbr0` for the IntPort, we still have to specify it in the Open vSwitch bridge definition or else the interface will never be started.

# CLI for Open vSwitch

Besides the option to create and edit Open vSwitch devices through the Proxmox GUI, Open vSwitch comes loaded with the command line options to manage and gather information of a particular bridge, bond, or interface. There are four types of commands in Open vSwitch:

- **ovs-appctl** : This is used to query and control the Open vSwitch daemon
- **ovs-vsctl**: This is used to manage the Open vSwitch configuration database
- **ovs-ofctl**: This is a tool used to monitor and manage the OpenFlow switch
- **ovs-dpctl**: This is used to manage Open vSwitch datapaths

It is beyond the scope of this book to go into the details of all the available commands of Open vSwitch. In this section, we will only take a look at the commands that may prove to be very helpful while managing the Proxmox cluster:

- To see a list of configured Open vSwitch bridges, ports, and interfaces, use the following commands:

  ```
  # ovs-vsctl list br
  # ovs-vsctl list port
  # ovs-vsctl list interface
  ```

- To see a list of all the interfaces in Open vSwitch, run the following command:

  ```
  # ovs-vsctl show
  ```

- To modify the options run time without rebooting the node:

  ```
  # ovs-vsctl set <interface_type> <interface_name> <option>
  ```

  For example, if we want to add more VLAN IDs to our Open vSwitch bonded interface, run the following command:

  ```
  # ovs-vsctl set port bond0 trunks=2,3,4,5,6,7
  ```

We have to mention all the existing VLAN IDs along with the new ones. Otherwise, the trunk configuration will get replaced with only the new ones while the old configuration will get replaced. We also have to add the new IDs to the `/etc/network/interfaces` file.

- To snoop and display traffic to and from the Open vSwitch bridge, run the following command:

  ```
  # ovs-ofctl snoop <bridge_name>
  ```

- To see the status of each of the Open vSwitch components, run this command:

  ```
  # ovs-ofct lshow <name>
  ```

- To dump OpenFlow flows, including hidden ones, run this command:

  ```
  # ovs-appctl bridge/dump-flows <bridge_name>
  ```

- To print the version of Open vSwitch, run the following command:

  ```
  # ovs-appctl version
  ```

For a complete list of the available Open vSwitch commands, visit http://www.pica8.com/document/v2.3/pdf/ovs-commands-reference.pdf.

# Practicing Open vSwitch

If you are using Open vSwitch for the first time, it may seem slightly complex at first. But with practice and exposure, it really gets easier to create and manage a complex virtual network fully powered by Open vSwitch. In this section, you are given a task to create a network configuration for a Proxmox node using all the network components that we learned so far. The full configuration is given in the following section but try to create it on your own first.

## Configuration requirements

The Proxmox node has three physical network interface ports `eth0`, `eth1`, and `eth2` and one Infiniband interface `ib0`.

We have to configure an LACP bonded Open vSwitch interface with two of the physical ports. The bridge needs to be configured as a trunk for VLAN 11, 12, 13, and 14. All VM tagged interfaces will connect to this bridge. The third physical interface will have to be configured for backup purposes on a separate subnet without VLAN.

The `infiniband` interface has to be configured to be used with Ceph on a separate subnet. The node must use VLAN 12 for all host-related communication utilizing the Open vSwitch bridge.

# Solutions

The following are the full network configurations for the given requirements:

```
auto lo
iface lo inet loopback

# LACP Bonded Open vSwitch Interface
allow-vmbr0 bond0
iface bond0 inet manual
  ovs_bridge vmbr0
  ovs_type OVSBond
  ovs_bonds eth0 eth1
  pre-up (ifconfig eth0 mtu 8996 && ifconfig eth1 mtu 8996)
  ovs_options bond_mode=balance-tcp lacp=active other_config:lacp-
time=fast trunks=11,12,13,14
  mtu 8996

# Creating Open vSwitch bridge
auto vmbr0
allow-ovs vmbr0
iface vmbr0 inet manual
  ovs_type OVSBridge
  ovs_ports bond0 vlan12
  mtu 8996

# Creating IntPort for physical node
allow-vmbr0 vlan12
iface vlan12 inet static
  ovs_type OVSIntPort
  ovs_bridge vmbr0
  ovs_options tag=12
  ovs_extra set interface ${IFACE} external-ids:iface-id=$(hostname
-s)-${IFACE}-vif
```

```
    address 172.16.0.171
    netmask 255.255.252.0
    gateway 172.16.3.254
    mtu 1500

# Creating Infiniband interface
auto ib0
iface ib0 inet static
    address 192.168.0.171
    netmask 255.255.255.0
    pre-up modprobe ib_ipoib
    pre-up echo connected > /sys/class/net/ib0/mode
    mtu 65520

# Creating dedicated interface for backup
auto eth2
iface eth2 inet static
    address 192.168.10.171
    netmask 255.255.255.0
```

# Sample virtual networks

At this stage, we have covered components of virtual networks within the Proxmox cluster environment. We know the components Proxmox uses to hold everything together.

We are going to take a look at a few virtual environment scenarios to solidify our understanding of networking in a Proxmox virtual environment. These are scenario-based network diagrams and some of them are taken from a real production environment.

# Network #1 – Proxmox in its simplest form

This is a small-scale Proxmox cluster with three nodes and two subnets within the virtual environment. Each Proxmox node has two NICs, and both the bridges vmbr0 and vmbr1 are attached to eth0 and eth1, respectively. Each bridge has three virtual machines attached to them. Outside the virtual environment, there is a physical switch, which connects Proxmox nodes, and an admin console for all management work. This is Proxmox in its simplest form in a production environment. This type of network can be used as a learning platform or in a very small business environment with less demanding work load. Internet connectivity is provided to the second subnet directly from the firewall with a second NIC, as shown in the following diagram:

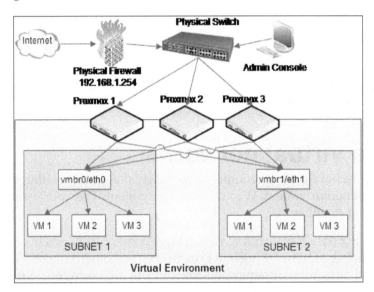

# Network #2 – the multitenant environment

This network setup is almost the same as the previous network with the added benefit of a fully multitenant virtual platform. In a physical firewall, we can only add a very small number of NICs to provide Internet connectivity to isolated subnets. Using a virtualized firewall, we can add as many firewalls or vNICs as we want. This setup is especially useful when multiple, isolated client subnets need to be hosted and each subnet requires its own firewall control for filtering purposes. In this example, vmbr0 is directly served by the physical firewall. The bridges vmbr1 and vmbr200 have their own virtualized firewalls. The firewalls also act as bridges between bridges. For example, the firewall for the subnet 2 has two vNICs. One of these setups was WAN, where vmbr0 acts as an Internet provider. The second vNIC is LAN-facing, which serves the subnet 2.

This is a common scenario for infrastructure service providers who host virtual networks for multiple clients. Since multiple companies can access their virtual networks remotely, it puts extra workload on the physical firewall. Single-point firewall failure should be avoided at all costs by creating a cluster of physical firewalls to provide load balance and failover firewall service.

Never use a virtualized firewall on the same cluster to connect to the Internet directly. Always use separate physical hardware as the main firewall to act as a barrier between the Internet and internal network.

For firewall virtualization, pfsense is a great choice to set up. It is easy to set up, yet extremely powerful and customizable. Get pfsense and more information from `https://www.pfsense.org`.

The following diagram is an example of a multitenant virtual environment:

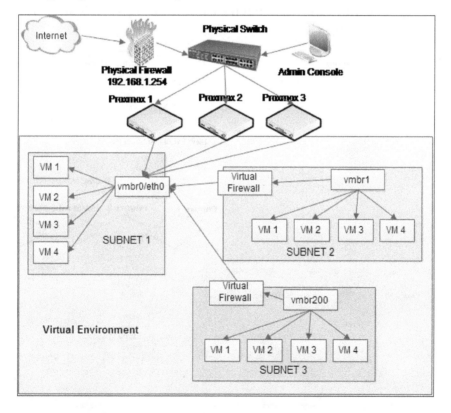

# Network #3 – academic institution

This network diagram is an example of an academic institution network. The following diagram shows network connectivity between the admin office, library, and a remote campus. There are two physical firewalls providing Internet connectivity redundancies. The main virtual network consists of the database server, file server, accounting server, and library catalog server. The database server and the file server are connected with the bridge, vmbr0. The accounting server is connected with the bridge vmbr10 and VLAN ID 10. The library server is connected with the bridge vmbr20 and VLAN ID 20. The main switch is set up with VLAN 10 and 20. The library switch is set up with VLAN 20. In this set up, accounting server data goes straight to the admin office and the library catalog server data goes to the library building without causing additional stress on the network. Remote campus students and staff can access the main campus network through VPN, thus eliminating the need to set up a separate virtual environment.

Of course, the following diagram is a very simplified form of the actual network topology of an academic institution. But the basics of using VLANs and bridges are the same for any network size:

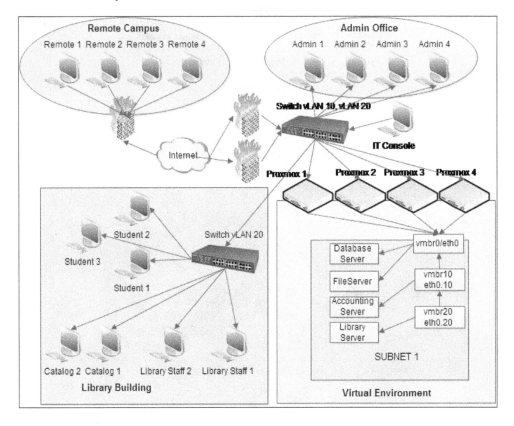

# A multitenant virtual environment

Multitenancy is a very frequently used word in the world of cloud computing, where a virtual environment is regularly used by different clients from different organizations set up with fully isolated networks. Multitenancy is an integral part for a service provider who provides **Infrastructure-as-a-Service (IaaS)** to many clients.

To know more about cloud computing, visit http://en.wikipedia. org/wiki/Cloud_computing.

In this type of setup, the service provider hosts or "rents out" computing time and storage space to their clients. Because of the standard monthly subscription or SLA-based payment method required for this type of service, the term multitenancy quickly gained popularity. Basically, a multitenant virtual environment is where several isolated networks coexist on the same platform without interfering with one another. Almost all public datacenters are multitenancy platforms.

Multitenancy is not new in the world of information. The first multitenant environment appeared back in the 1960s, when companies rented processing time and storage space on mainframe computers to reduce the giant expenses of mainframe operation. The virtual environment only augmented the same idea exponentially by leveraging all the virtualization features Proxmox provides. By combining virtualization with cloud computing, multitenancy is able to get a very strong footing to serve better and to more customers without increasing financial overheads. Prior to virtualization, the physical space and power requirements to host customers in an IAAS environment meant it was rare and cost prohibitive, thus not many people enjoyed its benefit.

The Proxmox hypervisor is capable of setting up a stable and scalable multitenant virtual environment. All the networking components we have seen so far, such as vNIC, virtual bridge, and VLAN, are the building blocks used to set up a multitenant virtual environment. Once we understand the relationships between virtual machines and virtual bridges, it is fairly easy to set up a multitenant virtual environment with Proxmox.

When setting up a multitenant virtual environment, it is very important to take special care so that one network traffic does not get intercepted by another network. Without a proper VLAN and subnet, it is possible for one network to sniff network packets on the entire virtual environment, thus stealing data from other tenant organizations on the network.

# A multitenant network diagram

The following is an example of a network diagram of a typical cloud service provider who provides IAAS to their clients. The entire client network is virtualized within the service provider's virtual environment:

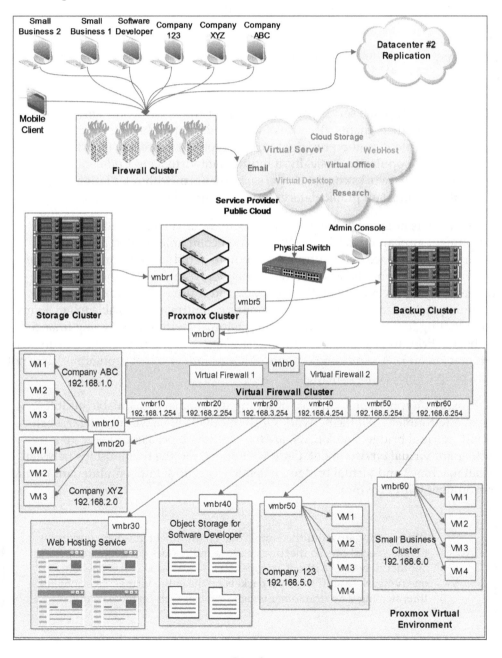

On the client side, they only have simple desktop computers and mobile devices to access their virtual cloud resources, such as desktop, storage, processing power, and so on. Clients access these resources through virtual means, such as **Virtual Network Computing (VNC)**, **SPICE**, or **Remote Desktop Protocol (RDP)**.

Virtual networks are isolated with separate subnets. VLANs are set up (not shown in the diagram) to reduce mass broadcast traffic. All virtual machine data is stored on a separate storage cluster with full redundancy. A backup cluster does a regular backup of all virtual machines, and granular file backup with histories is done with a third-party backup software. A virtual firewall cluster is set up in between the virtual environment and the host Ethernet interface to provide Internet connectivity to all client virtual machines. Each virtualized firewall has several vNICs to connect to each subnet. A typical virtual firewall with multiple vNICs will look this, as shown in the following screenshot:

| Add ▾ | Remove | Edit | Resize disk | Move disk | Disk Throttle |
|---|---|---|---|---|---|
| Keyboard Layout | Default | | | | |
| Memory | 256MB/1.00GB | | | | |
| Processors | 2 (1 sockets, 2 cores) | | | | |
| Display | Default | | | | |
| Hard Disk (ide0) | nfs-backup-02:2001/vm-2001-disk-1.raw,format= | | | | |
| CD/DVD Drive (ide2) | none,media=cdrom | | | | |
| Network Device (net0) | e1000=42:64:0F:B2:B4:64,bridge=vmbr0 | | | | |
| Network Device (net1) | e1000=D2:77:2E:BE:69:AC,bridge=vmbr2000 | | | | |
| Network Device (net10) | e1000=26:2A:1C:74:56:E1,bridge=vmbr2000 | | | | |
| Network Device (net11) | e1000=E6:65:9B:00:36:E6,bridge=vmbr2000 | | | | |
| Network Device (net12) | e1000=DE:9C:BE:8E:5D:04,bridge=vmbr2000 | | | | |
| Network Device (net2) | e1000=82:BE:65:B4:28:CB,bridge=vmbr2000 | | | | |
| Network Device (net3) | e1000=9E:EF:74:20:2F:FB,bridge=vmbr2000 | | | | |
| Network Device (net4) | e1000=4E:15:3F:25:A4:17,bridge=vmbr2000 | | | | |
| Network Device (net5) | e1000=B2:80:68:17:C8:D9,bridge=vmbr2000 | | | | |
| Network Device (net6) | e1000=5A:62:0B:EB:57:D7,bridge=vmbr2000 | | | | |
| Network Device (net7) | e1000=1A:81:2C:EB:B4:33,bridge=vmbr2000 | | | | |
| Network Device (net8) | e1000=B2:09:CA:31:89:FA,bridge=vmbr2000 | | | | |
| Network Device (net9) | e1000=36:77:5B:3D:B5:5E,bridge=vmbr2000 | | | | |

Since the firewall is virtualized, we can add any number of virtual network interfaces without worrying about running out of physical slots. A virtualized clustered firewall provides maximum uptime. Each company network in this example has its own virtual bridge, which only talks to that company's virtual machines and firewall interface, eliminating any chance of packet sniffing by other company networks.

> **Packet** sniffing is a process when data packets passing through a network interface are captured and analyzed. Packet sniffer software can be placed in a subnet to capture data. This is a common practice of someone with malicious intention to capture sensitive unencrypted data passing through, such as usernames and passwords in clear texts.

This environment is serving multiple clients or organizations, so uptime is a big concern. To eliminate this issue, the entire virtual environment is replicated to another datacenter for ensuring 99.9 percent uptime. The previous diagram is an overly simplified version of what really goes on inside a very busy Proxmox virtual environment. Studying this diagram will give a clear understanding of virtual network mechanics. From the previous diagram, we can see that this network environment heavily uses virtual bridges. So, it is imperative to understand the role of bridges and plan out a draft diagram before actually setting up this level of a complex virtual network.

> When working with a complex virtual network, always keep a network diagram handy and update it whenever you make any changes. An up-to-date network diagram will help greatly to have total control over a virtual network. Especially when an issue arises, it is easy to pinpoint the cause of the issue with a diagram.

# Summary

We were very busy in this lively chapter. We looked at the differences between physical and virtual networks. We learned about the Proxmox network components that make up a Proxmox-based virtual network. We also learned about Open vSwitch and its components to create a really complex virtual network. We even got to analyze a few network diagrams from the basic to the advanced to get a better understanding of how the Proxmox virtual network really comes to life.

Proxmox provides all the tools we need to build any level of virtual network. It is up to the network administrator's imagination, the company's budget, and the need to foresee how all pieces should come together to form a well-designed and efficient virtual network. The best part is that any mistake is easily correctable in a virtual environment. We can always go back and change things until we are satisfied. For this very reason, a virtual network is always evolving. Over time, a virtual network becomes an extension of the network administrator's mind. The configurations and design of a virtual network infrastructure can give us a window into how that administrator thinks and the logic they used to construct the environment.

In the next chapter, we are going to learn all about the built-in Proxmox firewall and learn how to protect from the whole cluster down to a single virtual machine.

# 8

# The Proxmox Firewall

The Proxmox VE firewall is a security feature that allows easy and effective protection of a virtual environment for both internal and external network traffic. By leveraging this firewall, we can protect VMs, host nodes, or the entire cluster by creating firewall rules. By creating rules at the virtual machine level, we can provide total isolation for VMs to VM network traffic, including VMs to external traffic. Prior to the Proxmox VE firewall, security and isolation was not possible at the hypervisor level. In this chapter, we will cover the following topics of the Proxmox VE firewall:

- Exploring the Proxmox VE firewall
- Configuring the cluster firewall rules
- Configuring the host firewall rules
- Configuring the VM firewall rules
- Integrating a Suricata IPS
- Enabling the IPv6 firewall
- Firewall CLI commands

## Exploring the Proxmox VE firewall

The Proxmox VE firewall leverages iptables of each Proxmox node for protection. Iptables is an application that allows you to manage rules tables for the Linux kernel firewall. All firewall rules and configurations are stored in the Proxmox cluster filesystem, thus allowing a distributed firewall system in the Proxmox cluster. The pre-firewall service provided by Proxmox of each node reads the rules and configurations from the cluster filesystem and automatically adjusts the local iptables. Rules can be fully created and maintained by the Proxmox GUI or CLI. The Proxmox firewall can be used in place of a virtualized firewall in the cluster.

Although the Proxmox firewall provides excellent protection, it is highly recommended that you have a physical firewall for the entire network. This firewall is also known as an edge firewall since it sits at the main entry point of the Internet. The Internet connection should not be directly connected to Proxmox nodes. A virtualized firewall should not be used as a physical firewall substitute.

# Components of the Proxmox firewall

There are several components that make up the Proxmox VE firewall. In order to effectively implement a firewall in a Proxmox cluster, it is important to know the components and their functions.

## Zones

The Proxmox firewall protection area is divided into the following three logical zones:

- **Datacenter**: Rules in this zone define traffic to and from all hosts and guests
- **Host**: Rules in this zone define traffic to and from a cluster and Proxmox nodes
- **VM**: Rules in this zone define traffic to and from each VM

All rules in the Datacenter and host zones are cascaded. This means that a rule created in the Datacenter zone will be applied to all hosts or nodes and all the VMs. While rules created in a host zone will be applied to all VMs in that host or Proxmox node, care must be taken when creating rules in the host zone for particular VMs. This is because when the VM is migrated to a different node, the rules in the previous node will not apply to the new node for the VM. These host-level rules must be created in the new host, and only then, will they be applied to the VMs. Rules created for a VM apply to that VM only. There is no rule cascading for the VM zone.

## Security Groups

This allows the grouping of several firewall rules into one rule. This is very helpful when the same multiple rules apply to several VMs. For example, we can create a security group named webserver and add multiple rules to open ports, such as 21, 22, 80, 443, and so on. Then, we can apply these **Security Groups** to any VMs used as a webserver. Similarly, we can create a security group to open ports for servers for e-mails only. The following screenshot shows an example of a webserver security group with rules to open ports for FTP, SSH, HTTP, and HTTPS:

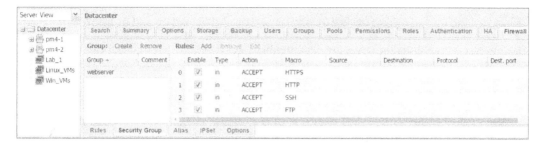

 It should be noted that **Security Groups** are only created in Datacenter zones. There are no security group creation options in the host or VM firewall zone.

**Security Groups** created in a Datacenter zone can be applied to any zones. Security groups make the creation of rules for multiple nodes or virtual machines much easier. Details on security group creation and management will be explained later in this chapter.

# IPSet

Sometimes, it is necessary to create firewall rules to restrict or allow traffic solely based on IP addresses. IPSet allows us to create firewall rules that may apply to multiple IP addresses or IP subnets. For example, we can create an **IPSet** to allow access to the Proxmox GUI from only a few limited IP addresses. The following screenshot shows an example of **IPSet** to allow the **proxmoxgui** access only from three IP addresses:

We can create rules based on individual IPs or the entire subnet using the CIDR format in the rules.

An IPSet can be created in both the Datacenter and VM zones as the option dialog boxes are also identical. An IPSet created in Datacenter zones can be applied to any hosts and VMs in the cluster. But the IPSet created under a VM zone is applicable to that VM only.

Another good example of IPSet usage is to create blacklists and whitelists of IP addresses in Datacenter zones. A whitelist will allow the defined traffic while a blacklist will block access to the defined IPs. Details on IPSet creation and management will be explained later in this chapter.

# Rules

Rules are the heart of a Proxmox firewall configuration. Rules define the flow and type of traffic that will be allowed or denied in the zones. There are two directions in which network traffic can flow:

- **IN**: This refers to traffic coming inbound from anywhere to any zones
- **OUT**: This refers to traffic outbound from any zones to anywhere

There are three types of action that a firewall rule can be applied to:

- **ACCEPT**: This allows traffic packets
- **REJECT**: Packets are rejected, and then an acknowledgement of rejection is sent to the sender
- **DENY**: Traffic packets are received and then silently dropped without sending any acknowledgement to the sender

A typical rule will contain the direction of traffic, the action to apply to the traffic, and and which port or protocol the rule affects. The following screenshot shows rules to block traffic on port 80 and allow on port 443 for an example VM in our cluster:

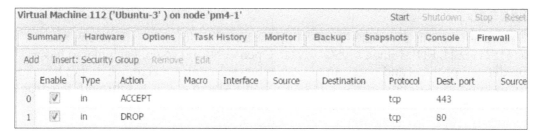

| | Enable | Type | Action | Macro | Interface | Source | Destination | Protocol | Dest. port | Source |
|---|---|---|---|---|---|---|---|---|---|---|
| 0 | ☑ | in | ACCEPT | | | | | tcp | 443 | |
| 1 | ☑ | in | DROP | | | | | tcp | 80 | |

# Protocols

In a Proxmox firewall, we can create rules based on various network protocols, such as TCP, UDP, ICMP, and so on. Depending on application requirements, different protocol selections may be necessary. For example, if we want to allow ping for a zone, we need to create a rule with the ICMP protocol. Predefined protocols are available for selection through the rules dialog box, as shown in the following screenshot:

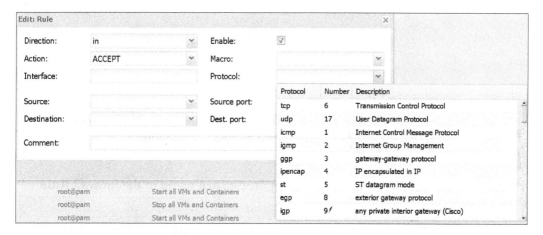

# Macros

Macros are various precreated port configurations for most known services, such as HTTP, SSH, FTP, Telnet, MySQL, NTP, OpenVPN, and so on. Each macro has a predefined protocol and port number. So, when selecting a macro, we do not have to define a protocol or port number. In fact, when a **Macro** is selected through the drop-down menu, the Proxmox dialog box automatically disables the protocol and port textboxes, as shown in the following screenshot:

 If we need to enter a custom port for any rule, then selecting the macro will not work. We have to manually define the port number and a proper protocol for the rule.

The following screenshot shows the **Macro** drop-down menu in the firewall **Rule** dialog box:

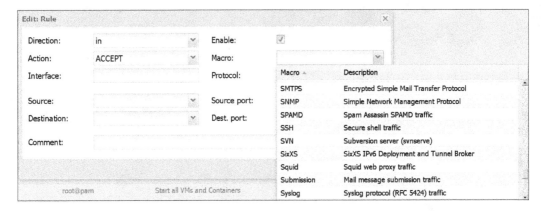

The firewall feature can be accessed through the firewall tab of all the three zones, such as Datacenter, Host, or Nodes and virtual machines of both KVM and LXC.

# The pve-firewall and pvefw-logger services

There are two services that enable the Proxmox firewall:

- **Pve-firewall**: This is the main service to run a firewall and it updates iptables rules
- **Pvefw-logger**: This is responsible for logging all firewall traffic when logging is enabled

The Pve-firewall service is started automatically when a node is rebooted. We can also manually start, stop, and restart the service using the following commands:

```
# pve-firewall start
# pve-firewall stop
# pve-firewall restart
```

To check the status of a firewall service, we can use the following command:

```
# pve-firewall status
```

When there are no issues in the firewall operation, the output of the status command will appear as follows:

```
Status: enabled/running
```

# Configuration files of a firewall

Although the Proxmox firewall can be managed entirely from the Proxmox GUI, at times accessing the rules from the CLI may be necessary especially when a cluster is locked out due to misconfiguration of firewall rules. All firewall configurations and rules follow the same naming format with the .fw extension. The firewall configuration and rule files are stored in two different directories for all the three zones:

```
/etc/pve/firewall/cluster.fw
```

This is the Datacenter configuration and zone rule file. All the other Datacenter-wide firewall information, such as **Security Groups** and IPSets are also stored in this single file. We can enable or disable the Datacenter-wide firewall by editing this configuration file:

```
/etc/pve/nodes/<node_name>/host.fw
```

**CAUTION!** Do not enable the Datacenter-wide firewall before reading the Configuring the datacenter-specific firewall section later in this chapter. This is the configuration and rules files for a Proxmox node or host:

`/etc/pve/firewall/<vm_id>.fw`

Each virtual machine whether it is KVM or LXC has a separate firewall configuration file with its VM ID stored in the same directory where the Datacenter firewall file is stored.

When new rules are created or edited through the Proxmox GUI, these are the files that get changed. Whether the changes are made through the GUI or CLI, all rules takes effect immediately. There are no reboots required or is restarting a firewall service required.

# Configuring the Datacenter-specific firewall

As mentioned earlier, Datacenter-specific firewall rules affect all resources, such as cluster, nodes, and virtual machines. Any rules created in this zone are cascaded to both hosts and VMs. This zone is also used to fully lock down a cluster to drop all incoming traffic and then only open what is required. In a freshly installed Proxmox cluster, the Datacenter-wide firewall option is disabled.

 **CAUTION!** Attention must be given to this section to prevent full cluster lock out.

# Configuring the Datacenter firewall through the GUI

The following screenshot shows the firewall option for the Datacenter zone through the Options tab by navigating to **Datacenter** | **Firewall** | **Options**:

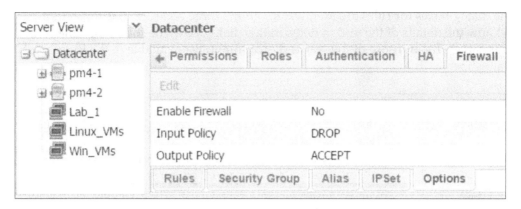

As we can see, in the preceding screenshot, the Proxmox firewall for the Datacenter zone is disabled by default, with **Input Policy** set to **Drop** and **Output Policy** set to Accept. If we did enable this firewall option right now, then all inbound access would be denied. You would have to be on the console to access the node. Before we enable this option, we must create two rules to allow the GUI on port 8006 and the SSH console on port 22.

# Creating the Datacenter firewall rules

To open the **Rule** creation dialog box, we need to click on **Add** by navigating to the **Datacenter** | **Firewall** | **Rules** tabbed menu. For the first rule, we are going to allow the Proxmox GUI on port 8006, as shown in the following screenshot:

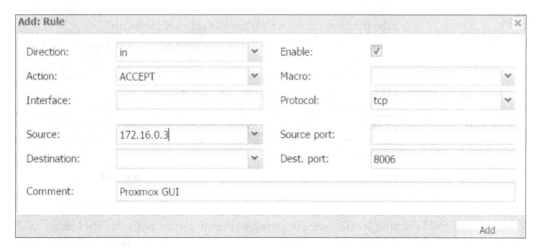

The dialog boxes for rules are identical for all the three zones, so it is important to know the details of the option items in this dialog box. The following table summarizes the purpose of the text and drop-down list available in the Rules dialog box:

| Items | Functions |
|---|---|
| **Direction** | This is a drop-down list used to select the direction of the traffic for the rule, and it is a required field. |
| **Action** | This is a drop-down list used to select actions that need to be taken, such as Accept, Drop, or Reject. This is a required field. |
| **Interface** | This is a textbox used to define the interface to apply this rule to. This does not apply to the datacenter zone. It is useful to define this for a VM with multiple interfaces. |
| **Source** | This is a drop-down list used to select a preconfigured IPSet or textbox to type in the IP address where the traffic originates from. We can also define a subnet in the CIDR format. When left blank, it accepts traffic from all the source IP addresses. |
| **Destination** | This is a drop-down list used to select a preconfigured IPSet or textbox to type in the IP address of the destination device in the cluster. When left blank, it accepts traffic from all the destination IP addresses. |
| **Enable** | This is a checkbox used to enable or disable the rule. |
| **Macro** | This is a drop-down list used to select preconfigured macros. We can also type the macro, which filters the list of macros. |
| **Protocol** | This is a drop-down list used to select protocols. We can also type the protocol name, which filters the list of protocols. |
| **Source port** | This is a textbox used to define the originating port number for the incoming traffic. When left blank, it accepts traffic from any ports. We can also define the port ranges separated by : in this field. This source port field is also used for the outgoing traffic when the traffic originates internally from a VM, node, or cluster. |
| **Dest. Port** | This is a textbox used to define the destination port of the incoming traffic. When left blank, it accepts traffic from any port. We can also define port ranges separated by : in this field. |
| **Comment** | This is a textbox used to write descriptions or any notes regarding the rule. |

To allow the SSH console traffic, we are going to create a rule with the SSH macro. The following screenshot shows the firewall feature of the Datacenter zone with two rules created to allow access to the Proxmox GUI and SSH:

 Note that the Proxmox GUI can only be accessed from one IP address, which is 172.16.0.3, whereas SSH can be accessed from any IP address. Remember that all Datacenter rules are cascaded down to hosts and VMs. In this scenario, SSH is open for all hosts and VMs in the cluster. In certain situations, we may need to block SSH for certain VMs in order to increase the security. If we keep the previous rule as it is, we will need to create a separate VM-level rule to drop SSH traffic for all VMs. However, this can become a tedious task since some VMs may require SSH access and there can be dozens of VMs. A revised advanced rule to allow SSH access to only Proxmox nodes would be to create an **IPSet** in **Datacenter** with IP addresses for Proxmox nodes only, and then assign the **IPSet** as the **Destination** for the rule.

# Creating the Datacenter IPSet

The following screenshot shows the IPSet named **proxmox_node_ips** with IP addresses for two nodes in our example cluster:

From the IPSet management page, we need to create the IPSet itself first, and then add IPs from the right-hand side IP/CIDR option. IP addresses can be added separately or defined in an entire block using the CIDR value. The IPSet name can only be alphanumeric with two special characters: – and _. But when Proxmox displays IPset in the drop-down list, it adds + as a prefix. This is not part of the IPset name. If a string is entered as capital letters, it automatically gets changed to small. The following screenshot shows the Rules dialog box where we selected an IPSet for Proxmox nodes in Destination to allow SSH only for Proxmox nodes:

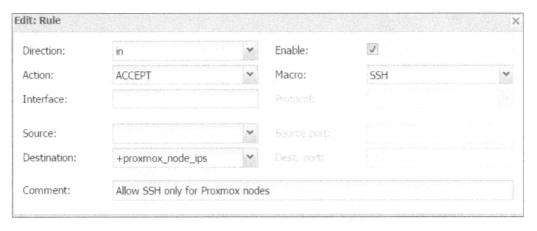

This revised rule will ensure that SSH is only enabled for Proxmox nodes and not VMs. As we can see, in the previous example, when creating rules in the Datacenter zone, it is very important to think about the cascading effect of the Datacenter rules and how it can affect nodes and VMs. It is best to use the Datacenter zone rules for cluster-related traffic and not VMs in any nodes.

After we have created rules to allow SSH and the Proxmox GUI, we are ready to enable the Datacenter-wide firewall through the Options menu. The following screenshot shows the menu with the firewall now enabled:

The preceding screenshot shows a policy that will drop all incoming traffic and outgoing traffic will be permitted. To have a fully locking-down secured cluster, both the policies should be set to **DROP**. Usually, outgoing traffic is considered safe. Alternatively, in a multitenant environment, outgoing traffic should be firewalled. This way, we can control the type of traffic that can leave out of a VM. An example of traffic that should be denied would be ICMP or Ping traffic, which will allow one VM to discover other devices in the network.

> If both the inbound and outbound firewall rules are set to Deny or Drop, you will likely have to configure all the allowed traffic, even updates and common traffic. If you are implementing **DROP** for the **Input Policy** in an already established Proxmox cluster, make sure that you first create all the necessary rules for all VMs and nodes before enabling the Datacenter-wide firewall. Failure to do so will cause all VMs and nodes to drop the connectivity.

## Creating aliases

Aliases make it simple to see what devices or group of devices are affected by a rule. We can create aliases to identify an IP address or a network. It is similar to an IPSet, but one alias only points to one IP address or network, whereas an IPSet holds multiple IP addresses or networks. For example, in a scenario where we have one Proxmox as `10.0.0.0/24` and an IP address `172.16.0.3` for a management interface. We can create two aliases using the **Alias** creation dialog box by clicking on **Add** from the **Alias** menu, as shown in the following screenshot:

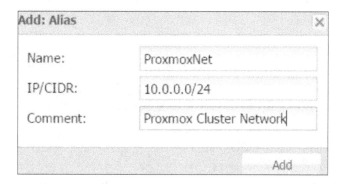

In the preceding screenshot, we created an alias named **ProxmoxNet** to identify the network 10.0.0.0/24. Using the same dialog box, we will create another alias named **Management** for IP 172.16.0.3. The following screenshot shows the **Alias** window with both the aliases created:

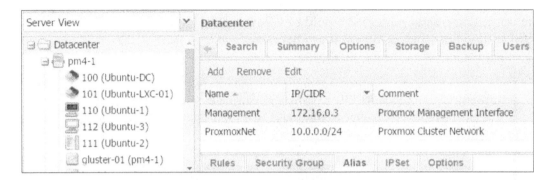

The advantage of having an **Alias** is that whenever we create rules, we can use these aliases instead of typing in the entire IP address. This is especially useful when using IPv6. Since IPv6 addresses are quite long, we can create an alias to call the IP address in a rule whenever we need them.

This is also another way to identify a numeric IP address with a text. Aliases are accessible through the drop-down list for both **Source** and **Destination** from the **Rules** dialog box. The following screenshot shows the rule creation dialog box with the aliases in the drop-down list for **Source**:

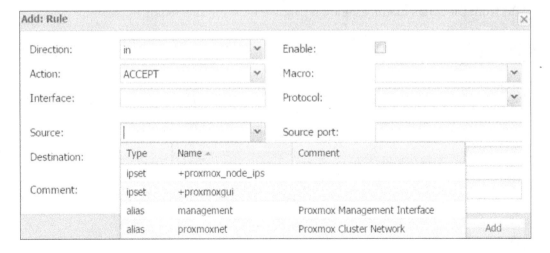

Aliases created in the Datacenter zone are useable throughout the cluster in both the host and VM zones.

# Configuring the Datacenter firewall through the CLI

The Proxmox firewall can also be managed entirely through the CLI by editing the firewall configuration and rules files directly. The content of the configuration and rule files are laid out in a very specific format. The following screenshot shows the `/etc/pve/firewall/cluster.fw` file of the Datacenter zone after adding rules from the previous section:

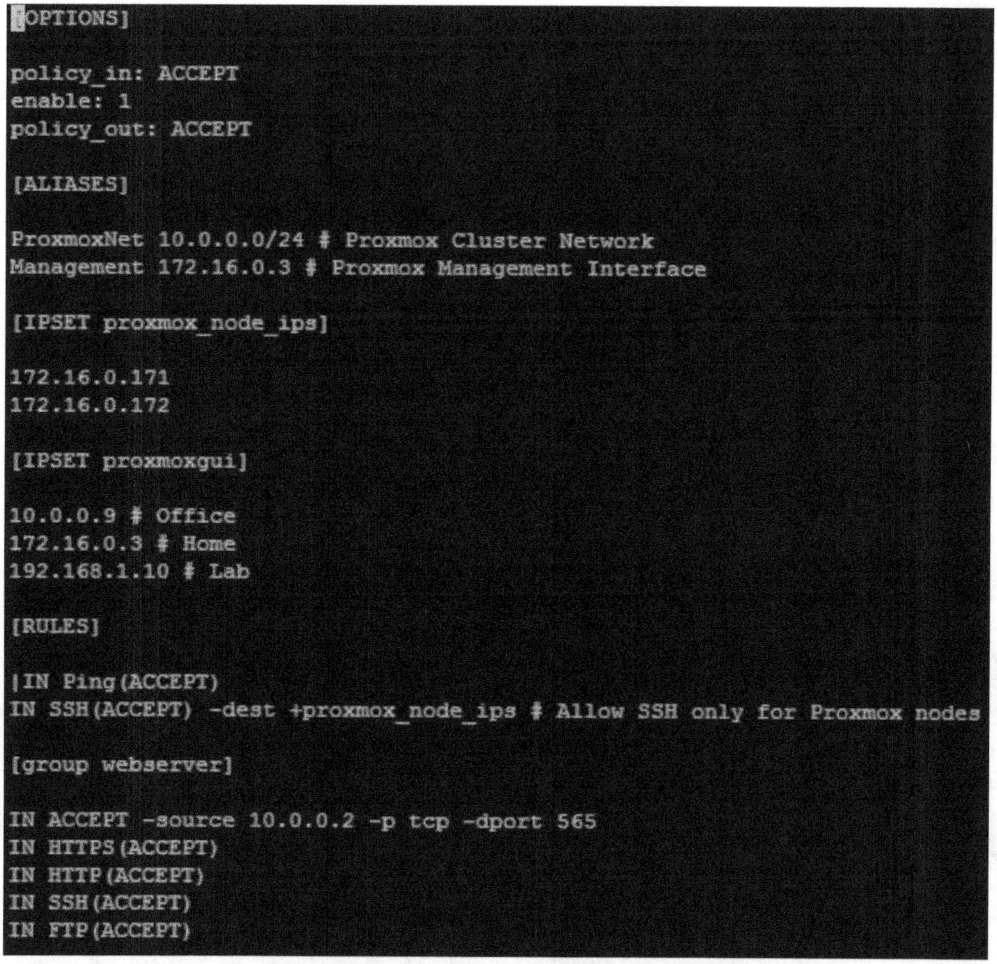

```
[OPTIONS]

policy_in: ACCEPT
enable: 1
policy_out: ACCEPT

[ALIASES]

ProxmoxNet 10.0.0.0/24 # Proxmox Cluster Network
Management 172.16.0.3 # Proxmox Management Interface

[IPSET proxmox_node_ips]

172.16.0.171
172.16.0.172

[IPSET proxmoxgui]

10.0.0.9 # Office
172.16.0.3 # Home
192.168.1.10 # Lab

[RULES]

|IN Ping(ACCEPT)
IN SSH(ACCEPT) -dest +proxmox_node_ips # Allow SSH only for Proxmox nodes

[group webserver]

IN ACCEPT -source 10.0.0.2 -p tcp -dport 565
IN HTTPS(ACCEPT)
IN HTTP(ACCEPT)
IN SSH(ACCEPT)
IN FTP(ACCEPT)
```

As we can see, in the preceding screenshot, there are four segments in the firewall configuration file for the Datacenter zone. They are as follows:

```
[OPTIONS]

. . . . . . . .

[ALIASES]

. . . . . . . .

[IPSET <name>]

. . . . . . . .

[RULES]

. . . . . . . .

[group <name>]

. . . . . . . .
```

# [OPTIONS]

This area is used to enable or disable a Datacenter-wide firewall. Currently, our example cluster has the default **Input/Output** policy, which is set to drop all incoming traffic while allowing all outgoing traffic. If we were to change the input policy to accept all incoming traffic, then the option segment would appear as follows:

```
[OPTIONS]

policy_in: ACCEPT

enable: 1
```

If, due to firewall rules misconfiguration, we locked ourselves out, we can disable the Datacenter-wide firewall using the following option on the console:

```
enable: 0
```

# [ALIASES]

This segment shows all the aliases created in the Datacenter zone. It shows the name of the alias and IP address or the network the alias belongs to. Each line is used for a separate alias entry.

# [IPSET <name>]

This segments clumps all IPSets created under the Datacenter zone. It shows the name of the IPSet and the IP addresses added in the set. In our example, we have two IPSets named proxmox_node_ips and proxmoxgui.

# [RULES]

This segment contains all the firewall rules, one on each line. To disable any rule, we simply need to put a | in front of the rule and save the configuration file. In the preceding screenshot, the rule to allow ping is disabled in this way.

# [group <name>]

This segment clumps all the **Security Groups** created in the Datacenter zone. It shows the name of the security group and the rule added to the group. In the preceding screenshot, we can see that we created a security group named webserver and added macro rules in order to allow the HTTPS, HTTP, SSH, and FTP traffic. We can also manually add rules in this segment by defining a protocol and port. For example, if we want to allow the TCP traffic to port 565 only from the IP address 10.0.0.2, we will add the following line of code to the security group webserver:

```
IN ACCEPT -source 10.0.0.2 -p tcp -dport 565
```

# Configuring a host-specific firewall

Any rules created in the host zone only apply to the node itself where the rule is created and the VMs are in that host node. Rules for one node do not get replicated to the other nodes although the rule files are stored in the Proxmox cluster filesystem. There are no options to create IPSet or **Security Groups** in the host zone. We can only create firewall rules. The following screenshot shows the Firewall feature for the host node **pm4-1** in our example cluster:

# Creating host firewall rules

The process of creating new rules for the Host zone is identical to the rule creation process that we have already discussed in the *Configuring a datacenter-specific* firewall section earlier in this chapter. Besides creating rules from scratch, we can also assign predefined rules in the form of a **Security Group** to a node. We cannot create a new **Security Group** under the host firewall menu, but we can assign it some predefined rules. For example, earlier in this chapter, we created a **Security Group** named webserver. If a Proxmox node is only going to host the VMs used for only webservers, then we can assign the **Security Group** webserver to that node, and all the rules will be cascaded into all the VMs in the host. Thus, we would save a lot of time from not having to create separate rules for each VM.

To open the dialog box to assign a security group, click on **Insert: Security Group**. The following screenshot shows the dialog box with webserver selected from the **Security Group** drop-down list:

We have to ensure that we enable the rule by clicking on the checkbox, and then we need to click on **Add** to assign the security group. The following screenshot shows the **Rule** added to the node **pm4-1**:

# Options for the host zone firewall

The Proxmox node firewall has several items under the **Options** tab. Most of the items can be left at their default values, as shown in the following screenshot. However, an understanding of this item will aid in combating security through the cluster. The following screenshot shows the **Option** items with default values for an unmodified **Proxmox** node:

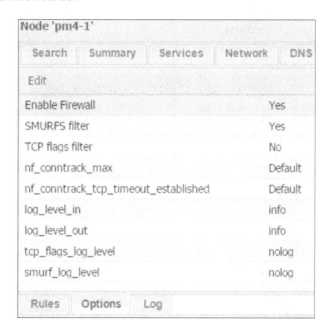

To change the settings of any option item, we need to select the line item, and then click on the **Edit** button.

## Enable a firewall

By default, all Proxmox nodes have the firewall option enabled. To disable a firewall for the node completely, select **No** for this option.

## The SMURFS filter

By default, the **SMURFS** filter is enabled. By nature, SMURF is a **distributed denial-of-service (DDoS)** attack. In this attack, an attacker sends a very large number of ICMP data packets with the victim's spoofed IP address as the source, and it is broadcasted to a network using the broadcast address. Generally, all network devices answer an ICMP ping. During a SMURF attack, the victim's device gets flooded by ICMP responses. If there are a large number of devices in the network, then the flooding become extreme, making the victimized device unresponsive. This is why this filter should remain enabled at all times.

# The TCP flags filter

In simple terms, TCP flags are control bits that indicate how TCP packets should be handled by the client. These control bits or indicators reside in the TCP header. There are a total of nine control bits with one bit for each flag. The full description of how exactly these TCP flags work is beyond the scope of this book since TCP is a vast subject of various complexities. Here, we will see what those TCP flags are and how the Proxmox firewall handles TCP flag filtering. The following table is a summary of the TCP flags and their functions:

| TCP Flag | Function |
|---|---|
| URG – 1 bit | This indicates that the TCP packet is urgent. |
| ACK – 1 bit | This indicates the `Acknowledgement` field. After the initial SYN for all packets, they are usually followed by this flag. |
| PSD – 1 bit | This flag asks for the buffer data to be pushed as soon as possible to the receiving side of the client application. |
| RST – 1 bit | This flag indicates the TCP connection reset. |
| SYN – 1 bit | This flag indicates a synchronized sequence number before initiating a TCP connection. Only the first packet that is sent from a source usually has this flag. |
| FIN – 1 bit | This flag indicates the end TCP packets. |

TCP flags are useful to detect and pinpoint oddly-behaved TCP packets and determine a possible intrusion. Arguments for TCP flags filtering are added to the firewall rules right after the -p syntax, as shown in the following code:

```
[RULES]
IN DROP -p tcp -tcp-flags SYN,ACK SYN -dport
```

 As of Proxmox VE 4.1, there are no options used to manually add TCP flags to filter through the GUI. We can add them through the CLI but this makes the rule disappear from the GUI.

By default, TCP flag filtering is disabled in the Proxmox VE. We can enable it to let the Proxmox firewall automatically filter odd packets with out-of-sync bits. All data packets traversing through the network have a uniformed SYN behavior. Odd packets usually indicate that they are from a bad source.

# nf_conntrack_max

This value defines the maximum size of a netfilter connection tracking table. This table keeps a record of all live connections and deletes them when a connection is closed. By default, the size of this table is 65,536 bytes. While for most of the nodes, this is perfectly fine, for high-volume connection servers, such as DNS or Webserver, this table may become full quickly. For a Proxmox node, which holds lots of high-traffic VMs, this value needs to be increased. We can check the current value of nf_conntrack_max using the following command:

```
# sysctl -a | grep nf_conntrack_max
```

The following command will show you the number of current live connections in the node:

```
# sysctl -a | grep nf_conntrack_count
```

The following screenshot shows the connection count for our example node **pm4-1**:

```
root@pm4-1:~# sysctl -a | grep nf_conntrack_count
sysctl: reading key "net.ipv6.conf.all.stable_secret"
sysctl: reading key "net.ipv6.conf.default.stable_secret"
sysctl: reading key "net.ipv6.conf.eth0.stable_secret"
sysctl: reading key "net.ipv6.conf.eth0/10.stable_secret"
sysctl: reading key "net.ipv6.conf.eth1.stable_secret"
sysctl: reading key "net.ipv6.conf.eth2.stable_secret"
sysctl: reading key "net.ipv6.conf.fwbr100i0.stable_secret"
sysctl: reading key "net.ipv6.conf.fwbr112i0.stable_secret"
sysctl: reading key "net.ipv6.conf.fwln100i0.stable_secret"
sysctl: reading key "net.ipv6.conf.fwln112i0.stable_secret"
sysctl: reading key "net.ipv6.conf.fwpr100p0.stable_secret"
sysctl: reading key "net.ipv6.conf.fwpr112p0.stable_secret"
sysctl: reading key "net.ipv6.conf.lo.stable_secret"
sysctl: reading key "net.ipv6.conf.tap112i0.stable_secret"
sysctl: reading key "net.ipv6.conf.veth100i0.stable_secret"
sysctl: reading key "net.ipv6.conf.vmbr0.stable_secret"
sysctl: reading key "net.ipv6.conf.vmbr0v10.stable_secret"
sysctl: reading key "net.ipv6.conf.vmbr1.stable_secret"
net.netfilter.nf_conntrack_count = 74
```

 Note that if the tracking table is full, due to many live connections, then the node will drop all new connection packets.

# nf_conntrack_tcp_timeout_established

This node only keeps track of the netfilter connections if they live. Dead connections are deleted automatically from the table. This deletion happens based on the set timeout period. The longer the timeout period, the longer the record of the connection will stay in the tracking table. The value of this option is in seconds. By default, the value is set to 4,32,000 seconds or 12 hours. We can check the current value using the following command:

```
# sysctl -a | grep nf_conntrack_tcp_timeout_established
```

By reducing this value, we can keep the tracking table lean-faster for a high-traffic node.

# log_level_in/out

A firewall is only as good as its logging capability. It is only by going through the log that we can see what is being blocked and what is not. Proxmox comes with a custom service named `pvefw-logger`, which is based on the netfilter logging daemon. The sole purpose of this service is to log a connection activity based on the set firewall rules. Through the firewall Option tab, we can set logging at various levels of verbosity. There are eight levels of logging available for the iptable-based firewall. The following table shows the iptable logging levels and their availability in the Proxmox firewall:

| Log Level | Type | |
|---|---|---|
| Level 0 | Emergency | Available in Proxmox |
| Level 1 | Alert | Available in Proxmox |
| Level 2 | Critical | Available in Proxmox |
| Level 3 | Error | Available in Proxmox |
| Level 4 | Warning | Available in Proxmox |
| Level 5 | Notice | Not available in Proxmox |
| Level 6 | Info | Available in Proxmox |
| Level 7 | Debug | Available in Proxmox |

In addition to these levels, Proxmox also has the `nolog` option. This disables all logging for a resource. The log-level info is mostly used as it logs all the good and bad connections. This way, we can see exactly what is being blocked and allowed. However, **Info log level** also creates many log entries in a very short period of time. As a good rule of thumb, always select some form of logging when enabling a firewall.

## tcp_flags_log_level

Similar to the standard log level, we can also enable different log levels for the `tcp` flags. If the TCP flags filter is not enabled, this will not produce any log entries. When enabled, we will see the `tcp` flags filter logged in the log window.

## smurf_log_level

Like the `tcp` flags log, this also shows log entries for the `smurf` attacks. This also follows various log levels.

# Configuring the host firewall through the CLI

We can also configure and manage the host zone firewall through the CLI. The firewall configuration file for the host is in `/etc/pve/local/host.fw`. The following screenshot shows the content of the `host.fw` file:

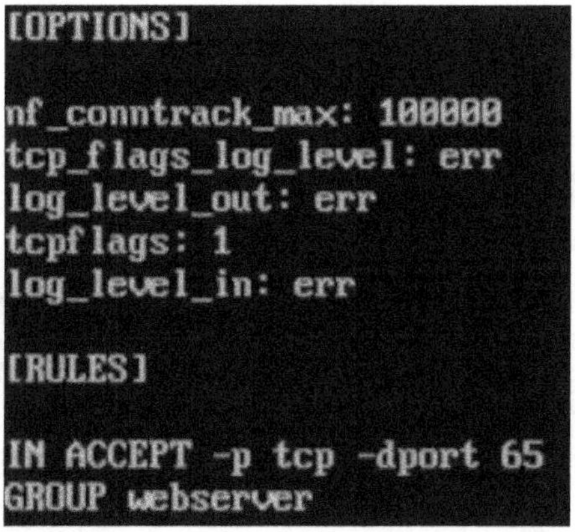

```
[OPTIONS]

nf_conntrack_max: 100000
tcp_flags_log_level: err
log_level_out: err
tcpflags: 1
log_level_in: err

[RULES]

IN ACCEPT -p tcp -dport 65
GROUP webserver
```

As we can see, in the preceding screenshot, there are only two segments in the firewall configuration file for the host zone. They are as follows:

[OPTIONS]

. . . . . . . .

[RULES]

. . . . . . . .

The functions of these segments are exactly the same as the segments in the *Configuring the Datacenter firewall through the CLI* section, as discussed earlier in this chapter. Note that there are no segments for Security Group or IPSet. This is because these features are not present for the host firewall zone.

# Configuring a VM-specific firewall

Rules created for a VM only apply to that particular virtual machine. Even when the virtual machine is moved to a different node, the firewall follows the VM throughout the cluster. There are no rules cascading from this zone. Under the VM firewall feature, we can create Rules, Aliases, and IPSets, but we cannot create any security group. The firewall management is the same for both the KVM virtual machines and LXC containers. We can go to the firewall feature of a VM by navigating to the **VM | Firewall** tab menu. The following screenshot shows the firewall feature of our example **VM #112**:

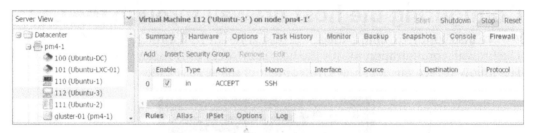

# Creating VM firewall rules

The process of creating new rules for a VM is identical to the rule creation process that we have already seen in the *Configuring the Datacenter firewall through the CLI* section earlier in this chapter. Besides creating rules from scratch, we can also assign predefined rules in the form of a Security Group to a VM. The preceding screenshot shows that our example VM has a firewall rule to allow the SSH console traffic.

# Creating Aliases

An **Alias** for a VM zone serves the same purpose as the Alias for the Datacenter zone. The Alias creation process is also identical to the *Configuring the Datacenter firewall through the CLI* section that we have seen earlier in this chapter. Alias created under a VM stays with that particular VM only. Alias for one VM can be used in another VM.

# Creating IPSet

Like an Alias for a VM, an **IPSet** created under a VM also stays with that particular VM. The IPSet creation process is identical to the IPSet for the Datacenter zone as we have already seen in the *Configuring the Datacenter firewall through the CLI* section earlier in this chapter.

# Options for a VM zone firewall

All the option items under the VM zone Option menu are the same as items for the Datacenter and host zone already described except for the **DHCP** and **MAC** filters. The following screenshot shows the Option items for our example **VM #112**:

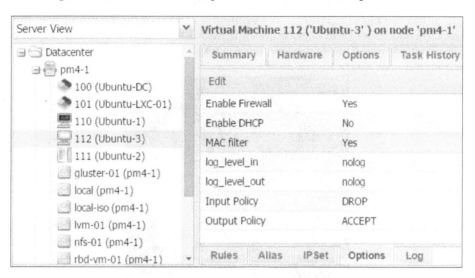

## Enable DHCP

This option is used for a VM that is configured as a DHCP server. A DHCP server uses the UDP ports 67 and 68 to complete IP requests from clients. Instead of manually opening these ports, we can enable this option to let all DHCP-related requests to pass to and from the VM. By default, the DHCP is disabled.

## The MAC filter

When this option is enabled, it prevents the VM user to spoof its own MAC address of the virtual network interface and sends out traffic. This filter will drop the packets from the spoofed MAC address. By default, this option is enabled.

# Configuring a VM-specific firewall through the CLI

As with other firewall zones in Proxmox, we can also configure and manage a virtual machine-specific firewall through the CLI. The configuration file for each VM is in /etc/pve/firewall/<vm_id>.fw. All segments in the configuration file are the same as the Datacenter or host zone configuration. The following screenshot shows the content of a firewall configuration file for **VM #112**:

```
[OPTIONS]

enable: 1
dhcp: 0

[ALIASES]

kvm-112Ubuntu 192.168.1.10

[RULES]

IN SSH(ACCEPT)
```

# Integrating a Suricata IDS/IPS

The security protection of the Proxmox VE firewall can be further enhanced by configuring an intrusion detection and prevention system such as Suricata. It is a high-performing IDS/IPS engine that is able to protect a virtual machine by rejecting traffic that are possible intrusions. Currently, Snort and Suricata are two open source main stream IDS/IPS available among a few others. One of the primary advantages of Suricata is that it is multithreaded, whereas Snort is single-threaded. Suricata is under rapid deployment and gaining popularity fast in the security community.

By default, Suricata is not installed on a Proxmox node, it needs to be manually installed and configured. As for Proxmox VE 4.1, Suricata can only be used to protect a virtual machine, not any Proxmox host nodes.

Do not try to manually download the Suricata package from any other source other than the Proxmox repository and install it on the Proxmox node. It may break the system. Always use the apt-get installer in Proxmox to install Suricata.

If you are new to Suricata, then visit the official Suricata site that will help you gain some knowledge on Suricata as an IDS/IPS at: `http://suricata-ids.org/`.

# Installing/configuring Suricata

We can install Suricata in a Proxmox node using the following command:

```
# apt-get install suricata
```

After Suricata is installed, we have to load the `netfilter` queue subsystem's `nfnetlink_queue` module using the following command:

```
# modprobe nfnetlink
```

To ensure that this modules gets loaded automatically whenever the node is rebooted, we need to add it to the `/etc/modules` file.

The installer installs all the necessary files for Suricata, including Oinkmaster rules. All IDS/IPS engines are heavily dependent on rules. These rules are precompiled and prepackaged in rule files. Oinkmaster is a script that allows us to easily update and manage rules. It is mainly used by Snort but is also supported by Suricata. Without these rules, Suricata will not perform anything. Visit the official Snort site for information on rules at: `https://www.snort.org/`.

There are no options to enable Suricata for a VM through the GUI. So, we have to manually enable it through the CLI by editing the VM firewall configuration file in `/etc/pve/firewall/<vm_id>.fw`. We need to add the following lines to the `[OPTIONS]` segment of the configuration file:

```
ips: 1
ips_queues: 0
```

Ips_queues binds to a specific CPU queue of the virtual machine due to its multithreaded nature. Available queues that Suricata should listen to are defined in `/etc/default/suricata`, as follows:

```
NFQUEUE=0
```

The value is usually set based on the number of CPUs. For example, to use four CPU cores for Suricata, we can use the value 3 for NFQUEUE. The default value **0** indicates that we only use the first CPU, which is CPU 0.

Suricata will only work when listening on `nfqueue`. This is configured by default when Suricata is installed on a Proxmox node. All traffic that is only accepted by the Proxmox firewall gets passed to Suricata for inspection. All the other dropped or rejected traffic does not get passed to Suricata. Suricata configuration files are in `/etc/suricata/suricata-debian.yaml`. The default configuration should work in most cases.

It is comparatively easier to write your own custom rules for Suricata than it is for Snort. You can refer to this excellent documentation on how to learn to write your own rules for Suricata at

`https://redmine.openinfosecfoundation.org/projects/suricata/wiki/ Suricata_Rules`.

We can start the Suricata service by running the following command:

```
# service suricata start
```

The following screenshot shows the command to check the status of the Suricata service and displays the status information:

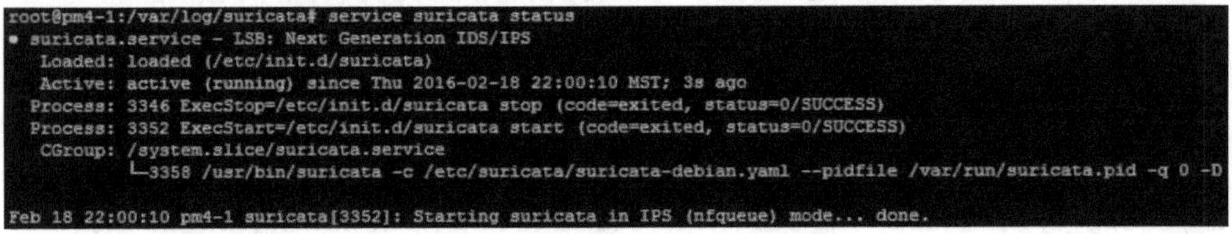

```
root@pm4-1:/var/log/suricata# service suricata status
● suricata.service - LSB: Next Generation IDS/IPS
   Loaded: loaded (/etc/init.d/suricata)
   Active: active (running) since Thu 2016-02-18 22:00:10 MST; 3s ago
  Process: 3346 ExecStop=/etc/init.d/suricata stop (code=exited, status=0/SUCCESS)
  Process: 3352 ExecStart=/etc/init.d/suricata start (code=exited, status=0/SUCCESS)
   CGroup: /system.slice/suricata.service
           └─3358 /usr/bin/suricata -c /etc/suricata/suricata-debian.yaml --pidfile /var/run/suricata.pid -q 0 -D

Feb 18 22:00:10 pm4-1 suricata[3352]: Starting suricata in IPS (nfqueue) mode... done.
```

# Limitation of Suricata in Proxmox

As mentioned earlier, there are no GUI options for Suricata in Proxmox. All configurations are done through the CLI. Without a proper knowledge on IDS/IPS rules, it is very difficult to create rules based on their own environments. Suricata cannot be used to protect any Proxmox nodes but only virtual machines. This limitation may be due to the fact that IDS/IPS can frequently consume a large amount of CPU resources. While for a dedicated firewall appliance, this may not be an issue, for a hypervisor, where the CPU is shared between the hypervisor itself and hosted virtual machines, this could be fatal due to CPU over consumption.

There are no dedicated log view options for Suricata as there is for the Proxmox firewall through the GUI. All Suricata logs are stored in the `/var/log/Suricata` directory by default. However, we can pass Suricata IPS logs to syslog by changing the configuration file in `/etc/pve/suricata/suricata-debian.yaml`. We have to make the following changes in order to pass the Suricata log to syslog:

```
# a line based alerts log similar to fast.log into syslog
syslog:
enabled: yes
identity: "Suricata"
level: Info
```

There are a few more options available to log the output in the same configuration file. Some Proxmox users try to pass Suricata logs to a third-party solution using Logstash and Kibana from Elastic (`www.elastic.co`). Suricata or any other IPS is a complex task to manage on a day-to-day basis. Suricata is still in its infancy in Proxmox. Over time, it may be integrated with the GUI for easier management, but for now, using a dedicated firewall appliance, such as pfSense may be a better option to integrate Suricata in a network. Suricata is fully supported in pfSense with a large amount of manageable features all through the pfSense GUI dashboard. Implementing an IDS/IPS system in a network is not optional but should be made mandatory to protect it from any sort of intrusion.

# Summary

In this chapter, we learned about one of the most powerful features of Proxmox, the built-in firewall. We learned what it is and how to implement it to protect the entire cluster, Proxmox host nodes, and virtual machines. We learned how to manage the firewall rules and configuration using both the GUI and CLI. Proxmox adds security where it is needed the most. By leveraging a flexible and granular firewall protection at a hypervisor level, we are now able to have a better, secured cluster.

In the next chapter, we are going to learn about the Proxmox High Availability feature for VMs, which has been completely redesigned from the ground up. The new changes have brought higher stability while making management and configuration a much simpler task.

# Proxmox High Availability

**9**

In this chapter, we are going to see one of the most prominent features that makes Proxmox an enterprise-class hypervisor. Proxmox High Availability or Proxmox HA allows the cluster to move or migrate virtual machines from a faulty node to a healthy node without any user interaction. We will take a look at the following topics:

- Understanding High Availability
- Requirements for HA
- Configuring Proxmox HA
- Configuring the Proxmox HA simulator

## Understanding High Availability

High Availability is a combination of components and configurations that allow continuous operation of a computational environment for a length of time on a regular basis. Basically, it means that even when unattended server hardware goes bad in a live environment, High Availability can manage the remaining servers on its own and keep a virtual environment running by automatically moving or migrating virtual machines from one node to another. A properly configured HA requires very little actual user interaction during a hardware failure. Without HA in place, all nodes will require constant monitoring by a network manager in order to manually move virtual machines to healthy nodes when a node goes bad.

In a small environment, manually moving VMs is not a major issue, but in a large environment of hundreds of virtual machines and nodes, constant monitoring can be very time consuming. Although there can be monitoring software in place to automatically alert administrators for any node failure, without HA the administrator will have to manually move or migrate any virtual machine from a faulty node. This can cause longer downtime due to the network staff response time. That's where the Proxmox HA feature comes in. HA takes operator intervention out of the equation by simply moving or migrating virtual machines to a node as soon as server hardware failure occurs.

# High Availability in Proxmox

To set up functional HA in Proxmox, it is important to have all the virtual machines on shared storage. It is crucial to understand that Proxmox HA only handles Proxmox nodes and virtual machines within the Proxmox cluster. These HA features are not to be confused with shared storage redundancy, which Proxmox can utilize for its HA deployment. HA in a shared storage is just as important as Proxmox VM's High Availability. A third-party shared storage can provide its own HA features. So, both the Proxmox cluster and shared storage will need to be configured to provide a truly High Availability environment. It is beyond the scope of this book to go in to the details of storage high availability.

There can be levels of redundancy in a Proxmox computing node, such as the use of RAID, a redundant power supply, an aggregated network link, or bond. HA in Proxmox is not a replacement for any of these layers. It just facilitates redundancy features for virtual machines to keep running during a node failure.

It should be noted that in a Proxmox node, a reboot due to an applied update will cause all HA-enabled virtual machines to shut down and moved to the next available Proxmox node and restart again. In such a situation, it may be necessary to manually live migrate virtual machines first before rebooting the node.

# How Proxmox HA works

When a node becomes unresponsive for various reasons, Proxmox HA waits for 60 seconds before fencing the faulty node. Fencing prevents cluster services to come online in that line. Then, HA moves the VM to the next available node in the HA member group. As of Proxmox VE 4.1, LXC containers cannot be live migrated. So, HA will stop all LXC containers, and then move them to the next node. Even if the node with VMs is still powered up but it loses the network connectivity, Proxmox HA will try to move all VMs out of the node to a different node.

Once the faulty node comes back online; however, HA will not automatically move the VMs back to the original node. This must be done manually. But a VM can only be moved manually if the HA is disabled for that VM. So, we have to disable the HA first, and then move to the original node and enable HA on the VM again. As we can see, Proxmox HA likes to manage everything on its own although it adds little annoyance to manually perform certain functions. HA is focused on maintaining uptime which is a job it does suitably. Later in this chapter, we will see how to configure HA for virtual machines.

# Requirements for HA setup

From Proxmox 4.0 and later, the High Availability feature has been completely redesigned from the ground up making it much simpler to configure and use. There are a few requirements that the environment must meet before configuring Proxmox HA. They are as follows:

- Minimum three nodes
- Shared storage
- Fencing

## Minimum three nodes

HA must be configured in a cluster with a minimum of three nodes because with three nodes or more, achieving a Quorum is possible. A Quorum is the minimum number of votes required for a Proxmox cluster operation. This minimum number is the total vote by a majority of the nodes. For example, in a cluster of three Proxmox nodes, a minimum vote of two Proxmox nodes is required to form a Quorum. Or, in a cluster with eight nodes, a minimum vote of five Proxmox nodes is required to form a Quorum. With just two nodes, the ratio of vote remains at 1:1, so no Quorum is possible.

## Shared storage

During a node failure, VMs are moved to the next member node in the HA. This migration usually happens live. A VM cannot be live migrated when the disk image is not stored on a shared storage.

 Do not try to enable HA for any locally stored VMs. The HA will forcefully move the VM configuration file and not update the location of the disk image.

# Fencing

Fencing is the concept of isolating a node or its resources during a node failure so that other nodes cannot access the same resources putting them at risk for data corruption. In Proxmox, fencing prevents multiple nodes from running on the same virtual machine or cluster-specific services. Fencing ensures data integrity during a node failure by preventing all nodes from running on the same virtual machine or cluster services at the same time.

As of Proxmox VE 4.1, a separate **Fencing** device used to configure Proxmox HA is no longer required. Fencing now uses hardware-based watchdog or Linux softdog. Linux softdog is a software version of a traditional watchdog. Most modern server BIOSs have the watchdog functionality, but it is normally disabled by default. When enabled, this will reboot server nodes after a certain period of inactivity. Proxmox HA will always check whether there is a hardware watchdog, and if not, it will automatically use softdog. The use of softdog now allows HA to be implemented in a nested virtual environment. This is helpful to set up a virtualized Proxmox environment to learn and test Proxmox HA without affecting changes on the main systems.

# BIOS power on feature

Before we set up fencing and Proxmox HA, we have to make sure that nodes can boot immediately after a power cycle or power loss. Usually, this feature is disabled by default. The following screenshot shows this BIOS feature:

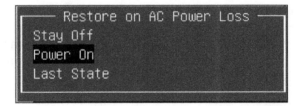

It is important that the BIOS power on functionality should be tested and verified. To do so, unplug the power cord, then plug it back again to see whether the node powers up. Without this feature enabled, the node will not be able to auto boot or power cycle by Proxmox HA fencing.

# Configuring Proxmox HA

All configurations of Proxmox HA can be done from the GUI. Thanks to the new version of HA in Proxmox. The HA feature is available by navigating to **Datacenter | HA**. This is the menu where we will perform all HA-related configurations and management. The following screenshot shows the Proxmox HA management interface:

As we can see, in the preceding screenshot, the **HA** interface has four submenus.

## Status menu

This menu shows the **Status** of the HA configuration. There are no management options in this menu. A clean installed Proxmox cluster will show only one line item for a healthy quorum. Once the new member nodes are added to the HA configuration, this status menu will show the running states of all the nodes and the virtual machines that have HA enabled.

# Groups menu

This menu is to used create and manage different groups of Proxmox for HA. The most relevant use of groups is some software solutions, or infrastructure VMs should always be running together for continuous functionality in the event of a failure. For example, a domain controller, file server, and so on. We can create multiple groups through this menu. A VM assigned to a particular group will only be moved within the member nodes in that group. For example, if we have six nodes, out of which three nodes are resourceful enough to run the database virtual server, the other three nodes run virtual desktops or VDI solutions. We can create two groups for which the database virtual servers will only be moved within the nodes that we have assigned for that group. This ensures that a VM is moved to a correct node, which will be able to run the VMs. We need a minimum of one group to enable HA for a VM. To open the group creation dialog box, simply click on **Create** in the **Groups** submenu. The following screenshot shows the groups dialog box for our example group named Pmx_2ndEd_HA:

The following are the items available on the **HA Group** dialog box.

## ID

This is a textbox used to enter a name for the **HA Group**. The **ID** string can be an alphanumeric text with only underscore or _ as special characters.

 Note that once we create a group, we cannot change the group name. We will have to delete the group and create a new one with a proper ID if we need to change the group name.

# Node

This is a drop-down list used to assign Proxmox nodes in the group. We can select multiple nodes in the list. In order to create the group, we need to select at least one node. Unlike the ID textbox, we can change the assigned member nodes for the group even after the group has been created.

# Restricted

This is a checkbox used to allow VMs to be moved by Proxmox HA only within the available member nodes in the HA group. If there are no available member nodes, then the VMs will be stopped automatically. This option is not enabled by default.

# Nofailback

This is also a checkbox used to prevent the group from automatic failback when a new node joins the cluster. This is not enabled by default. Unless there is a strict requirement, this option should not be enabled.

The following screenshot shows the **Group** submenu interface with our example group created:

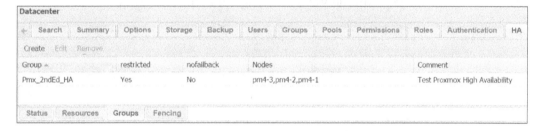

| Group ▲ | restricted | nofailback | Nodes | Comment |
| --- | --- | --- | --- | --- |
| Pmx_2ndEd_HA | Yes | No | pm4-3,pm4-2,pm4-1 | Test Proxmox High Availability |

# Resources menu

This is the menu where we enable HA for a virtual machine or container. Click on **Add** to open the VM resource dialog box. This is a very simple dialog box where we only need to select a VM and the HA group the VM will belong to. The following screenshot shows that we are adding our example VM #112 to the new HA group that we created in the previous section:

Through the **Resource** menu dialog box, we can also disable HA for a VM instead of deleting the resource assignment. This is useful when we want to temporarily disable the resource, and we can may use it in future. The following screenshot shows the resource menu with the example VM #112 assigned to the HA group:

# Fencing menu

As of Proxmox 4.1, there is no function for this menu. It only informs the fencing device being used by Proxmox HA. Proxmox uses the hardware watchdog and Linux software watchdog for fencing. The following screenshot shows the Fencing `tabbed` menu interface:

At this point, we created a Proxmox HA group and added a VM to the group to be managed by HA. Our VM is currently in the pmx4-1 node and is ready to be managed by Proxmox HA. The following screenshot shows the **Status** menu of HA:

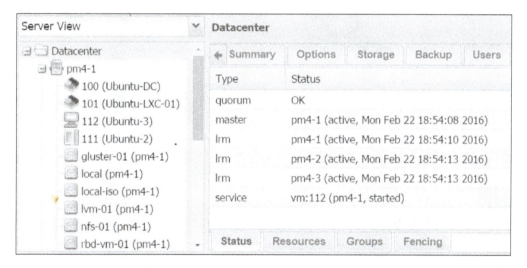

As we can see, in the preceding screenshot, the **Status** menu shows the current state of the entire HA feature. For our example cluster, it shows the following vital information:

- The cluster quorum is established
- The master node pm4-1 of the HA group is active and the timestamp of the last heartbeat is checked
- All the three member nodes of the HA group are active and the timestamp of the last heartbeat is checked
- The VM service for #112 is currently running on the first node pm4-1

# Testing Proxmox HA configuration

To test whether the HA is really working, we will disconnect the network connectivity for the node pm4-1 and observe the **Status** window for HA changes. The **Status** window displays the states of resources in real time as they occur. The following screenshot shows the **HA** status after interrupting the network connectivity:

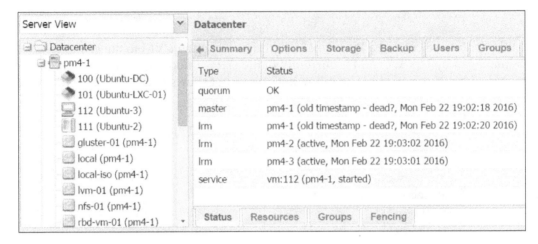

In the preceding screenshot, we can see that our example node pm4-1 is no longer connected to the cluster, and HA does not get any acknowledgement from the node. After 60 seconds, Proxmox HA promotes the next available node in the HA group as the master, as shown in the following screenshot:

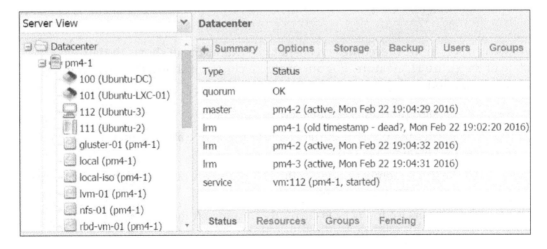

After Proxmox HA promotes a new master for the HA group, it then starts fencing the VM resources to prepare them in order to move them to another node. During fencing, all services related to the VM are fenced, which means that even if the failed node comes back online at this stage, the VM will not be able to resume its normal operation. The following screenshot shows the VM status in the fenced state:

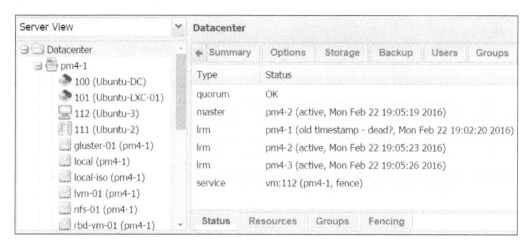

After the VM resources are fenced, in the next stage, the VM is fully stopped. Since the node itself is down, the VM cannot be live migrated because the memory state of the running VM cannot be retrieved from the down node. The following screenshot shows the VM resource in the stopped state:

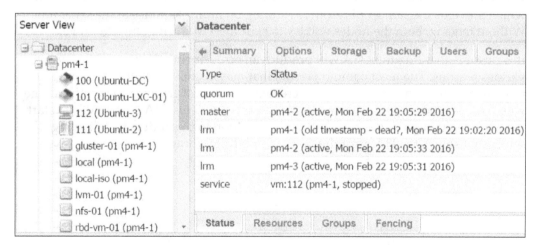

After the VM is stopped, it is moved to the next available node in the HA group and started automatically. The following screenshot shows that the VM is now moved to the node pm4-2 and has been started:

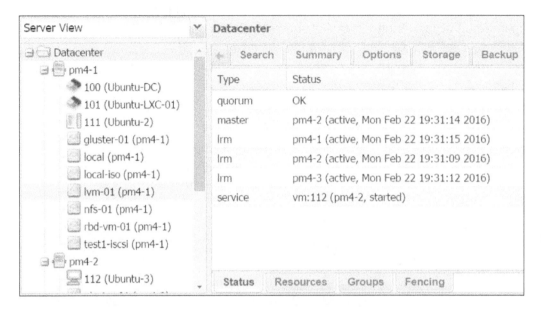

We can also see, in the preceding screenshot, that even though the first node pm4-1 did come back online after the network connectivity was restored, the HA continued with the VM resource to move to the next available node. This is because of fencing, which prevents the same VM resource running on multiple nodes at the same time. Without fencing, both the nodes will try to start the VM during the VM move.

It is possible that Proxmox HA will produce an error during the auto VM move for various reasons. The most common errors that may occur due to shared storage misconfiguration. In our example, we created an artificial error for the Ceph storage where the second node pm4-2 could not read storage. Thus, HA was unable to start the VM even though it moved the VM configuration to the node. The following screenshot shows the HA error due to the Ceph RBD storage:

After any error, Proxmox HA will make several attempts with the **restart** and **relocate** policy to recover from the error. If all attempts fail, Proxmox HA puts the resource in the error state and will not perform any automated tasks for it. For this reason, even after the error has been addressed and fixed, HA will not automatically start the VM. We will manually have to start the VM by temporarily disabling HA for the VM, and then enable it after the VM is started. This is one of the unintended side effects of enabling Proxmox HA where it may not behave as expected after any error has occurred.

If the VM is automatically moved after a node failure and then restarted on a new node, this completes the entire process of the Proxmox HA configuration.

# The Proxmox HA simulator

Although Proxmox HA has become far easier to configure and manage, it is still a complex topic to grasp. With the use of software-based watchdog, it is entirely possible to configure, test, and learn Proxmox HA in a virtualized environment before implementing it in a production cluster. There is also a simulator for Proxmox HA that we can use to see HA in action without setting up a cluster. The simulator allows us to see the HA configuration in action and see how the states change at different stages.

# Configuring the Proxmox HA simulator

The Proxmox HA simulator is not shipped with the distribution that it needs to be manually installed. Along with the simulator package, we also need `xorg` and `xuath` because the simulator requires X11 redirection, which is also known as X11 forwarding. We can use the following commands to install the packages:

```
# apt-get install pve-ha-simulator
```

```
# apt-get install xorg
```

```
# apt-get install xauth
```

We can access the simulator from both the Linux and Windows operating systems. If we log in from Linux, use the standard SSH command with the `-Y` option, as shown in the following command:

```
# ssh root@<pmx_node> -Y
```

For Windows, we can use the advanced terminal, such as MobaXterm, which can be downloaded from `http://mobaxterm.mobatek.net/`.

After we access the Proxmox node through Linux or Windows, we need to create a directory, which will be used as the working data directory for the simulator. After the directory is created, we can run the simulator pointing to the working directory. The following screenshot shows the SSH console with the directory created and simulator started using the Mobaxterm program:

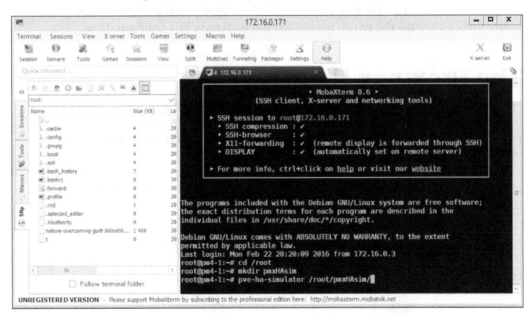

After the command is executed, the Proxmox HA simulator is started in a graphical interface, as shown in the following screenshot:

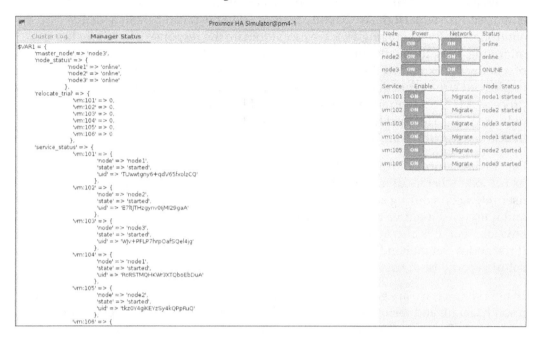

As we can see, in the preceding screenshot, the simulator provides a three node HA setup with two VMs per node. We can simulate a node or network failure using the **Power** or **Network** button and watch HA in action. Before HA takes action, we have to enable HA for each of the VMs. We will see that as various HA states change, the configuration entries of the HA also change in real time. This simulator will aid in understanding Proxmox HA better through practice.

# Summary

In this chapter, we learned the different aspects of the recently redesigned and enhanced Proxmox High Availability feature and how it can benefit a virtual environment. By leveraging HA, we can automate the response to a failure by auto migrating VMs, thus reducing the down time during the node or network failure of a node. We explained the requirements the infrastructure must meet in order to implement a fully functional High Availability feature. We walked you through the process of HA configuration and finally tested HA by creating a simulating device failure. We also learned how to install and use the Proxmox HA simulator to see HA in action without setting up a cluster.

Due to the nature of Proxmox HA it is highly recommended to test this feature to its full extent before diving into implementing it in production cluster. HA can limit user interaction during some operations. The need for HA should be evaluated and if used it should be thoroughly tested before implementing it in a production environment. It is also quite important to group and size the HA solution properly. If the nodes cannot handle the load of virtual machines that HA requires, the entire solution could be at risk when a failure occurs, compounding the issue.

In next chapter, we are going to see how to prepare for a data disaster by implanting a solid backup and restore strategy. We will look at the backup and restore option available in Proxmox itself and how to implement backup schedules.

# 10
# Backup/Restore VMs

A good backup strategy is the last line of defense against disasters, such as hardware failure, environmental damage, accidental deletions, or misconfigurations. In a virtual environment, a backup strategy can turn into a daunting task because of the number of virtual machines needed to be backed up. In a busy production environment, a new virtual machine can come and go any time. Without a proper backup plan, the entire backup task can become difficult to manage. Gone are those days when we only had a few servers' hardware to deal with, and backing them up was an easy task. In today's virtual environments, a backup solution has to deal with several dozens or possibly several hundred virtual machines.

Depending on the business requirement, an administrator may have to backup all the virtual machines regularly instead of just the files inside VMs. Backing up an entire virtual machine takes up a very large amount of space after a while, depending on how many previous backups there are. A granular file backup helps you quickly restore just the file needed but can be a bad choice if the virtual server is badly damaged to a point that it becomes inaccessible.

A restore plan along with a backup strategy is also equally important, because a backup is only useful when we can successfully restore data in a timely and proper manner after a disaster. In this chapter, we will cover the following topics:

- Exploring Proxmox backup options
- Configuring backups
- Configuring snapshots
- Restoring VMs
- Backing up a configuration file

# Proxmox backup options

As of Proxmox VE 4.1, there are two backup options included out of the box:

- **Full backup**: This backs up the entire virtual machine
- **Snapshots**: This freezes the state of a VM at a point in time

Proxmox 4.1 can only do a full backup and cannot do any granular file backup from inside a virtual machine. Proxmox also does not use any backup agent.

# A full backup

A full backup is a complete compressed backup of a virtual machine, including its configuration file. We can take this backup and restore it locally to the same cluster or to an entirely different Proxmox cluster. We can potentially set up a full backup everyday or on a different schedule up to one week. Since a full backup commits the complete backup of the entire virtual machine, including all the virtual disk images in it, it is the slowest backup option. It is also the safest since the final backup file is not dependent on the original VM. Two of the most important components of a full backup are backup modes and compression level.

# Full backup modes

Various backup modes offer different data assurance and speed. There are three types of modes available for a full backup.

## Snapshot

A snapshot for a full backup is not the same as snapshots for virtual machines where it freezes the state of the VM in a point in time. A full snapshot backup is when it is committed without powering off the VM or temporarily suspending it. This is also known as **Live backup**. Since a backup occurs while the VM is running, there is no downtime for this mode, but it also has the longest backup time. On rare occasions, files in use can cause backup errors due to file locks.

## Suspend

In this mode, a backup occurs after temporarily suspending or freezing the VM. There is no need to completely power off the VM, thus the downtime is moderate during a backup. After a backup is completed, the VM resumes its regular operation. This mode has much less chances of errors during a backup since a VM is suspended.

## Stop

In this mode, running VMs are automatically powered off or stopped and then powered on after the backup has been completed. This provides the maximum assurance or zero errors in the backup since the VM is not running at all. This is also the fastest backup mode.

# Backup compression

In Proxmox, we can commit a backup with different compression levels. The higher the level, the less space is used to store backup files, but it also consumes higher CPU resources to perform compression. There are three compression levels in a Proxmox backup.

## None

When this level is selected, no compression occurs for the backup task. While this will take the least amount of CPUs during a backup task, do keep in mind that this will significantly take up a large amount of space to store backup files. Proxmox virtual disk images are sparsed, which means that an allocated disk image only uses some space of the actual data. The rest of the allocation is sparsed or filled with zeros.

A backup with no compression will save the disk image as it is trying to compress the empty spaces. This will cause the backup file to take up as much as room as the disk image itself. Use this option with care and ensure that the backup storage has enough storage space to hold uncompressed backup files.

## LZO

This is the default compression level in Proxmox. LZO provides a balance between speed and compression. It also has the fastest decompression rate, making the restore of a VM much faster.

## GZIP

This level provides a much higher compression ratio but also takes a longer time to back up. Due to an increased compression rate, this level consumes much more CPUs and memory resources. We need to ensure that backup nodes have sufficient processing ability before we enable this level.

# Snapshots

Snapshots freeze or capture the state of a virtual machine at a point in time. This is not a full backup of a VM since the snapshots are fully dependent on the original VM. We cannot move snapshots elsewhere for safekeeping. Snapshots are used to roll back to a previous state. Since snapshots do not back up the entire virtual machine with disk images, it is the fastest backup option to quickly save the state of the VM. In Proxmox, we can take snapshots of a running VM; in which case, the content of the running memory also gets saved. This way, we can revert to the earlier VM exactly as it was running when a snapshot was taken.

A good case of using this backup is when testing software or applying updates. We can take snapshots of a VM prior to installing any software or applying updates, so, if something goes wrong after the installation, we can simply revert to the previous state in a matter of minutes instead of reinstalling the entire virtual machine. This is much faster and cleaner than uninstalling the tested software itself.

 A full backup should never be substituted for snapshots. Always include a full backup in a primary disaster recovery strategy.

As with Proxmox VE 4.1, there is no snapshots scheduling option. All snapshots must be performed manually. In an environment with several dozen virtual machines, manual snapshots can become a time-consuming task. It is possible to set up snapshot scheduling using bash, cron, and qm, but these methods can be flawed and they are known to be somewhat unstable; and therefore they are not recommended for a production environment.

If a full backup is performed on a virtual machine that has snapshots applied, the snapshots do not get placed in the backup file. A full backup task ignores all the snapshot images. Also, when a virtual machine is deleted, all the snapshots belonging to the virtual machine also get deleted.

# Configuring backup storage

A sound backup strategy has a dedicated shared storage for the backup images instead of local storage that is used for the disk images themselves. This way, we can centralize the backup location and restore them even in the event of a Proxmox node failure. If the backup is stored locally on the same node, during hardware failures, that node may become completely inaccessible causing a VM restoration delay.

One of the most popular options for a backup storage node is NFS. In an enterprise or mission-critical environment, a cluster with built in redundancy dedicated to backups is a recommended practice. In smaller environments, good redundancy can still be achieved using storage options, such as Gluster or DRBD. With the addition of ZFS and Gluster in Proxmox VE, it is now a viable option to turn a Proxmox node into a backup using Gluster on top of ZFS, and still manage the node through the Proxmox GUI. Unfortunately, we cannot store backup files on the Ceph RBD storage.

For a single backup storage node, FreeNAS is a great option without cluster redundancy. Regardless of which storage system is used, the primary goal is to store a backup on a separate node instead of the computing node. Refer to *Chapter 4, Storage Systems,* for information on how to attach various storage systems with Proxmox. Once a storage is set up and attached to Proxmox, we need to ensure that the content type for the storage is configured in order to store backup files and backup rotation quantity. There are two options in the storage dialog box to select the content type and to define the backup rotation quantity. The following screenshot shows the storage dialog box for a NFS storage in our example cluster:

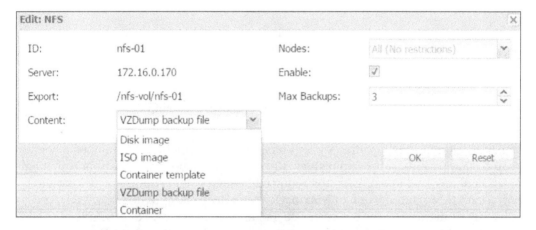

In the preceding screenshot, we selected the **VZDump backup file** from the drop-down list and typed in **3** in the **Max backups** or backup rotation quantity tab. This means that the storage will allow you to store backup files and three recent backups will always be kept. Older backups will be automatically deleted. This will only happen automatically when the backup is handled by a backup schedule.

When performing manual backups, this quantity value will actually prevent you from committing manual backups if there are already three backups stored in the storage for a VM. In such cases, we will have to manually delete older backups or increase this value to accommodate new manual backups. We can delete backup files for the VM through the Backup tab menu of the VM, or directly from the storage device in the content tab. We need to select the backup file that we need to delete, and then click on Remove. The following screenshot shows the backup tab menu for our container **#101**:

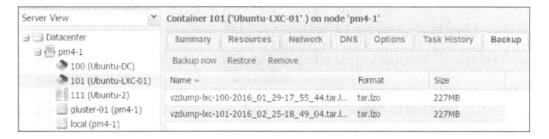

 Make sure that you set appropriate values for Max Backups, because higher values will keep more backup files, consuming a lot more space of the storage node. Too many backup files and not enough space will cause new backup tasks to fail. We can also set up two storage nodes and use one to store frequent backups, for example, weekly, while the other one can be used to store longer interval backups, for example, bi-annually.

Depending on the backup strategy and business requirement, there may be a need to keep certain periods of backup history. Proxmox allows both automatic and manual deletion of any backups outside the required history range. Automatic deletion is performed through the value of **Max backups** in the backup dialog box. We can enter any numeric number between 0 to 365 as **Max backups**. For example, our NFS storage has **Max Backups** of **3**. This means that during a full backup, Proxmox will keep the three newest backups of each virtual machine and delete anything older.

If we are to commit to daily backup, we could potentially keep 365 days or 1 year worth of backups at any given time. If we did backup every other day, then it would be 2 years worth of backup.

# Configuring full backup

All full backups are in the `tar` format containing both the configuration file and virtual disk image file. The backup files are all you need to restore a virtual machine on any nodes and on any storage. Full backup files are named based on the several following formats for both KVM and LXC virtual machines:

```
vzdump-lxc-<ct_id>-YYYY_MM_DD-HH_MM_SS.tar
vzdump-lxc-<ct_id>-YYYY_MM_DD-HH_MM_SS.tar.lzo
vzdump-lxc-<ct_id>-YYYY_MM_DD-HH_MM_SS.tar.gz

vzdump-qemu-<vm_id>-YYYY_MM_DD-HH_MM_SS.vma
vzdump-qemu-<vm_id>-YYYY_MM_DD-HH_MM_SS.vma.lzo
vzdump-qemu-<vm_id>-YYYY_MM_DD-HH_MM_SS.vma.fz
```

The following screenshot shows a list of backup files in a backup storage node, as seen from the Proxmox GUI:

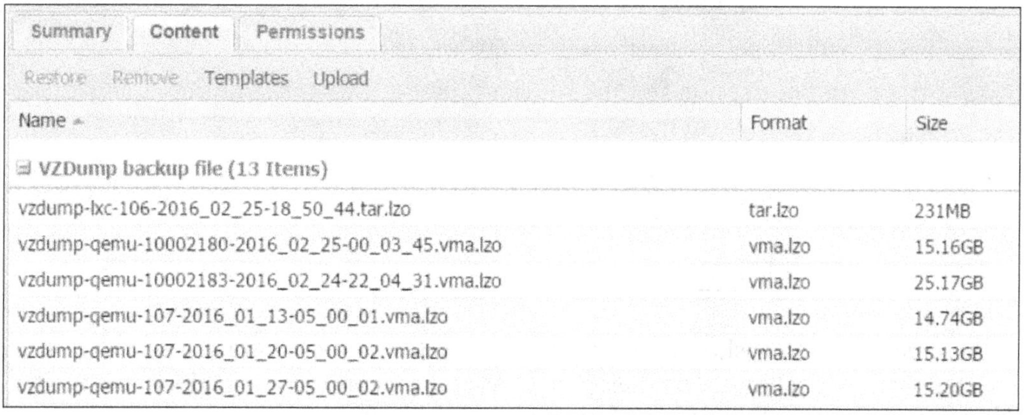

| Summary | Content | Permissions | | |
|---------|---------|-------------|--|--|
| Restore | Remove | Templates | Upload | |
| Name ▲ | | | Format | Size |
| ⊟ VZDump backup file (13 Items) | | | | |
| vzdump-lxc-106-2016_02_25-18_50_44.tar.lzo | | | tar.lzo | 231MB |
| vzdump-qemu-10002180-2016_02_25-00_03_45.vma.lzo | | | vma.lzo | 15.16GB |
| vzdump-qemu-10002183-2016_02_24-22_04_31.vma.lzo | | | vma.lzo | 25.17GB |
| vzdump-qemu-107-2016_01_13-05_00_01.vma.lzo | | | vma.lzo | 14.74GB |
| vzdump-qemu-107-2016_01_20-05_00_02.vma.lzo | | | vma.lzo | 15.13GB |
| vzdump-qemu-107-2016_01_27-05_00_02.vma.lzo | | | vma.lzo | 15.20GB |

In Proxmox, we can schedule automated backup tasks or commit manual backups for each virtual machine. Whether scheduled or manual, the backup process is the same for both KVM and LXC virtual machines.

# Creating a schedule for Backup

Schedules can be created from the **Backup** option under the Datacenter tabbed menu. We will see each option box in detail in the following sections. The backup option shows a list of already created **Backup** schedules along with options to **Add**, **Remove**, and **Edit** tasks. The schedule dialog box is the same for adding, removing, and editing backup tasks. We can click on add, to open the dialog box, as shown in the following screenshot:

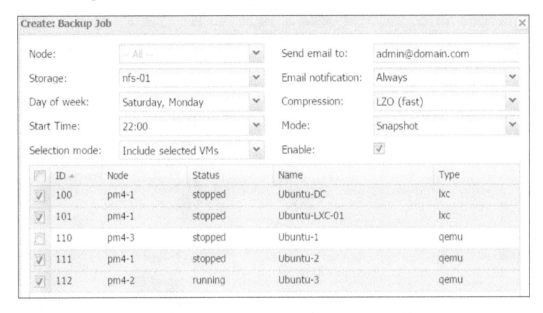

In the preceding screenshot, we created a backup task to perform twice a week for selected virtual machines. The dialog box has several components, which need to be defined in order to schedule a backup task.

## Node

This is a drop-down list used to select a Proxmox node to only show the virtual machines in that node. This also sets the task to apply to that node only. For example, if we select a particular node and a VM in it to commit a backup, and we later move that VM to another node, no backup task will be performed since the VM is no longer in the original node. By default, all nodes are selected. In our example, we have selected all nodes.

# Storage

This is a drop-down list used to select a backup storage destination where all full backups will be stored. Typically, an NFS server is used for backup storage. They are easy to set up and do not require a lot of upfront investment due to their lower performance requirements.

Backup servers are much leaner than computing nodes since they do not have to run any virtual machines. Some storage nodes, such as ZFS, do need a lot of memory to operate adequately. For example, we have selected an NFS storage.

## Day of week

This is a drop-down list used to select which day or days the backup task applies to. We can select multiple days in this list. In order to create a daily backup task, all days need to be selected. As with Proxmox VE 4.1, we can create monthly or yearly backup tasks.

## Start Time

Unlike for **Day of week**, only one time slot can be selected. Multiple selections of time to backup different times of the day are not possible.

 If the backup needs to run multiple times a day, create a separate task for each time slot.

## Selection mode

This is a drop-down list used to define how VMs are selected for backups. There are three options available to select from. The **All** mode will select all the virtual machines within the whole Proxmox cluster or node, depending on the selection in the Node drop-down list. The **Exclude selected VMs** mode will back up all VMs except the ones selected. **Include selected VMs** will back up only the ones selected. For example, we have selected include selected VMs.

## Send e-mail to

Enter a valid e-mail address here so that the Proxmox backup task can send an e-mail upon backup task completion, or if there was any issue during backup. The e-mail includes the entire log of the backup tasks.

It is highly recommended that you enter an e-mail address here so that an administrator or backup operator can receive backup task feedback e-mails. This will allow us to find out if there was an issue during backup or how much time it actually takes to see if any performance issue occurred during backup.

# E-mail notification

This is a drop-down list used to define when the backup task should send automated e-mails. We can select this option to always send an e-mail or only send an e-mail when there is an error or a failure.

# Compression

This is a drop-down list used to select the compression level for the backup task. Refer to the *Backup compression* section earlier in this chapter to see the difference between the various compression levels. By default, the LZO compression method is selected.

# Mode

This is a drop-down list used to define the backup mode for the task. Refer to the *Full backup modes* section earlier in this chapter to see the difference between backup modes. By default, all running virtual machine backups occur with the snapshot option.

# Enable

This is a checkbox used to enable or disable a backup task. This has been newly added in the recent Proxmox version. With this option, we can disable a backup task temporarily instead of deleting and creating from scratch, as was the case in the previous Proxmox versions.

The following shows the **Backup** option with our newly created backup task listed:

# Creating a manual backup

A manual backup can be performed on a particular virtual machine at any time through the Proxmox GUI. The Manual backup option is accessible through the Backup tabbed menu of the virtual machine. From the same Backup menu, we can back up, restore, and delete backup files.

To open the backup creation dialog box, we need to click on the **Backup now** button. The **Manual** backup dialog box is extremely simple. We only need to select the destination **Storage** node, backup **Mode**, and **Compression** level, as shown in the following screenshot:

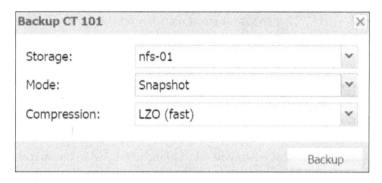

# Creating snapshots

Snapshots are a great way to preserve the state of a virtual machine. It is much faster than a full backup since it does not copy all the data. Snapshot is not really a backup in this way and does not perform granular level backup. It captures the state in a point in time and allows rollback to that previous state.

Snapshot is a great feature to be used in between full backups. The Snapshot option can be found under the Snapshots tabbed menu of the virtual machine. A newly installed VM without any Snapshots will appear under the Snapshots menu, as shown in the following screenshot:

The actual snapshot creation process is very straightforward. Click on **Take Snapshot** to open the dialog box, and then just enter a **Name**, select or deselect the **RAM** content, and type in some description. The **Name** textbox does not allow any spaces and the name must start with a letter of the alphabet. The following screenshot shows the **Snapshots** creation dialog box for our example **VM #112**:

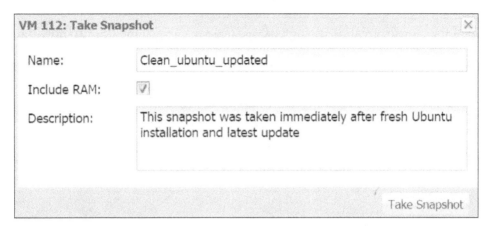

 Keep in mind that when you select to include RAM in the snapshot, the bigger the RAM allocation is for the virtual machine, the longer it will take to create a snapshot. But it is still much faster than a full backup.

The **Snapshot** feature is available for both KVM and LXC virtual machines. The following screenshot shows the Snapshot option with our newly created snapshot:

If we want to go back to the snapshot image, just select the snapshot to go back to and click on **Rollback**. It will prompt to ask if we really want to rollback, as shown in the following screenshot:

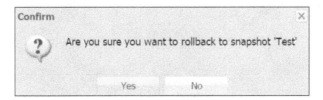

Keep in mind that when you roll back to the earlier virtual machine state, it will erase all the changes that happened to the virtual machine between the time of rolling back and the snapshot being rolled back to.

# Restoring a VM

Like Backup, we can also restore virtual machines through the Proxmox GUI. VMs can be restored through the Backup menu tab of the VM or by selecting a backup file through the storage content list. If restore is selected through the VM backup option, then the VM ID cannot be changed. To understand this better, let's take a look at the following example:

In the preceding screenshot, we are under the **Backup** option for **VM #112**. Since the backup option shows a list of all backup files stored in that backup storage node, we can see the backup files for **VM #110**. If we select the backup file and then click on **Restore**, we will not be able to restore the **VM #110** on its own. Instead, it will actually replace **VM #112**. The following screenshot shows the **Restore** dialog box where the destination **VM ID** is not definable:

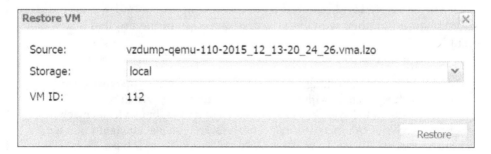

In order to restore a backup file with its original **VM ID**, we need to select the backup file from the storage content tab menu, as shown in the following screenshot:

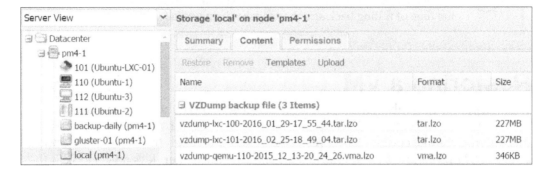

If we select the backup file for **VM #110** from the storage content list and then click on **Restore**, we will be able to define a **VM ID** in the **Restore** dialog box, as shown in the following screenshot:

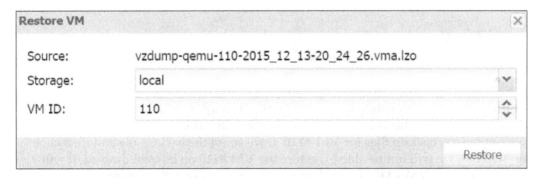

If the same **VM ID** is kept, then the existing virtual machine in the cluster with the same ID will be deleted and restored from the backup version. If we use a different ID before restoring it, then we will have an exact copy of the original VM with a different VM ID.

One important thing to remember is that a full backup created for a virtual machine with the qcow2 or vmdk image format can only be restored to local, CephFS, or NFS-like storages, but a virtual machine with the RAW image format can be restored on just about any storage system. RBD or LVM storages do not support image types such as qcow2 or vmdk.

Also, there is no restoration for snapshot images. The snapshots can only be rolled back to the previous state.

# Backup/restore through the CLI

In Proxmox, the entire backup and restore process can be managed from the command line in case the GUI becomes inaccessible.

## Backup using the CLI

The command to commit backup for both KVM and LXC virtual machines is the same. The following is the command format for backup:

```
# vzdump <vmid> <options>
```

There is a long list of vzdump options that can be used with the command.
The following are just a few of the most commonly used ones:

| Options | Description |
|---------|-------------|
| -all | The default value is 0. This option will back up all available virtual machines in a Proxmox node. |
| -bwlimit | This adjusts the backup bandwidth in KBPS. |
| -compress | The default value is LZO. This sets the compression type or disables compression. The available options are 0, 1, gzip, and lzo. |
| -mailto | This is the e-mail address used to send a backup report. |
| -maxfiles | This contains an integer number. This sets the maximum number of backup files to be kept. |
| -mode | The default value is Stop. This sets backup mode. The available options are snapshot, stop, and suspend. |
| -remove | The default value is 1. This removes older backups if the value entered is more than in maxfiles. |
| -lockwait | This is the maximum time in minutes to wait for a global lock. The default value is 180. |
| -storage | This is the storage ID of the destination backup storage. |
| -tmpdir | This specifies a temporary directory to store files during backup. This is optional. |

# Restore using the CLI

Although the same command can be used to perform a backup for both KVM and LXC, there are two separate commands available to restore the KVM and LXC virtual machines:

- qmrestore: To restore KVM-based VMs
- pct restore: To restore LXC containers

The following command format will restore KVM VMs through the command line:

```
#qmrestore <backup_file> <new/old_vmid> <options>
```

Based on the previous command, if we want to restore our example **KVM #110** from a backup onto local storage, it will appear as follows:

```
#qmrestore /var/lib/vz/dump/vzdump-qemu-110-2015_12_13-20_24_26.vma.lzo
110 -storage local
```

The following options can be used with the qmrestore command:

| Options | Description |
|---|---|
| -force <int> | The Boolean value is 0 or 1. This option allows overwriting the existing VM. Use this option with caution. |
| -unique <int> | The Boolean value is 0 or 1. This assigns a unique random Ethernet address to the virtual network interface. |
| -pool <string> | This is the name of the pool to add the VM to. |
| -storage <string> | This is the storage ID of the destination storage where the VM disk image will be restored. |

The following command format will restore LXC containers through the command line:

```
#pct restore <ct_id> <backupfile> <options>
```

Based on the previous command, if we want to restore our example container **#101** onto local storage, it will appear as follows:

```
#pct restore 101 /var/lib/vz/dump/vzdump-lxc-101-2016_02_25-18_49_04.tar.lzo -storage local
```

The following options can be used with the `pct restore` command:

| Options | Description |
| --- | --- |
| `-force <int>` | The default value is 0 or 1. This option allows overwriting the existing VM. Use this option with caution. |
| `-cpulimit <int>` | The value range is from 0 to 128 with the default value as 0. This defines the number of CPUs or CPU time. Value 0 defines no CPU limit. |
| `-cpuunits <int>` | The value range is from 0 to 500,000 with the default value as 1,024. This defines the CPU weight of the VM in relation to other VMs. |
| `-console <int>` | The default value is 1. This defines the number of consoles to be attached to the container. |
| `-force <int>` | The Boolean value is 0 or 1. This allows overwriting of the existing container with the restored one. |
| `-hostname <string>` | This sets the hostname of the container after a restore command. |
| `-memory <int>` | The default value is 512. This defines the amount of memory allocated for the container. |
| `-swap <int>` | The default value is 512. This defines the amount of swap space for the container. |
| `-password <string>` | This sets the root password in the container after a restore command. |
| `-storage <string>` | This defines the destination storage ID where the container will be restored. |

# Unlocking a VM after a backup error

At times, any backup process can be interrupted before it is finished due to various issues, such as backup storage node failure, loss of network connectivity, very large virtual disk images, and so on. Prior to starting the actual backup process, Proxmox puts a global lock on the VM so that multiple backup tasks cannot be run on the same node. If the backup is not finished successfully, this lock sometimes remains in place and is not automatically removed. If we try to start/stop the VM, we may see an error message that informs us that the VM is locked.

In such cases, we need to manually unlock the VM to resume the normal operation. The unlocking cannot be done from the Proxmox GUI but only through the CLI. The command will need to be run in the node where the VM is. The following command will unlock a locked VM in a Proxmox node:

```
# qm unlock <vm_id>
```

# Back up a configuration file

The backup configuration file in Proxmox allows more advanced options to be used. For example, if we want to limit the backup speed so that the backup task does not consume all of the available network bandwidth, we can limit it with the `bwlimit` option. As of Proxmox VE 4.1, the configuration file cannot be edited from the GUI. It has to be done from the CLI using an editor. The backup configuration file can be found in `/etc/vzdump.conf`. The following is the default `vzdump.conf` file on a new Proxmox cluster:

```
# tmpdir: DIR
# dumpdir: DIR
# storage: STORAGE_ID
# mode: snapshot|suspend|stop
# bwlimit: KBPS
# ionice: PRI
# lockwait: MINUTES
# stopwait: MINUTES
# size: MB
# maxfiles: N
# script: FILENAME
# exclude-path: PATHLIST
# pigz: N:
```

All the options are commented by default in the file because Proxmox has a set of default options already encoded in the operating system. Changing the `vzdump.conf` file overwrites the default settings and allows us to customize the Proxmox backup.

# #bwlimit

The most common option to edit in `vzdump.conf` is to adjust the backup speed. This is usually done in case of remotely stored backups and interface saturation if the backup interface is the same used for the VM production traffic. The value must be defined in KB/s or Kilo Bytes per second. For example, to limit backup to 200 MB/s, make the following adjustment:

```
bwlimit: 200000
```

# #lockwait

The Proxmox backup uses a global lock file to prevent multiple instances running simultaneously. More instances put an extra load on the server. The default lock wait in Proxmox is 180 minutes. Depending on different virtual environments and the number of virtual machines, the lock wait time may need to be increased. If the limit needs to be 10 hours or 600 minutes, adjust the option as follows:

```
lockwait: 600
```

The lock prevents the VM from migrating or shutting down while the backup task is running.

# #stopwait

This is the maximum time in minutes the backup will wait until a VM is stopped. A use case scenario is a VM, which takes much longer to shut down; for example, an exchange server or a database server. If a VM is not stopped within the allocated time, backup is skipped for that VM.

# #script

It is possible to create backup scripts and hook them with a backup task. This script is basically a set of instructions that can be called upon during the entire backup tasks to accomplish various backup-related tasks, such as to start/stop a backup, shutdown/suspend VM, and so on. We can add customized scripts as follows:

```
script: /etc/pve/script/my-script.pl
```

# #exclude-path

To ignore certain folders from backing up, use the exclude-path option. All paths must be entered on one line without breaks. Keep in mind that this option is only for OpenVZ containers:

```
exclude-path: "/log/.+" "/var/cache/.+"
```

The previous example will exclude all the files and directories under /log and /var/cache. To manually exclude other directories from being backed up, simply use the following format:

```
exclude-path: "/<directory_tree>/.+"
```

# #pigz

In simple terms, pigz allows multiple threads on multiple cores during the `gzip` compression backup. The standard `gzip` backup process uses a single core, which is why the backup is slower. Using the `pigz` package, we can notify the backup process to use multiple cores, thus speeding up the backup and restore process. Pigz is basically a gzip but with multi core support. It is not installed in Proxmox by default. We can install it using the following command:

```
# apt-get install pigz
```

In order to enable `pigz` for backup, we need to select the `gzip` compression level for the backup task in GUI. Then, the following `pigz` option in the backup configuration file enables the pigz feature:

```
pigz: 1
```

By default, this value is 0 and is used to disable the use of pigz. The value of 1 uses half of the total core in the node while any value greater than 1, creates a number of threads based on the value. The value should not exceed the maximum number of CPU cores of the node.

 It is worth noting here that pigz is not faster or superior than the lzo compression level, but when using the maximum compression, such as gzip, then the use of pigz will significantly reduce the backup time while compressing backup at the maximum level.

# Summary

In this chapter, we looked at the backup and restore features in Proxmox, how to configure them, and how to use them to create a good data disaster plan. There are no substitutes for data backup to face any disasters where data may be at risk. As much as backup is important, the ability to restore is also equally important, since backup files will not mean anything if restore is not possible in the time of need. Although Proxmox does not provide everything you need for backup such as a granular file backup, backing up a virtual machine is very helpful. Backup features in the Proxmox platform have proven to be reliable in production environments and during actual disaster scenarios.

In the next chapter, we are going to take a look at the necessity of an up-to-date Proxmox cluster and how to apply new releases or patches regularly.

# 11
# Updating and Upgrading Proxmox

There is no such thing as a perfect piece of software. All software matures as it progresses through time by getting new features and finding and fixing hidden bugs. By releasing regular updates and upgrades, a developer can ensure that their software does not become obsolete owing to the rapid pace of software and hardware. In this chapter, we will see how to update and upgrade a Proxmox node to keep it up to date. We will cover the following topics:

- Introducing the Proxmox update
- Updating Proxmox through the GUI
- Updating Proxmox through the CLI
- Updating after subscription change
- Rebooting dilemma after updates

## Introducing Proxmox update

The Proxmox update keeps a node up to date with the latest stable packages, patches security vulnerabilities, and introduces new features. Each node checks for the latest updates and alerts administrators through e-mails if there are any available updates. It is vital to keep all Proxmox nodes up to date especially when security patches are released. Proxmox developers are very prompt to close vulnerabilities through updates in a timely manner.

The number and nature of updates varies depending on your Proxmox subscription level. For example, a Proxmox free version without a subscription receives the most up-to-date stable updates while a node with a subscription level receives updates, which are not so cutting edge and go through an additional layer of testing. Delaying the new package releases for subscription levels creates a buffer to address any issues that may have not been identified during the initial release.

This is not to say that a node without a subscription is not as stable as a paid version. Both offer a very high-level of stability and performance. The only difference is that the delay allows subscribed updates to receive bug fixes, which may not have been noticed during the initial release of the update in a no subscription free version of Proxmox.

A Proxmox node can be updated through both the GUI and CLI. There is no strict recommendation on which one to use. But, in the recent release, an incident occurred when upgrading through the Proxmox GUI Shell caused a grub issue, making the node unbootable. The issue would not have occurred if the upgrading was done through the CLI by accessing the node through SSH or by logging in directly into the node console. Proxmox developers were extremely fast to address this issue and provided a workaround until the next update release was ready. If you are using an older version, such as Proxmox 3.2 or below, it is highly recommended that you choose Proxmox 4.1 as the next upgrade path.

# Updating Proxmox through the GUI

In this section, we will see how to update a Proxmox node through the GUI. Proxmox checks for daily updates and displays relevant packages for which updates are available based on subscription levels. The update menu in the Proxmox GUI can be accessed by selecting the node and clicking on the Update tabbed menu. The following screenshot shows the available update packages for our example node **pm4-1**:

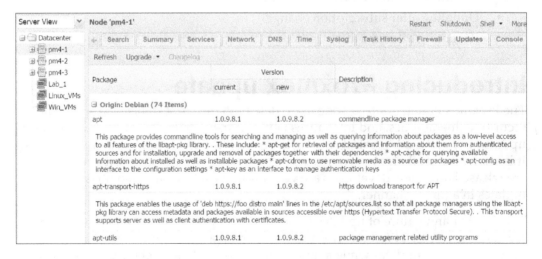

In the preceding screenshot, we can see that the node **pm4-1** has **74** updates available. The update feature shows the name of the package, the current version installed, the new available version, and the description of the package. To start the update or upgrade process, we simply need to click on **Upgrade**. It will open the node shell on the default console, such as noVNC, and will start the update process. Depending on the packages being updated, it may be necessary to act on some prompts. The following screenshot shows a typical prompt waiting for a response during the update process:

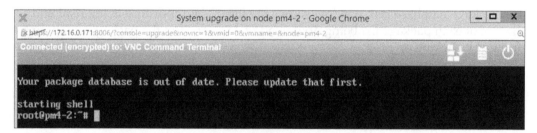

If the package list is old and has not been refreshed, it will notify you that the package database is out of date, as shown in the following screenshot:

We can update the package list by clicking on **Refresh** through the GUI. To restart the update process, click on the **Upgrade** button again on the GUI. The following screenshot shows the updated interface in the GUI after clicking on Refresh:

The package database task window shows the list of the repository being read and the size of each package list being downloaded. We can stop the package database update by clicking on **Stop**.

Proxmox downloads or refreshes the updated package list daily, and sends an e-mail to the root e-mail address. The Proxmox GUI update menu visually displays the list. If there are no updates available, the list will be empty with no messages, as shown in the following screenshot:

# Updating Proxmox through the CLI

As mentioned earlier in this chapter, in the recent Proxmox release, owing to a bug in the software, upgrading through the GUI caused some issues. The GUI is basically the frontend of the behind the scene commands that are run through Proxmox scripts. But still, updating or upgrading Proxmox through the CLI seems to be the safest path.

There are no special Proxmox-specific commands to update a Proxmox node. The standard apt-get for all debian-based distributions is used for the updating process. Log in to the Proxmox node directly on the node or through SSH, and then run the following command to update the list of new packages, as follows:

```
# apt-get update
```

After the package database is up to date, we can start the update process using the following command:

```
# apt-get dist-upgrade
```

# Difference between upgrade and dist-upgrade

Besides the dist-upgrade command, there is another option available for upgrade. It is as follows:

```
# apt-get upgrade
```

This is also the standard debian-based Linux distribution command. However, there is a big difference between these two commands.

The apt-get upgrade command will only update the already installed packages without installing any new ones or making significant changes to the package, such as removing. This will also not satisfy any dependency issues. If any packages require dependency to be resolved, this command will simply leave it alone. The main benefit of this package is that it will very rarely break the system. On the downside, it will also not update or patch everything that is necessary to bring a node up to date.

The apt-get dist-upgrade command, on the other hand, will upgrade all the packages and remove any unneeded packages dictated by the package maintainer. This command will also intelligently satisfy almost all of the required dependencies for a package being updated or marked for a new installation.

Based on the previous explanation of these two update commands, we can see that both these commands have advantages and disadvantages, but to keep a Proxmox node up to date, the apt-get dist-command command seems to be the right way to go. Proxmox is not just another Linux distribution but a highly specialized hypervisor, so, packages that are included in a distribution are carefully chosen by Proxmox developers. Also, there is no mention of the apt-get upgrade command anywhere in Proxmox Wiki.

# Recovering from the grub2 update issue

Due to the latest grub2 update, there may be some instances when updating a Proxmox node through the GUI causes issues, breaking packages. This is specifically true for an earlier release such as Proxmox 3.4. All the newer versions of Proxmox seem to have this issue fixed. To prevent this issue from happening, it is best to upgrade a node, through SSH, or console by logging in directly on the node and not through the GUI. If the upgrade has already been applied through the GUI and there are unconfigured packages due to issues, perform the following steps to fix the issue:

- Check package status with:

  ```
  # pveversion -v
  ```

- Before configuring grub, we need to know the device where Proxmox is installed. We can find the device by running the following command:

  ```
  # parted -l
  ```

- If there are incorrect packages, run the following commands to kill the background dpkg process and configure all the packages, including the new grub2:

  ```
  # killall dpkg
  ```

  ```
  # dpkg --configure -a
  ```

- Select the Proxmox device name when prompted during the grub2 installation.

- Reboot the node.

It is also possible to manually install grub2 on the **Master Boot Record** or **MBR**. Run the following command to install grub2 on the boot device:

```
# grub-install /dev/sdX
```

# Updating after a subscription change

The Proxmox subscription level for a node can be changed at any time by simply applying a subscription key through the GUI. Different subscription levels have different natures of package updates. If a node has started with no subscription, it can always be changed to any paid subscription at any given time. After the subscription level changes, it is important to update the node accordingly so that updates related to the subscription level can be applied. In this section, we will see how to update a node if the subscription level of the node changes at any time. For example, we are assuming that the node is on no subscription and we are adding a paid-level subscription. We can upload a subscription key through the Subscription tabbed menu for a node on the Proxmox GUI. But the modification that needs to be made to activate the repository for subscription needs to be done through the CLI. To disable the free subscription-level repository, we are going to comment out the following command in the /etc/apt/sources.list file:

```
# deb http://download.proxmox.com/debian jessie pve-no-subscription
```

After this, we need to uncomment the following line of code in /etc/apt/sources.list.d/pve-enterprise.list to enable the subscription-level repository:

```
deb https://enterprise .proxmox.com/debian Jessie pve-enterprise
```

After these modifications are made, we can update the Proxmox GUI by following the steps in the *Updating Proxmox through the GUI* section in this chapter.

To update through the command line, we can follow the steps in the *Updating Proxmox through the CLI* section in this chapter.

The same enterprise repository works for all paid subscription levels, such as **Community**, **Basic**, **Standard**, and **Premium**. All paid subscriptions receive the same type of updates.

# Rebooting dilemma after Proxmox updates

After any update, all administrators face the question of whether the node should be rebooted or not. The Proxmox upgrade process is usually very informative and tells us whether the node really needs a reboot. Most of the updates do not require any reboot. They are simply package updates, but some upgrades, such as kernel releases, newer grubs, and so on will require a node reboot every time. The exact method of rebooting depends on each environment, number, and nature of VMs that are stored per node. In this section, we will see the most widely used method, which is by no means the only a method.

For minimal virtual machine downtime, we can live migrate all the VMs from a node to a different node, and then migrate them back to the original node. As with Proxmox VE 4.1, there is a nice GUI feature addition to instruct all VM migrations with a menu instead of selecting and migrating one VM at a time. The feature is under the **More** drop-down menu in the top-right hand corner of the GUI, as shown in the following screenshot:

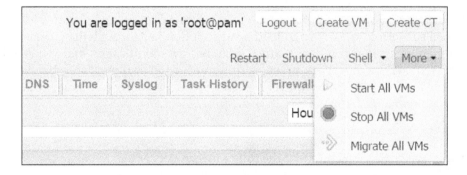

As we can see, in the preceding screenshot, we can also start or stop all virtual machines. The selected action will only take place on a selected node from the left navigation pane of the GUI. If the Proxmox cluster environment is not very mission-critical and some downtime is allowed, then we can shut down all VMs in the node and then restart. Simply click on Stop All VMs from the More drop-down menu to shut down all VMs in the node, and then restart the node. After the node restarts, start all VMs by clicking on **Start All VMs** under the More drop-down menu.

Always check and read all major or minor Proxmox update releases before applying them to a node. This gives a good idea of what is being updated and their importance. If the importance or seriousness is not critical, we can always prolong the update to avoid any node reboot. You can refer to the Proxmox Roadmap, which is a good place to find out new feature additions, bug fixes, or simply information on changes at `http://pve.proxmox.com/wiki/Roadmap#Roadmap`.

The official Proxmox forum is also a great place to hang out to get information on issues due to updates. This is also a great place to learn about fixes posted by Proxmox developers if there are any issues with the released update. Visit the official Proxmox forum at `https://forum.proxmox.com`.

# Summary

In this chapter, we learned about the importance of keeping Proxmox nodes up to date in a cluster and how to properly update and upgrade a node through both the GUI and CLI. We also covered when to reboot or not reboot a node after an upgrade.

In the next chapter, we will see how to configure an enterprise-class network monitoring system to monitor not only a Proxmox or Ceph cluster but also the entire network.

# 12
# Monitoring a Proxmox Cluster

Monitoring a network environment of any size is mandatory to ensure a healthy operation and timely response to any issues. In this chapter, we will see how to monitor and configure notifications, so that when something goes wrong in the cluster, we can know about it right away and take the necessary action. We will cover the following topics in this chapter:

- An introduction to monitoring
- Zabbix as a monitoring solution
- Proxmox built-in monitoring
- Configuring the Disk Health notification
- Configuring SNMP in Proxmox
- Monitoring the Proxmox cluster with Zabbix
- Monitoring the Ceph cluster with the Ceph dashboard

## An introduction to monitoring

In a network of any size, it is only a matter of time before an issue arises owing to intentional or unintentional circumstances. The root cause for an issue can be owing to hardware failures, software issues, human errors, or just about any other environmental factor, which causes loss of network or data. Network monitoring is a practice in which an administrator can check a pulse of the network components in a network environment.

There is no system to monitor everything. A good monitoring system is usually put together with various tools and some types of notification options to send alerts automatically. The Proxmox cluster is a sum of switches, network cables, physical nodes acting as hosts, and virtual machines. A monitoring system should be able to monitor all of these components and automatically send notifications via a medium, such as an e-mail or SMS to responsible parties. There are wide ranges of network monitoring tools available today, such as, Icinga, Zabbix, Nagios, OpenNMS, Pandora FMS, Zenoss, and so on. There are many more options, both paid, and free open source. In this chapter, we will see how to use Zabbix to monitor the Proxmox cluster. Zabbix has a user friendly GUI, graphing ability, and many more features out of the box. It is very easy to learn for novice and network professionals alike. Once Zabbix is installed, all the configuration and monitoring can be done through the GUI.

A monitoring node should be a standalone reliable machine. For learning and testing purposes, it can be set up as a virtual machine. However, to monitor a production-level cluster, a separate node outside the main cluster is an ideal solution. This will ensure that even if the internal network is down, the monitoring system can still send out notifications.

# Proxmox built-in monitoring

Proxmox has limited monitoring capabilities built into the GUI; however, it does lack the extensive and robust monitoring usually found in a complete monitoring solution. Proxmox comes with built-in RRD-based graphs to show the historical resource usage and performance data up to 1 year. Using this tool, we can analyze the performance trend of a resource over a period of time. All consumption and performance data are under the Summary tab menu for both Proxmox nodes and virtual machines. We can view data on a per hour, day, week, and yearly basis.

The following screenshot shows the **Summary** page of the **Node pm4-1** with the drop-down list to select a period of data:

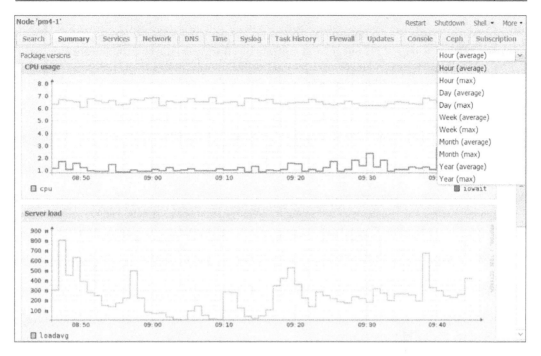

There are also ways to display a list of all the nodes and virtual machines in the cluster and sort them by consumption to get quick information on the highest or lowest resource consuming entity. We can see the list by navigating to **Datacenter | Search**. The following screenshot shows the list of Proxmox nodes and virtual machines sorted by the highest memory consuming entity:

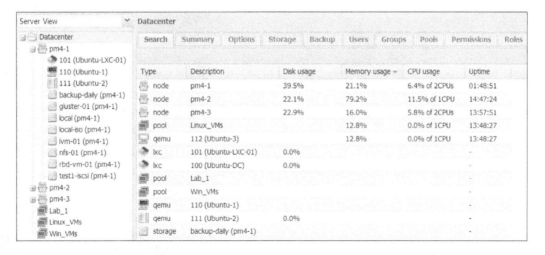

We can sort this list by **Type**, **Description**, **Disk usage**, **Memory usage**, **CPU usage**, and **Uptime** by clicking on the column header. There is no historical data in this list. It only shows the resource consumption in real time.

We can leverage S.M.A.R.T. for disk drives to receive automated e-mails by the Proxmox node when there are any major issues occurring in any disk drives in the node. For this, we will need to install Smart monitor tools using the following command:

```
# apt-get install smartmontools
```

 Make sure that you install this in all the Proxmox nodes in the cluster. There is no other configuration needed to receive the e-mail except ensuring that the correct e-mail address is entered for the root user in Proxmox.

We can check the correctness of the e-mail address from the User details dialog box, as shown in the following screenshot:

Whenever there is a major issue on any disk drive in the Proxmox node, it will send out an automated e-mail with the name of the node where the issue originated and the nature of the failures or issues for the disk drive. The e-mail also shows the details of the drive itself, such as the serial number and the device ID of the drive. The following screenshot shows the sample of an e-mail received from the node pm4-1 with the sector error for the device /dev/sda with the serial number V1FA516P:

```
This message was generated by the smartd daemon running on:

   host name:  pm4-1
   DNS domain: domain.com

The following warning/error was logged by the smartd daemon:

Device: /dev/sda [SAT], 8 Offline uncorrectable sectors

Device info:
ST2000DM001-1CH164, S/N:V1FA516P, WWN:5-000c50-06040e51c, FW:CC26, 2.00 TB

For details see host's SYSLOG.

You can also use the smartctl utility for further investigation.
The original message about this issue was sent at Sat Feb 13 09:01:14 2016 MST
Another message will be sent in 24 hours if the problem persists.
```

If the same error continues to occur, the Proxmox node will send this e-mail every 24 hours. Based on the information provided in the e-mail, we can pinpoint the drive and replace it if necessary.

As we can see, Proxmox really does not have a robust monitoring system and it's very unlikely that it ever will be. Its strength lies with being a great hypervisor, not a monitoring system. However, we can easily fill the gap using a third-party monitoring system, such as Zabbix.

# Zabbix as a monitoring solution

Zabbix, released in 2004, is a robust web-based network monitoring tool capable of monitoring many hundreds of hosts and running thousands of checks per host at any set time. Zabbix is completely open source and does not have enterprise or paid versions. Zabbix takes just a few minutes to install, even by a beginner, and it can be fully configured through a web-based interface. The following screenshot shows the Zabbix 3.0 dashboard after logging in through the web GUI:

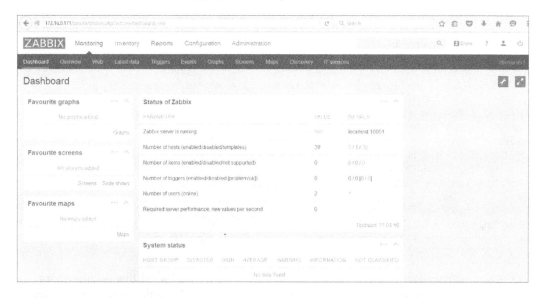

Zabbix has a very active community and many downloadable templates used to monitor a variety of devices or equipment. It is also comparatively easy to create our own custom Zabbix template for nonstandard devices. More details on Zabbix can be found on the official Zabbix site at: http://www.zabbix.com/.

It can easily be argued to give preference to Zabbix over main stream monitoring systems, such as Nagios, or Icinga, or any other solution currently available. The reason is simplicity without sacrificing any of the features that make a great monitoring system. Zabbix is fully managed through the GUI without requiring to edit any script file through the CLI. This eases the burden of device configuration through the script file, such as in the case of the Nagios-based monitoring system. Whether it is a small network environment or a large one spread across regions, Zabbix is up to the challenge with ease.

# Installing Zabbix

In this section, we will see how to install Zabbix and configure it to monitor the Proxmox cluster and network devices. We are going to install the Zabbix version 3.0 on CentOS 7. Zabbix can be installed very easily on other major distributions, such as Debian or Ubuntu.

For stability and performance when monitoring a large production environment, using CentOS as the base operating system is highly recommended.

Always make sure that you set up a separate node or a virtual machine to offer maximum performance. A fully configured Zabbix with thousands of items will run frequent checks, which is resource heavy. Using Zabbix in a node or VM, which serves other roles, will greatly affect the performance.

Zabbix also provides preinstalled and preconfigured downloadable appliances for evaluation purposes. It is useful for learning and testing purposes but not recommended for production use. Zabbix appliances can be downloaded from http://www.zabbix.com/download.php.

Zabbix will still work without a Zabbix agent installed on the host to be monitored, but an agent can gather much more data from the host. There are agents available for all major operating systems, including Linux, Windows, FreeBSD, AIX, Solaris, and HP-UX. For devices where an agent installation is not possible, such as a managed switch or other network equipment, Zabbix is able to monitor them through SNMP. After the Zabbix server installation is completed, install Zabbix agents on hosts to be monitored.

A Zabbix agent can capture much more data than SNMP. Use an agent whenever possible over SNMP. This reduces the complexity of configuring SNMP while creating a lot more custom checks. Agents are a great option for Proxmox host nodes.

The Zabbix official documentation has excellent instructions to install Zabbix on various Linux distributions. Refer to the documentation for instructions on how to install the Zabbix 3.0 server and agent at: https://www.zabbix.com/documentation/3.0/manual/installation/install_from_packages.

After the installation is complete, the Zabbix server can be accessed through the link format available at: http://<node_ip>/zabbix.

By default, the username password to log in to the Zabbix web GUI is Admin:Zabbix where the username is case sensitive. It is recommended that you change the password right away after logging in. Go to **Administration | Users,** then click on the **Admin** (Zabbix Administrator) member, or click on the **User Profile** icon in top-right corner of the GUI to change the administrative password, as shown in the following screenshot:

If you are using CentOS 7 for the Zabbix server, after accessing the Zabbix GUI, you may notice that the status informs that the Zabbix server is not running, as shown in the following screenshot, even though the Zabbix service is running:

| Status of Zabbix | | |
|---|---|---|
| PARAMETER | VALUE | DETAILS |
| Zabbix server is running | No | localhost:10051 |
| Number of hosts (enabled/disabled/templates) | 39 | 0 / 1 / 38 |
| Number of items (enabled/disabled/not supported) | 0 | 0 / 0 / 0 |

This is due to the `httpd_can_connect_network` argument in the SELinux firewall configuration. The argument needs to be enabled in order to let Zabbix access the network. Run the following command to check whether it is off or disabled:

```
# getsebool httpd_can_network_connect
```

If the result shows up, then enable it by running the following command:

```
# setsebool httpd_can_network_connect on
```

The Zabbix GUI now shows that the server is running.

# Configuring Zabbix

After the Zabbix server is installed and functioning, we have to set up e-mails so that we get automated e-mails whenever there is an issue. Zabbix 3.0 is able to send e-mails through SMTP. We can figure it out by navigating to the **Administation | Media types** menu and changing the SMTP information under **Email**. After the e-mail is configured, it is time to add some hosts or devices to start monitoring.

# Configuring a host to monitor

In this section, we will see how to add a host, whether it is a Proxmox node or a virtual machine, to the Zabbix monitoring server. This procedure is the same for adding any host with a Zabbix agent installed. By default, the Zabbix server is added to the monitoring host. We are now going to add our example Proxmox node pm4-2 in Zabbix in order to be monitored. The following steps show how to add the host to Zabbix:

1. Go to **Configuration | Hosts** and click on **Create Host**.
2. Type in the **Hostname** and **Visible** name. The hostname must match with the hostname entered in the host Zabbix agent configuration file. We will configure the agent after we add the host in the Zabbix server. The visible name can be anything.
3. Select an appropriate **Group**. Since we are adding a Proxmox host node, we need to select **Hypervisors as Group**.

4. If we are adding a host with the agent installed, type in the IP address of the host in the **Agent interfaces** box. By default, the agent listens on port `10050`. If we are using a different port, type in the port here. Make sure that you open the ports in the firewall if the host is behind any firewall. The following screenshot shows the **host** configuration page after adding the necessary information:

5. Click on the **Templates** tab to add a template to the host. Templates in Zabbix are preconfigured groups of checks. By assigning a template to a host, we apply multiple checks at once instead of manually adding each checks.

6. Type in a template name in the **Link new templates** textbox, or select one by clicking on the **Select** button. The textbox is a self-search box, so the value does not need to be the exact name of the template. For example, we have typed in Linux, which pulled two possible templates. We are going to select Template OS Linux, as shown in the following screenshot:

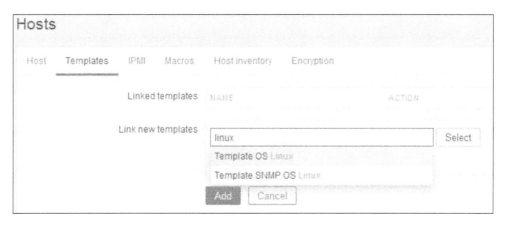

We can also assign an SNMP device using the same template page. Refer to the Configuring SNMP in Proxmox section later in this chapter on how to install and configure SNMP in Proxmox nodes, and then perform the following steps to add a host using SNMP templates:

1. Click on **Add** to assign the template to the host.

2. Click on **Host inventory**, and then select **Automatic** so that the Zabbix agent can pull relevant information about the host, such as the host brand, serial number, OS installed, and so on. We can also manually enter data, such as Longitude, Latitude, Hardware and Software installed in the node. This is helpful to build an inventory list.

3. Click on **Save** to finish adding the host.

The following steps need to be performed to configure the Zabbix agent in a host:

- Open the Zabbix agent configuration file in /etc/zabbix/zabbix_agentd.conf of the host.

- Make the changes for the following option lines:

  ```
  Server=172.16.0.172 //IP of Zabbix Server
  ServerActive=172.16.0.171:10051 //IP_Server:Server_Port
  Hostname=pm4-2  //must be same as Hostname typed in Zabbix Server
  for the host
  Save and exit the editor.
  ```

- Run the following command to restart the Zabbix agent in the host:

  ```
  # service zabbix-agent restart
  ```

Within a minute or so after adding the host, the Zabbix server will run auto checks and will discover that the host now has a live agent in the host. The following screenshot shows the Hosts list in the Zabbix server after adding the host and configuring the agent:

From the list, we can also see that the template added 32 **Items**, **15 Triggers**, and **5 Graphs** to the host. Items are what are being checked by Zabbix and triggers are what initiate certain actions, such as sending auto notifications for any event. The template has two discovery items, which automatically gather information of installed and configured disk drives and partitions in the node. The following screenshot shows the **Triggers** page for the **host pm4-2**:

The expression column in the Triggers page shows when an event is triggered. For example, the expression {pm4-2:system.cpu.util[,iowait].avg(5m)}>20 for Disk I/O overload will trigger a warning when the I/O wait exceeds 20 for 5 minutes in the host. Another example trigger {pm4-2:proc.num[].avg(5m)}>300 for processes may trigger when the number of running processes exceeds 300 for 5 minutes. Modern servers can run many more processes at once. So, for a node or host that hosts many virtual machines, this process limit of 300 may not be enough and will trigger a warning frequently. We can change the trigger, for example, to 900 to increase the limit. To learn more about triggers, refer to https://www.zabbix.com/documentation/2.2/manual/config/triggers/expression.

We can also add each virtual machine as a host and then monitor them through Zabbix. For this, we need to install the Zabbix agent inside the virtual machine, and add it as a host in Zabbix. To clump all the virtual machines, we need to create a group named Virtual Machine in Zabbix and assign all VMs to be monitored in that group.

# Displaying data using a graph

Zabbix comes with an excellent graphing ability out of the box without any manual configuration. As soon as data is pulled from a resource, the graphing utility starts plotting using the raw data. Almost all of the built-in templates in Zabbix have some graphing items predefined. We can have graphs of monitored items by navigating to **Monitoring | Graphs** in the Zabbix GUI. The following screenshot shows the graph of the **CPU load** over a period of 15 minutes for the host pm4-2 in our example cluster:

We can also create our own graph items through a few clicks for any host or device being monitored. For example, let's create a graph to visualize data for the CPU iowait overtime. For this, we need to go to **Configuration | Hosts**, and then click on the **node**. Once inside the node, click on the **Graphs** menu to open the graph editor page, as shown in the following screenshot:

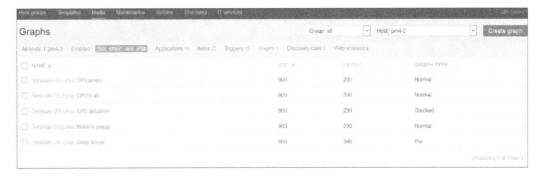

In the preceding screenshot, we can see that there are five graphs items that have already been created. We are going to add a new item to the CPU iowait time. Click on the **Create Graph** button to open a new graph item page. Type in an easily understandable name for the graph item. We are going to name it CPU IOWait Time. From the Items box below, click on **Add** to open a list of available items to choose from. We are going to select CPU iowait time for this example. We can configure the color and type of the graph being created. Click on the **Add** button when you are satisfied with the configuration. The following screenshot shows the graph creation page for our example of CPU iowait time:

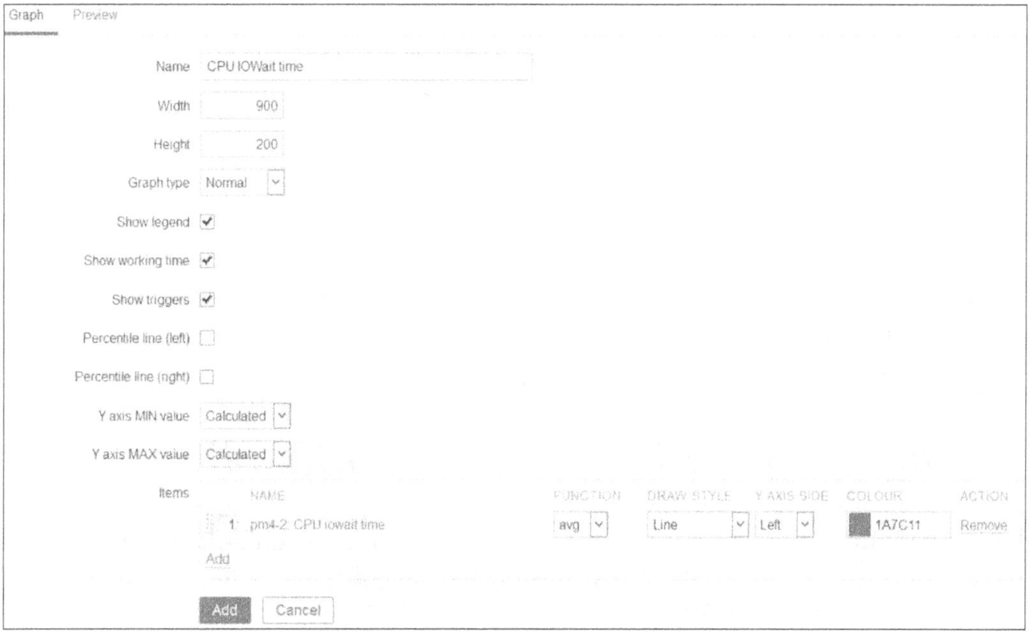

| Graph | Preview |

| | | |
|---|---|---|
| Name | CPU IOWait time | |
| Width | 900 | |
| Height | 200 | |
| Graph type | Normal | |
| Show legend | ✔ | |
| Show working time | ✔ | |
| Show triggers | ✔ | |
| Percentile line (left) | ☐ | |
| Percentile line (right) | ☐ | |
| Y axis MIN value | Calculated | |
| Y axis MAX value | Calculated | |

| Items | NAME | FUNCTION | DRAW STYLE | Y AXIS SIDE | COLOUR | ACTION |
|---|---|---|---|---|---|---|
| | 1: pm4-2: CPU iowait time | avg | Line | Left | 1A7C11 | Remove |
| | Add | | | | | |

Add   Cancel

To see the newly created graph item, we need to go to **Monitoring | Graphs,** and select the item for the node. The following screenshot shows the graph for the gathered CPU iowait time over a period of 15 minutes:

In the preceding screenshot, we can see that the IOwait time in shown in the color green, and if there are any trigger events due to the IOwait time being greater than 20%, it will show in the color yellow.

# Configuring the Disk Health notification

In the *Proxmox built-in monitoring* section, as discussed earlier in the chapter, we have seen how we can leverage S.M.A.R.T. to receive automated e-mails if there are any issues for any disk drives. In this section, we are going to accomplish the same but with Zabbix and with an additional feature, such as graphing. A great use case of a graph for a disk drive is monitoring data for temperature. High temperature is a bad thing for all spinning drives. Using the Zabbix graph, we can see the exact temperature trend of the storage cluster down to a single drive and take actions accordingly. Zabbix can also send automated e-mails when there are any issues in any of the drives, such as read or write, due to a bad sector or any other S.M.A.R.T. event.

Almost all HDDs or SSDs nowadays have the S.M.A.R.T. ability, which can gather valuable data for the disk drive health. Using the S.M.A.R.T. monitoring tool, we can avoid premature drive failure by detecting potential problems early on. We can configure each Proxmox node to send e-mail alerts when any problem is detected in any attached drives.

Note that if drives are connected to RAID controllers and configured as some form of arrays, then the S.M.A.R.T. tool will not be able to retrieve the drive's health data.

## Installing smart monitor tools

We need to install smartmontools in our storage using the following command:

```
#apt-get install smartmontools
```

Retrieve a list of all the attached drives using the following command:

```
# fdisk -l
```

Verify that each attached drive has the S.M.A.R.T. feature and it is tuned on using the following command:

```
#smartctl -a /dev/sdX
```

If the drive has the S.M.A.R.T. feature and it is enabled, it will appear, as shown in the following screenshot:

```
smartctl 6.4 2014-10-07 r4002 [x86_64-linux-4.2.8-1-pve] (local build)
Copyright (C) 2002-14, Bruce Allen, Christian Franke, www.smartmontools.org

ATA device successfully opened

Use 'smartctl -a' (or '-x') to print SMART (and more) information
```

If the feature is available but disabled for any reason, we can enable it using the following command:

```
#smartctl -s on -a /dev/sdX
```

## Configuring the Zabbix agent

Adding the disk drive monitoring into Zabbix is a two-step process. In the first step, we need to add arguments in the Zabbix agent configuration file, and then add the drive items in the Zabbix server for each host. These special arguments are known as user parameters. It works similar to a script where we can define commands to be run on the host, and then the Zabbix agent passes the data to the Zabbix server.

In this example, we are going to add user parameters to pull data for the serial number and drive temperature. The following two lines need to be added at the end of the agent configuration file in `/etc/zabbix/zabbix_agentd.conf`:

```
UserParameter=hdd.temp[*],smartctl -A /dev/$1 | grep -E -i '^[ ]*($2)[ ]' | cut -c88-90
UserParameter=hdd.serial[*],smartctl -i /dev/$1 | grep 'Serial Number' |cut -c19-
```

After adding the lines, we need to restart the Zabbix agent using the following command:

```
# service zabbix_agentd restart
```

## Creating a Zabbix item in the GUI

After the user parameters are added, we need to create new items in the Zabbix server for the host. First, we will add an item to gather data for the drive temperature. Go to **Configuration** | **Hosts** | **Items**, and then click on the **Create item** to open a new item page. The following screenshot shows the page with the necessary configuration:

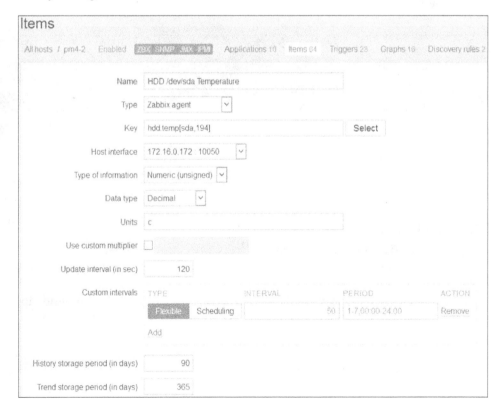

The name of the item can be any text string. Since we are pulling data through user parameters of the Zabbix agent, we need to select the agent as Type. The Key box is the most important here as this is where we define what data we are pulling. The key entered, as shown in the preceding screenshot, tells Zabbix to pull the drive temperature for the device sda. The numeric value of 194 in the key is for the temperature information. Each smart monitor attribute has a unique numeric ID. For example, if we want to gather data for an uncorrectable sector count, the code would be 197. To view a complete list of smart monitor attribute codes, refer to `https://en.wikipedia.org/wiki/S.M.A.R.T.#Known_ATA_S.M.A.R.T._attributes`.

Type of information is a drop-down list used to select the nature of data being collected. Since the temperature is a numeric value, we will select the Numeric type. To increase the temperature accuracy, we need to select **Decimal** as **Data type**.

**Update** interval is a textbox used to enter seconds, which needs careful attention. This is the interval that Zabbix will run checks for each item. By default, Zabbix uses an interval of 30 seconds. When adding high-volume checks, such as disk drive's data, the higher the number of disk drives present in a node, the volume of checks will increase exponentially. For example, if we want to gather drive data for a Ceph node with 12 drives, Zabbix will run checks every 30 seconds for all the 12 drives and that will accumulate to hundreds of checks per hour. To reduce the check bottleneck, we can set it to a higher interval. In our example, we are using 2 minutes or 120 seconds for a drive check. Click on Add to finish creating the item.

> Note that we need to create separate new items for each drive that needs to be monitored. Change the device ID for each item, such as sdb, sdc, and so on.

# Creating a trigger in the GUI

After the item is created, we need to create a trigger so that Zabbix can send auto notification e-mails if the temperature goes beyond a threshold. To create a trigger, go to **Configuration | Hosts | Trigger,** and click on the **Create trigger** button. The following screenshot shows the new trigger creation page with the necessary information entered:

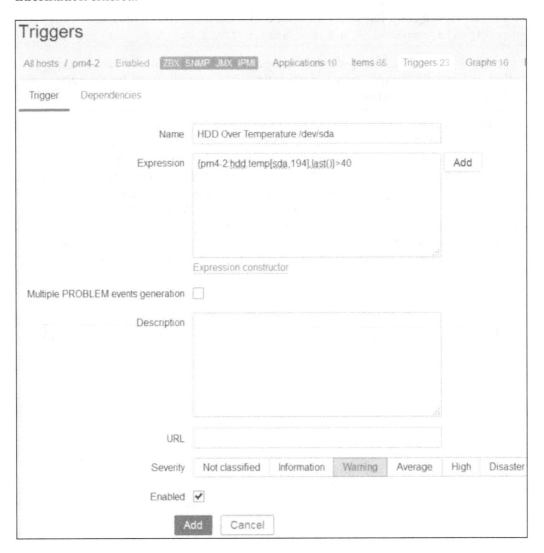

Type in a name to identify the trigger, and then enter an expression for the trigger. The expression is used to set a threshold beyond which Zabbix will trigger an event, such as sending an e-mail. In our example, as shown in the preceding screenshot, our expression shows that if the last temperature gathered is above 40 degree Celsius, Zabbix will send an alert e-mail.

In order to identify the importance of the trigger, we need to select the **Severity** level. For example, we have selected **Warning** as the severity of the trigger. Select the appropriate severity depending on the trigger. This creates color coded information throughout Zabbix to identify how serious the issue is. Click on **Add** to finish creating the trigger. Like triggers, each drive will need a separate trigger item.

## Creating graphs in the GUI

Following the instructions to display data using a graph, as discussed earlier in this chapter, we are now going to create a new graph item to show the drive temperature data visually. Unlike triggers and items, we do not need to create separate graph items. We can configure one graph item to show multiple drive data by simply adding the drive items in the same graph item. The following screenshot shows the drive temperature graph for a Ceph node with seven disk drives over a 6 hour period:

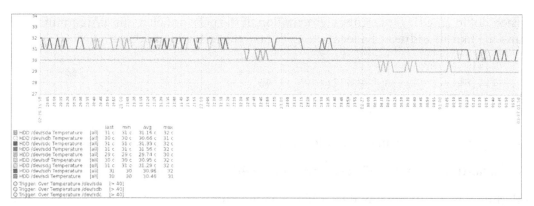

# Configuring SNMP in Proxmox

**Simple Network Management Protocol (SNMP)** is a network management protocol used to monitor a wide variety of network devices. It is especially useful when a full network monitoring agent installation is not possible, such as switches, routers, printers, IP-based devices, and so on. Almost all network monitoring programs support some level of SNMP.

If the choice of monitoring a package does not have any agents, SNMP is the best option to monitor those devices. SNMP is fully configurable in Linux distributions, and since Proxmox is based on Debian, it inherits all the benefits of SNMP. To learn more about SNMP, refer to: `https://en.wikipedia.org/wiki/Simple_Network_Management_Protocol`.

There are a few components of SNMP worth mentioning here since we will be using them to configure SNMP. They are as follows:

- **OID**; Object Identifier
- **MIB**; Management Information Base

# OIDs

OIDs or Object Identifiers are objects that the SNMP queries to gather information from a device. An object can be a network interface status, disk storage usage, device name, and so on. These object identifiers are extremely structured in a hierarchical tree manner. Each OID is specifically numbered. For example, the OID of the object, which gathers the device name is `1.3.6.1.2.1.1.5.0`. OIDs always have numerical values. OIDs can be compared with IP addresses where numeric values are used to identify a device in a network.

Each dot in an OID represents segmentation of the network element. We can think of an OID like an address of a location. Let's take the following address:

```
Wasim Ahmed
111 Server Street, 4th Floor
    Calgary, AB 111-222
    Canada
```

If we put this address in the OID format, it will look like the following:

Canada.AB.Calgary.111-222.Server Street.111.4th Floor.Wasim Ahmed

Putting this in a formula will look like the following:

Country.Province.City.Postal code.Street name.Street number.Unit number.Contact name

As with the address example, the OIDs also follow a strict hierarchy, as follows:

```
1 = ISO
1.3 = Organization
1.3.6 = US Department of Defense
1.3.6.1 = Internet
1.3.6.1.2 = IETF Management
1.3.6.1.2.X = Management-related OIDs
```

To look up management-related OIDs, refer to: `http://www.alvestrand.no/objectid/1.3.6.1.2.1.html`.

# MIB

There are databases where objects are stored. MIB acts as a translator, which allows an SNMP server to query an object using a textual instead of numeric OID. For example, to retrieve a device name through SNMP queries, we can use the OID 1.3.6.1.2.1.1.5.0 or OID SNMPv2-MIB::sysName.0. Both of them will give you the exact same result. But the textual OID is easier to understand than a numeric OID. We can compare MIB to OID as we would a domain name to an IP address. Some manufacturers provide their own MIB since they do not exist in the standard MIB. It is important to know the MIBs when configuring unsupported device with monitoring tools. There are a number of MIBs ready to be downloaded. Proxmox does not install any MIB by default. It has to be manually installed. For more details on MIB, refer to: `https://en.wikipedia.org/wiki/Management_information_base`.

There are three versions of SNMP currently available. Before implementing an SNMP infrastructure, it is important to know which version to use. The three versions are as follows:

- **SNMP version 1**: This is the oldest SNMP version, which only supports 32-bit counters and has no security at all. A community string is sent as plain text in this SNMP.

- **SNMP version 2**: This has all the features of version 1 with added features to support 64-bit counters. Most devices nowadays support version 2.

- **SNMP version 3**: This has all the features of version 1 and 2 with added benefits of security. Both encryption and authentication are added to counters. If security is the biggest concern, this is the SNMP version that should be used.

SNMP is not installed by default in Proxmox. The following steps show how to install SNMP in Proxmox and how to configure it:

Run the following command to install SNMP on Proxmox nodes:

```
# apt-get install snmpd snmp
```

Add the following repository in /etc/apt/sources.list of the Proxmox node. This is used to add a repository to install SNMP MIBs:

```
deb http://http.us.debian.org/debian/wheezy main non-free
```

Run the following commands to install SNMP MIBs:

```
# apt-get update
# apt-get install snmp-mibs-downloader
```

Open the SNMP /etc/snmp/snmpd.conf configuration file using an editor.

Ensure that the following line is uncommented. We can specify the node IP address. SNMP listens on port 161. Change it here if required:

```
agentAddress udp:127.0.0.1:161
```

Add the following line to the SNMP configuration file:

```
rocommunity <secret_string> <IP/CIDR>
```

In our example, we have added the following line:

```
rocommunity    SecretSNMP    172.16.0.0/24
```

Save the file and restart SNMP using the following command:

```
#service snmpd restart
```

# Adding an SNMP device in Zabbix

Adding an SNMP device in Zabbix is a similar process to adding a host except that we have to select SNMP interfaces instead of agent interfaces, as shown in the following screenshot:

By default, SNMP devices listen on port 161. Zabbix comes with prebuilt SNMP templates, which can gather a vast amount of data for devices where the agent installation is not possible or desired. A common example of an SNMP device is a network switch. Zabbix has excellent support for switch monitoring through the SNMP template.

In this example, we will add a Netgear 48 port switch using the SNMP interface. Go to **Configuration | Hosts,** and click on the **Create host** button to open a new host creation page. Besides using the SNMP interface in the host creation page, we need to select the SNMP Device template and type in SNMP v2 Community string under Macros, as shown in the following screenshot:

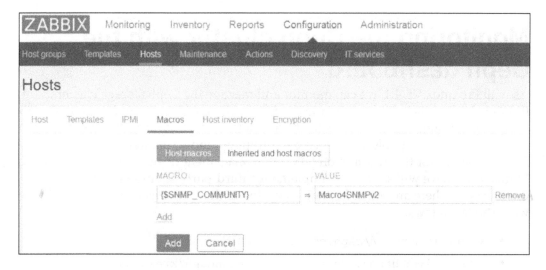

The {$SNMP_COMMUNITY} macro is used to pass a community secret string, which is used by the SNMP version 2. The value of this macro must match with the value entered in the monitored device itself.

After the host or device is added, Zabbix will start checks on the switch in a few minutes and start gathering data. The SNMP Device template has auto discovery configured, which will automatically scan the switch for the number of ports and show data for both incoming and outgoing traffic on each port. The template also has a graph item configured to show you the visual data of each port.

The following screenshot shows the graph of incoming and outgoing traffic usage for port 1 of the Netgear 48 port switch over the 1 hour period:

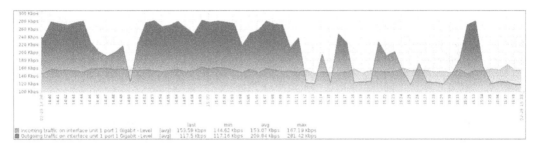

Like the switch, we can add just about any network device with the SNMP capability to Zabbix to monitor at all times.

# Monitoring the Ceph cluster with the Ceph dashboard

As with Proxmox VE 4.1, we can monitor and manage the Ceph storage cluster through the Proxmox GUI. Under the Ceph tabbed menu of each node, you will see a great amount of data such as the health status of the Ceph cluster, the number of OSDs, the MONs, pools, the Ceph configurations, and so on. Refer to *Chapter 4*, *Storage Systems*, for the information on Ceph management through the Proxmox GUI. In this section, we will see how to implement a third-party solution to monitor the Ceph cluster. There are several options used to monitor a Ceph cluster graphically, which are as follows:

- Calamari: https://ceph.com/category/calamari/
- Kraken Dash: https://github.com/krakendash/krakendash
- The Ceph dashboard: https://github.com/Crapworks/ceph-dash

All the three options are viable options used to monitor the Ceph cluster. But owing to the simplicity and effectiveness of this chapter, we are going to see how to install the Ceph dashboard. This is the only free monitoring dashboard, which is read-only without any management ability. This is also safer since an unauthorized user cannot make Ceph changes. Ceph Calamari and Kraken Dashboard are both equally challenging to install and configure.

The Ceph dashboard can be installed on any Ceph nodes or Proxmox+Ceph node in the cluster. As long as it can read the `ceph.conf` file, it will function just fine. The Ceph dashboard does not require any web server or any other services to function. We can download the Ceph Dashboard package from Git. By default, `git` is not installed in the Proxmox node. We can install it using the following command:

```
# apt-get install git
```

Next, we need to clone the Ceph dashboard github repository using the following command:

```
# git clone https://github.com/Crapworks/ceph-dash
```

After the download is complete, we need to add the IP address of the node where the dashboard will be started. We need to make changes in the following line in the `ceph-dash.py` file:

```
app.run(host='ip_address',debug=True)
```

To start the dashboard after making the changes, simply run the following command:

```
# <dashboard_directory>/ceph_dash.py
```

We can access the dashboard by pointing to the node, as follows: `http://ip_address:5000`.

The following screenshot shows the status of our example cluster using the Ceph dashboard:

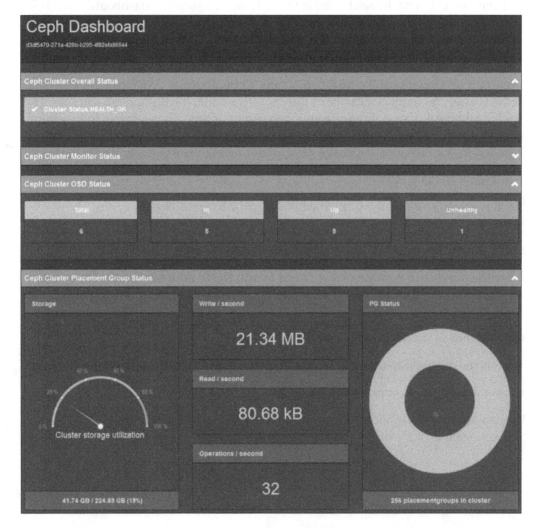

The Ceph dashboard displays the following information of a Ceph cluster:

- The Ceph cluster key
- The overall health status
- The monitor status

- The OSD status

- The Placement Group (PG) status

- The storage utilization percentage

- The total available space and used space

- Read/Write speed per second

- Operations per second

Refer to *Chapter 4, Storage Systems*, for information on Ceph components, such as MON, OSD, PG, and so on. All the data is automatically updated at regular intervals. During any faults within the cluster, the dashboard will show related information in a color coded format. Using port forwarding in the firewall, we can also monitor a Ceph cluster remotely.

# Summary

In this chapter, we saw how we can monitor a Proxmox cluster network using powerful monitoring systems, such as Zabbix. By no means is Zabbix the only monitoring option available in the main stream choice. But it does have many advantages over other solutions. The out-of-box features, such as graphing, template, SNMP, auto notification, and so on, are just the tip of the iceberg of what Zabbix has to offer. Whether it is a small environment or a large cloud service provider spanned over multiple regions, Zabbix can monitor them all. A good network administrator will try a few solutions and find the one that suits their environment best.

In the next chapter, we will see some complex production level virtual network environments leveraging Proxmox as a hypervisor. We will take a look at a scenario-based network diagram to gain knowledge on what Proxmox can do.

# 13
# Proxmox Production-Level Setup

So far in this book, we have seen the internal workings of Proxmox. We now know how to properly set up a fully functional Proxmox cluster. We discussed Ceph—a robust and redundant shared storage system—and how we can connect it with Proxmox. We also saw what a virtual network is and how it works with the Proxmox cluster.

In this chapter, we are going to see which components play a crucial part in making a Proxmox cluster production-ready with multi-layer redundancy, good performance, and stability. We are going to cover the following topics:

- The definition of production level
- Key components of a production-level setup
- Entry-level and advanced-level hardware requirements

Throughout this chapter, you will notice that we have used user-built hardware configurations instead of readymade brand servers. The purpose of this is to show you what sort of node configuration is possible using off-the-shelf commodity hardware to cut cost while setting up a stable Proxmox cluster. All example configurations shown in this chapter are not theoretical scenarios but taken from various live clusters in service. Use the information in this chapter purely as a guideline so that you can select proper hardware for your environment at any budget.

# Defining production level

Production level is a scenario where a company's cluster environment is fully functional and actively serving its users or clients on a regular basis. It is no longer considered as a platform to learn Proxmox or a test platform to test different things on. A production-level setup requires much advanced planning and preparation because once the setup is complete and cluster has been brought online, it just cannot be taken offline completely at moment's notice when users are dependent on it. A properly planned production-level setup can save hours or days of headache. If you are still learning Proxmox, you might want to set aside hardware to practice on so that you can hone your skillset before attempting a production-level setup. In this section, we are going to cover some of the key components or characteristics of a production-level environment.

# Key components

The following key components should be kept in mind while planning for a production-level cluster setup due to stability and performance requirements:

- Stable and scalable hardware
- Redundancy
- Current load versus future growth
- Budget
- Simplicity
- Hardware inventory tracking

## Stable and scalable hardware

Stable hardware means minimum downtime. Without quality hardware, it is not unusual to have randomized hardware failure in a cluster environment causing massive, unnecessary downtime. It is very important to select a hardware brand with a good reputation and support behind it. For example, Intel's server class components are well known for their superb stability and support. It is true that you pay more for Intel products. But sometimes, the stability outweighs the higher cost per hardware. AMD is also an excellent choice. But statistically, AMD-based hardware has more stability issues.

For budget-conscious enterprise environment, we can mix both Intel- and AMD-based hardware in the same cluster. Since Proxmox provides full migration option, we can have Intel nodes serving full time, while AMD nodes act as failover only. This reduces the cost without slashing stability. Throughout this chapter, we are going to stay primarily with Intel-based hardware. At the end of this chapter, we will see some proven AMD-based clusters to give you some idea of how viable AMD is in a Proxmox cluster environment.

When choosing between Intel and AMD, apart from stability, the following two criteria are also deciding factors:

- Energy Cost
- Heat Generation

Intel CPUs uses less energy and run much cooler than their AMD counterpart. Increased heat generation in AMD servers means increased requirement for cooling, thus increased utility bills. By design, AMD CPUs use much higher wattage per CPU, which is direct cause of high heat generation.

Another deciding factor of hardware is scalability and availability. Hardware components used in server nodes must be easily available when they need to be replaced. Using difficult-to-find components, even if they cost much less, only prolongs downtime when something needs to be replaced. A common practice is to use identical hardware for groups of servers based on their workload. This makes hardware management easier and also allows in-hand stock build up to quickly replace a node when needed. This is extremely difficult in an environment where a cluster has been put together using all sort of different brands, models, and configurations.

# Redundancy

The need to have redundancy in different layers in a production environment cannot be stressed enough. There must be redundancy in different levels of components.

## Node level

Node-level redundancy usually includes redundant power supply, network cards, RAID, and so on. This redundancy is confined in the node itself. With redundant power supply, the node can be connected to two different power sources, thus ensuring continuous operation during power failure. Always use mirrored SSD drive as the operating system drive. This will ensure that the operating system itself will run uninterrupted even if a drive fails entirely.

# Utility level

In order for the cluster nodes to keep running during power loss, we need to provide some sort of backup power either by means of UPS, generator, or large battery bank.

# Network level

The network-level redundancy includes network infrastructure such as switches and cables. By using multiple switches and multiple network paths, we can ensure that network connectivity will not be interrupted during a switch or cable failure. Use of Layer 3 managed switches such as stackable switches are the correct components to create truly redundant network paths.

# HVAC level

Proper cooling with a backup plan for continued cooling in the event the HVAC system goes down is often overlooked. Depending on the number of server nodes, switches, and so on, each network environment creates enormous amount of heat. If there is no redundancy in place, failure of the cooling system can result in failure of extreme heat generation components. Whether it is air or liquid cooled, there must be a contingency in the cooling system to prevent any damages. Damage of components also means loss of connectivity and increased cost.

# Storage level

Storage plays important role for any virtual environment and deserves the same level of redundancy attention as the rest of the cluster. There is no point in implementing redundancy in all Proxmox host nodes, network, or power supply, and putting virtual disk images on a single NAS storage without any redundancy. If the single node storage fails, even though it is considered shared storage, all VMs stored on it will be completely unusable. In a production environment, use of enterprise-grade storage systems such as Ceph, Gluster, and so on is critical. This type of storage has redundancy built into the firmware or operating system. We still need to ensure that these storage nodes have node, utility, network, and HVAC-level redundancy in place.

# Current load versus future growth

When designing a cluster, you should always think of future growth, at least the growth for the foreseeable future. An enterprise cluster must be able to grow with the company and adapt to the increased workloads and computational requirements. At the very least, plan in such a way that you do not exceed your resources within a few months of your deployment. Both the Proxmox and Ceph clusters have the ability to grow at any time to any size. This provides the ability to simply add new hardware nodes to expand cluster size and increase resources required by the virtual machines.

When provisioning your node memory configuration, take failover load into account. You will likely need to have 50 percent capacity available for a single node failure. If two nodes of a three-node cluster were to fail, you would want each machine to utilize only 33 percent of the available memory. For example, let's say all six nodes in a Proxmox cluster have 64 GB memory and 60 GB is consumed at all times by all the virtual machines. If node 1 fails, you will not be able to migrate all virtual machines from node 1 to the other five nodes, because there is not enough memory to go around. We could just add another spare node and migrate all the virtual machines. However, we have to make sure that there are enough power outlets to even plug in the new node.

# Budget

Budgetary concerns always play a role in decision making, no matter what kind of network environment we are dealing with. The true fact is that a setup can be adaptable to just about any budget with some clever and creative planning. Administrators often need to work with very small IT budget. Hopefully, this chapter will help you to find that missing thread to connect a budget with proper hardware components. By using commodity equipment over complete brand servers, we can easily set up a full Proxmox cluster on a very lean budget. Proxmox works very well on quality commodity hardware components.

# Simplicity

Simplicity is often overlooked in a network environment. A lot of times, it just happens naturally. If we are not mindful about simplicity, we can very quickly make a network unnecessarily complex. By mixing hardware RAID with software RAID, putting RAID within another RAID, or through a multi-drive setup to protect OS, we can cause a cluster's performance to drop to an almost unusable or unstable state. Both Proxmox and Ceph can run on high-grade commodity hardware as well as common server hardware. For example, just by selecting desktop-class i7 over server-class Xeon, we can slash cost in half, while providing a very stable and simple cluster setup — unless the task specifically calls for multi-Xeon setup.

# Tracking hardware inventory

An administrator should have access to key information about hardware being used in a network: information such as the brand, model, and serial number of a hardware component; when was it purchased; who was the vendor; when is it due for replacement; and so on. A proper tracking system can save a lot of time when any of this information needs to be retrieved. Each company is different, thus tracking system could be different. But the responsibility of gathering this information solely falls on the network manager or administrator. If there is no system in place, then simply creating a simple spreadsheet can be enough to keep track of all hardware information.

# Hardware selection

Several factors affect what type of hardware to select, such as, is the cluster going to support many virtual machines with smaller resources or will it serve few virtual machines with high resources. A cluster focused on many virtual machines needs to have much more processor core count, so our goal should be to put as many cores as possible per node. While a cluster is focused on few virtual machines, with a lot more users per virtual machines we need to have a large memory. Thus, a system with smaller core but a greater amount of memory is much more appropriate. Also, a cluster can focus on both types and create a hybrid cluster environment. A hybrid environment usually starts with entry-level hardware setup and then matures into an advanced-level setup as the company grows and a larger budget is available. For example, a small company can start its cluster infrastructure with stable desktop-class hardware, and then gradually replace them with a server-class platform such as Xeon to accommodate company expansion.

# Sizing CPU and memory

A question often asked when it comes to creating virtual environment is how much CPU or memory will be needed in each node and how much to allocate per virtual machine. This is one of those questions that are very open ended because their answer varies greatly from environment to environment. However, there are a few pointers that need to be kept in mind to avoid over-allocation or under-allocation.

It is a fact that we will and often do run out of memory much sooner than CPU for a given Proxmox or any other host node. From the usage of each VM on the Proxmox nodes, we can determine the RAM and CPU requirement on that node. In this section, we are going to go over the factors that will help us to decide on CPU and memory needs.

## Single socket versus multi-socket

A multi-socket node will always have better performance than a single socket regardless of the number of cores per CPU. They work much efficiently distributing VM work load. This is true for both Intel and AMD architectures. If budget is available, a quad socket node will provide the maximum performance in any other socket configuration node.

## Hyper-threading – enable versus disable

One of the major differences between Intel and AMD is hyper-threading. All cores in AMD CPUs are true cores, whereas all Intel CPUs have hyper-threading that creates two virtual cores per physical core. Another question that is asked far too often is whether to enable to disable hyper-threading. From hundreds of reports and testing, it appears that it is better to leave it on for newer Intel servers. The fear of performance degradation due to hyper-threading is no longer valid, as it has gone through decades of development and all the initial issues have been resolved. It is also best not to count all hyper-threading cores as real core since they are still virtual. When counting the number of total cores available in a node, take a conservative approach and count slightly less than the total cores.

# Start small with VM resources

A virtual machine is completely different from a physical machine and it needs to be treated as such. They do not consume CPU and memory like a physical node does. Best practice, always provision CPU and memory resources sparingly, and then increase them as you see the application's performance. This allows the VM to use allocated resources efficiently, which in turn makes all the VMs run efficiently in the node. By overprovisioning CPU and memory for all VMs in the node, we degrade node performance because all VMs will be fighting to have more CPU time. Always start with one virtual CPU (vCPU) for most of the VMs. Start from two vCPU for processor intensive VMs such as database servers, exchange servers, and so on. Monitor the VM's resource utilization and adjust accordingly. A quick way to see which VM is using the most CPU or memory is through the **Datacenter** or **Node Search** menu. The following screenshot shows the list of all entities in the example cluster sorted by highest CPU consumer:

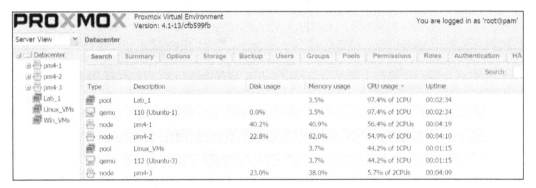

When allocating vCPU for a single VM, never exceed the total number of cores in the node. This will degrade performance of the entire node and all VMs in it. Keep in mind that in a virtual environment, more CPU and memory for a virtual machine does not mean better performance.

# Balancing node resources

Always ensure that each Proxmox node in a cluster has similar CPU and memory resources. If some nodes end up with more than the others, it will cause an issue when trying to move or migrate VMs from a high-resource node to a low-resource node. The node with fewer resources will not be able to handle all VMs, thus causing longer downtime during node failure. This issue can be mitigated by using combination of a few high-resource nodes and more low-resource nodes.

# Production Ceph cluster

As mentioned throughout this book, Ceph is a very resilient distributed storage system that pairs well with Proxmox to store virtual disk images. There are a few key factors that make Ceph cluster a good choice for production-level virtual environment.

## Forget about hardware RAID

When it comes to Ceph node and cluster, we can forget about hardware-based RAID. Instead, we have to think multi-node or clustered RAID. That is because of the distributed nature of Ceph and how data is dispersed in all the drives in the cluster regardless in which node the drive is. With Ceph, we no longer need to worry about a device failure in a particular node. Ceph performs best when it is given access to each drive directly without any RAID in the middle. If we are to place drives in RAID per node, we will actually hurt Ceph immensely and take away everything that makes Ceph great. We can, however, still use the RAID interface card to implement JBOD configuration or to be able to connect many drives per node.

## SSD for Ceph Journal

Incoming data for the Ceph cluster gets written to journal first before it gets passed down to the OSDs themselves. So, a dedicated drive such as SSD will increase write speed greatly, since they can achieve extreme write speed over standard SATA or SAS drive. Even the fastest 15,000 rpm enterprise-grade disk drive does not come close to the performance of SSD. When selecting SSD for Ceph journal, care must be taken with brand or model selection.

Not all SSD will perform well for Ceph journal. Currently, the only SSD that can withstand the rigorous load of Ceph, while providing great write speed and power loss protection, is Intel DC S3700 or S3500. There are other SSDs that can also perform well, but the ones mentioned here have a much longer lifespan. Their built-in power loss protection also prevents Journal data corruption, which may lead to corrupt data in OSDs. Visit the following link for an article on how to test suitable SSD for Ceph and list of possible SSDs for the Ceph cluster:

```
http://www.sebastien-han.fr/blog/2014/10/10/ceph-how-to-test-if-your-
ssd-is-suitable-as-a-journal-device/.
```

Instead of standard SATA SSD, we can also use PCI-based SSD, which can provide extreme performance increase over that of standard SATA SSDs. If there is a drive bay limitation for dedicated SSD, then this is the perfect choice. The following link specifies Intel PCI-E SSDs that can be considered as Ceph journal:

`http://www.intel.com/content/www/us/en/solid-state-drives/solid-state-drives-750-series.html.`

Ceph can still be used without the use of dedicated SSD journal drive. We can configure Ceph OSDs to store journal on same spinning drive. But due to the low speed of mechanical drives, we will see high IO wait time in the Proxmox nodes. Use of enterprise-grade SATA or SAS drive will lessen this IO wait time but not as much as a dedicated SSD.

 Never put dedicated journal whether SSD or HDD on any sort of RAID. This will reduce journal performance, which in turn will affect the Ceph overall performance.

# Network bandwidth

Having ample network bandwidth is crucial for Ceph or any other storage. The more bandwidth that is dedicated, the VM's performance and latency will benefit greatly. Note here that when dedicated journal such as SSD is used, the requirement of network bandwidth will increase significantly because more data will traverse in the Ceph cluster for replication and distribution. For a Ceph cluster where SSD is used as dedicated journal, gigabit network should not be used for Ceph cluster network. At the very least, 10 GB would be ideal network. We can also use Infiniband as an alternative network solution on lower budget. If neither is possible, then multiple bonded gigabit would also work. On a single gigabit, the network will become the bottleneck causing cluster wide performance degradation.

Also, Ceph cluster sync should be on its own dedicated network while the Ceph public facing network is on another. Ceph uses cluster network to commit all syncs in between OSDs. This prevents unnecessary load on public-side network since that is the only server to request data from Ceph storage.

# Liquid cooling

In this solution, computer equipment is cooled using liquid for heat transfer instead of air. Liquid is 1000 times better at heat transfer than air. We can effectively remove heat directly from IT equipment and transfer it with great ease out of the facility. Liquid cooling takes away the hassle of running large HVAC system, thus saving enormous costs and reducing noise significantly. Liquid cooling requires no internal fans, thus we can increase server density per rack 10 fold. Liquid cooling is the future as more and more IT facilities are realizing its full potential. By using liquid cooling, we can also decrease our energy consumption—reducing carbon footprint enormously. There are different liquid cooling solutions available on the market.

# Total immersion in oil

IT equipment is totally submerged in mineral oil. Hot oil is pumped through liquid-to-liquid heat exchanger, where the heat is carried away using water to an outside cooling tower. Water and oil never have full contact only heat transfer. This is not only the most cost-effective liquid cooling solution today, but also the messiest as servers are dipped in oil. It also requires more space, since all racks are laid on their backs. However, this extra space can easily be compensated by increased density per node. Currently, Green Revolution Cooling pioneers this technology. Visit the following links for their official site and great video showing the technology in action:

```
http://www.grcooling.com/
```

```
https://www.youtube.com/watch?v=7LgbN0cIu8k
```

There is another technology worth mentioning here that is similar to immersion but the immersion is isolated in the server node itself. Liquid cool solutions has a unique approach of filling up a sealed server chassis with mineral oil to remove heat. Visit the following link for more info on this approach:

```
http://www.liquidcoolsolutions.com/?page_id=86
```

# Total immersion in 3M Novec

Similar to oil immersion cooling, this is also a total immersion technology where 3M Novec Engineered Fluid is used instead of mineral oil. The advantage of this option is zero mess. Unlike oil, this fluid does not stick to any equipment and does not require a heat exchanger or pump to move the fluid itself. This fluid has boiling temperature of 60 degree Celsius, at which it becomes vapor. When the vapor hits the cold coil on top of the container it turns to liquid and drops back down to the tank. Only pump is needed to circulate water through the coil, thus it needs only half of the equipment needed for oil-based cooling. Visit the following link for a video presentation of the technology:

```
https://www.youtube.com/watch?v=a6ErbZtpL88
```

# Direct contact liquid cooling

Heat is removed directly from heat source, such as CPU and memory, using cold plate and liquid coolant such as water or any other coolant agent. Since no equipment is immersed, this technology can be used with existing infrastructure with major modification, while still increasing node density per node and reduced energy consumption. This is not unique technology as this type of liquid cooling solution had been in use for several years. Consumer class liquid cooling solutions uses this off-the-shelf technology. Asetek is known for a desktop liquid cooling solution for desktop users. Visit their official site through the following link:

```
http://www.asetek.com/
```

Another direct contact liquid cooling solution provider worth mentioning here is CoolIT Systems. They also take the cold plate approach to cool equipment through liquid cooling. Some of their solutions can be implemented directly in the rack as standard mounted cooling unit without the need to have a facility for water or cooling tower. Visit the following link for more information on their solution:

```
http://www.coolitsystems.com/
```

# Real-world Proxmox scenarios

Equipped with all the knowledge we have gathered from the previous chapters in this book, we are now ready to put all the pieces together to form complex virtual environment for just about any scenario that we are going to be called for. Some set of scenarios are given in the next section to build networks using Proxmox for various industries. At the end of the chapter, you will find network diagrams of each scenario given in first part of the chapter.

Some scenarios have been taken from real-life production environments, while some are theoretical to show how complex networks are possible with Proxmox. You can take these network models and use them as they are or modify them to make them even better.

We hope that through these network scenarios and models, you will start seeing Proxmox from a whole new point of view and be fully prepared to face any level of virtual infrastructure you are challenged with.

> While analyzing these scenarios, keep in mind that the solutions and diagrams provided in this chapter are one of the many ways the network infrastructure could be set up. To fit the diagrams within the confinement of the book, some non-vital components might have been omitted. All network and identification information used in the network diagrams is fictional.

The network diagrams show the relationship between components within the infrastructure, such as virtual environment, cluster of nodes, and overall network connectivity. They also represent virtual network components such as bridges relates to each other, network segmentation, and so on.

# Scenario 1 – an academic institution

This scenario is for a typical academic institution with multiple networks and multiple campus and multiple building setups, along with both private and public networks.

**Key requirements**:

- Network isolation to protect sensitive data.
- Ability to have centralized management for network infrastructure.
- Professors should be on separate Wi-Fi only accessible by them. This Wi-Fi should give professors the ability to log in to the campus main server to retrieve their files for lectures.
- Students should have on-campus Wi-Fi access and wired Internet connection to their dormitories. These subnets must be separated from main campus network.
- The library should be on separate subnet with own server.
- Classrooms, admin offices, and professors should be on the main isolated network. Professors should have the ability to retrieve their files from file server on classroom computers during lectures.

This is a scenario for a typical academic institution campus network. Thanks to Proxmox, we can have all main server equipment and virtual environment in one place to have centralized management. There are five subnets in this network:

| Subnet | Network description |
|---|---|
| 10.170.10.0 | Wired network for the dormitory. Firewall provides DHCP. This subnet does not need to go through main network. |
| 10.180.10.0 | Student and Public Wi-Fi on campus. Firewall provides DHCP. This subnet does not need to go through the main network. |
| 10.160.10.0 | Main administrative and professors' Network. Private Wi-Fi for professors is an extension of this network to allow professors to retrieve their files wirelessly. All classrooms are also on this network to provide in-class access of files for professors. |
| 10.110.10.0 | Storage Cluster. |
| 10.190.10.0 | Library subnet. DHCP provided by virtualized library server. This server is for library only. A separate LAN (eth2) is used to connect the virtual machine with library building. |

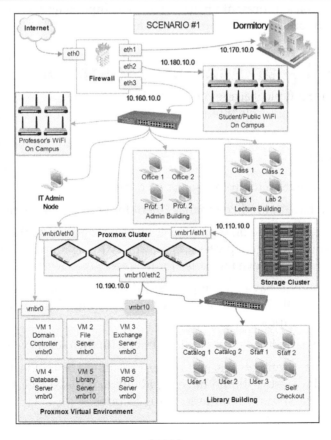

# Scenario 2 – multi-tier storage cluster with a Proxmox cluster

**Key requirements**:

- Need separate storage clusters for SSD, Hybrid HDD and HDD
- Storage clusters should be on separate subnets
- Storage should be distributed with high availability and high scalability

For this scenario, each Proxmox node must have at least four network interface cards: three to connect to three storage clusters subnet and one to connect to the virtual environment. This example is for six virtual machines to have access to three different performing storages. Following are the three Ceph clusters and their performance categories:

| Subnet | Network description |
|---|---|
| 192.168.10.0:6789 | CEPH cluster #1 with SSDs for all OSDs. This subnet is connected with Proxmox nodes through eth1.This storage is used by VM6. |
| 192.168.20.0:6790 | CEPH cluster #2 with Hybrid HDDs for all OSDs. This subnet is connected with Proxmox nodes through eth2. This storage is used by VM5. |
| 192.168.30.0:6791 | CEPH Cluster #3 with HDDs for all OSDs. This subnet is connected with Proxmox nodes through eth3. This storage are used by VM1, VM2, VM3, and VM4. |
| 10.160.10.0 | This is the main subnet for all virtual machines. |

A multi-tiered infrastructure is very typical for datacenters where there are different levels of SLA-based clients with various requirements for storage performance:

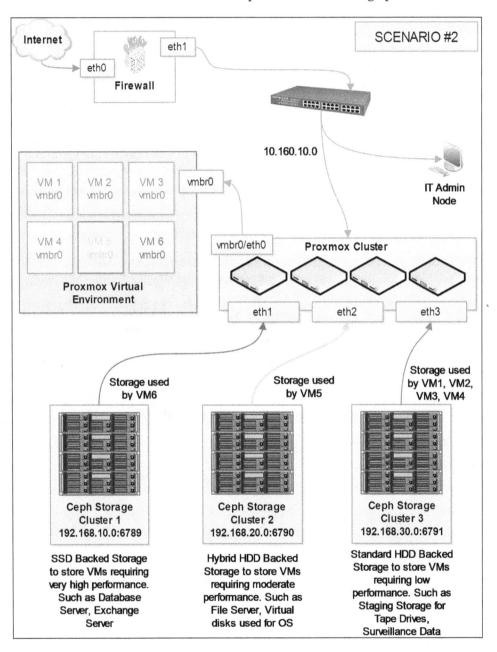

# Scenario 3 – virtual infrastructure for a multi-tenant cloud service provider

**Key requirements**:

- There should be firewall cluster for Edge firewalls
- Each client network must be fully isolated from each other
- Separate storage cluster for backup is required
- Client users must be able to access their company virtual desktops via RDP
- There must be bandwidth control ability for the client's network Internet connectivity
- Replicate all data to another datacenter

In this scenario, virtualized firewall and virtual bridges are used to separate traffic between each client network. Virtual firewall has seven virtual network interfaces to connect six client networks within a virtual environment and to provide WAN connectivity. Internet bandwidth is controlled through virtual firewall for each vNIC. Virtual firewall is connected to WAN through main virtual bridge vmbr0. Proxmox cluster has nine virtual bridges:

| Subnet | Network description |
|--------|---------------------|
| vmbr0 | Main virtual bridge to provide WAN connection to the virtual firewall |
| vmbr1 | Connects main storage cluster |
| vmbr5 | Connects storage cluster for backup |
| vmbr10 | Bridge for company ABC subnet 10.10.10.0 |
| vmbr20 | Bridge for company XYZ subnet 10.20.20.0 |
| vmbr30 | Bridge for LXC containers for web hosting instances |
| vmbr40 | Bridge for object storage instances to be used by software developer |
| vmbr50 | Bridge for company 123 subnet 10.50.50.0 |
| vmbr60 | Bridge for a small business virtual cluster |

Each bridge connects the client company's virtual machines together and creates an isolated internal network for respective clients:

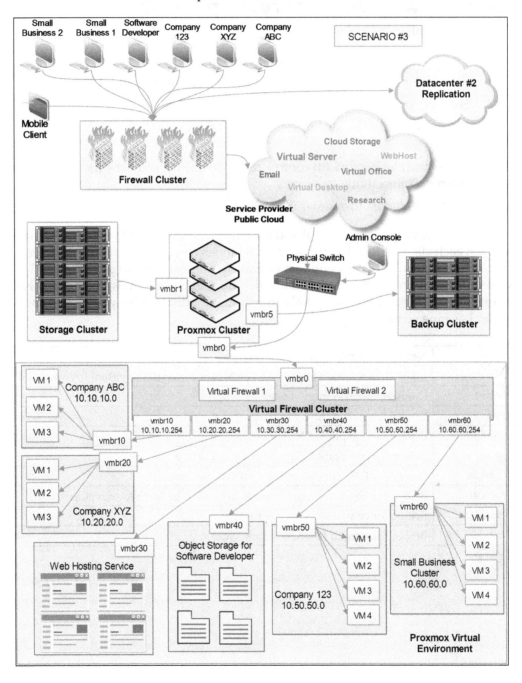

# Scenario 4 – nested virtual environment for a software development company

**Key requirements**:

- Developer must have nested virtual environment to test software
- Outsourced developer should have access to nested virtual environment using RDP
- Developer must have control to create or delete virtual cluster
- Nested virtual environment must be fully isolated from main company network

In this scenario, a nested Proxmox virtual cluster is created inside the main cluster mainly for software testing purpose for a software development company. Since virtual clusters can be created and taken down at any time, it reduces cost and time of setting up the entire hardware and setup process. A virtual firewall is used to direct traffic between nested and main virtual environment. All developers access their nested virtual machines through RDP port forwarding. Outsourced developers also need to connect to nested virtual environment using RDP. The main firewall does port forwarding to virtual firewall. Then, virtual firewall does port forwarding to nested virtual machines. Four subnets are used in this example:

| Subnet | Network description |
|---|---|
| 10.160.10.0 | This is the main company subnet. All staff including developers are on this subnet. |
| 10.160.20.0 | Main storage cluster subnet. It is connected to main cluster with vmbr1. |
| 10.170.10.0 | Nested cluster subnet. It is isolated from main cluster with vmbr2 which is only connected to virtual firewall. |
| 10.170.20.0 | Nested storage cluster subnet. |

Virtual machines VM Proxmox 1, VM Proxmox 2, and VM Proxmox 3 are used to create a nested Proxmox cluster while VM Storage 1, VM Storage 2, and VM Storage 3 virtual machines are used to create a nested storage cluster:

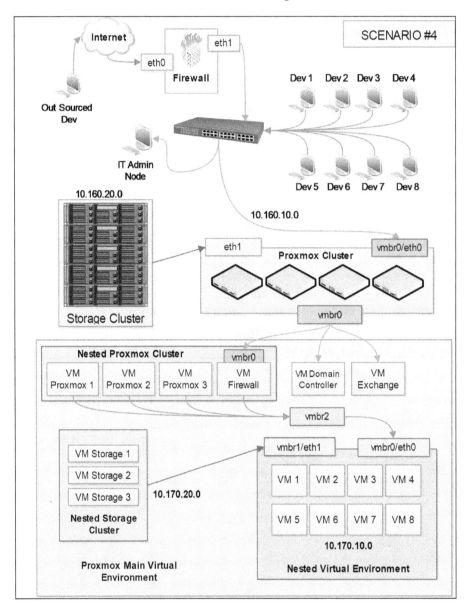

# Scenario 5 – virtual infrastructure for a public library

**Key requirements**:

- Catalog consoles should be on separate subnet along with main admin subnet
- Public Wi-Fi and consoles for public internet usage should be on same separate subnet
- Kiosks for self-check-in and check-out books and media
- Online access to the library catalog
- Public Internet traffic must be monitored for any Internet usage policy violations.
- Public computers should have printer access

This is a typical scenario for public library network system. Since a public library is a public place with access to computers for public usage, it is very important to isolates sensitive networks. In this example, the network is isolated using two subnets:

| Subnet | Network description |
|---|---|
| 10.16.10.0 | Main network for library staff and protected consoles only such as Catalog, Kiosks, staff printers, and self-check-in and check-out. |
| 10.20.10.0 | This public subnet for public Wi-Fi, internet consoles, and printers with payment system. |

The network 10.20.10.0 is controlled, managed, and isolated using a virtual firewall VM5. The virtual firewall has two vNICs, one for WAN connection through vmbr3 and the other to connect to a dedicated NIC on the Proxmox node through vmbr4. Eth2 of the Proxmox node is connected to a separate LAN switch to only connect public devices. Virtual firewall provides the ability to monitor internet traffic to keep in line with any violations of the library Internet usage policy.

Each Proxmox nodes has four network interface cards, `eth0`, `eth1`, `eth2`, and `eth3`, and the cluster has three virtual bridges, `vmbr0`, `vmbr2`, and `vmbr4`. The main storage cluster is connected to the Proxmox node through `eth1` and backup cluster is connected to `eth3`:

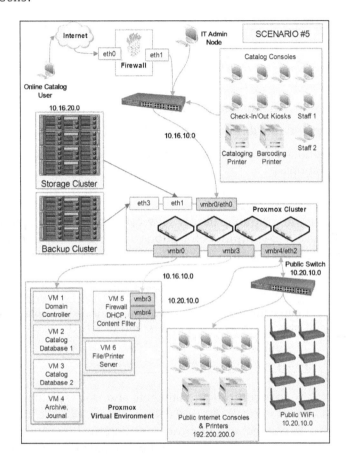

# Scenario 6 – multi-floor office virtual infrastructure with virtual desktops

**Key requirements**:

- All staff members should be on virtual desktops
- Redundant internet connectivity
- Each department should have their own Remote Desktop Server
- Accounting department network traffic should only be directed to their department

This is a common scenario for an office building where departments are on different floors of the building. Since accounting department requires data isolation, we are going to use a vLAN to isolate their data. Administrative offices, copy room, and main server room are in 4th floor. The HR department is in 5th floor, marketing is in 6th, and the accounting department is in 7th floor. The 5th, 6th, and 7th floors have their own LAN switches. So, we could easily use vLAN for other floors if it was required. We only need to setup vLAN on the switch in 4th floor.

Each Proxmox node has two network interfaces. `eth1` is to connect storage clusters and eth0 is to connect all virtual machines to their departments. `vlan0.10` is used to separate accounting traffic only direct to 7th floor.

All department staff use virtual desktops through RDP. Each department's virtual server acts as Remote Desktop servers and department's main server:

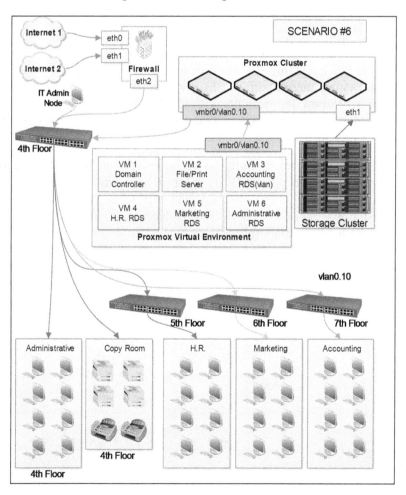

# Scenario 7 – virtual infrastructure for the hotel industry

**Key requirements**:

- Centralized IT infrastructure management.

- Dedicated secured Wi-Fi access for guests.

- Secured private Wi-Fi access in restaurant and bar for menu tablets only. The Wi-Fi need to talk to restaurant and bar server.

- All staff must have Remote Desktops for day-to-day work.

- The video surveillance system should be integrated with the virtual environment.

This is a scenario for a typical hotel establishment with in-house restaurant. This example uses a central virtualized database server to store all information. Although it is an unconventional way to connect all departments with a single database (including surveillance system), it is possible to use all-in-one single solution to reduce cost and management overhead. In a typical scenario, separate software is used to handle different departments without data portability. In this example, unified management software connects all departments with a single database and a customized user interface for each department.

Secured non-filtered Wi-Fi connectivity provided for all guests. DHCP is provided directly by firewall. Secured private Wi-Fi is set up for restaurant menu tablets only. All menu tablets only connect to the restaurant or bar virtual server with IP 10.190.1.5. All department thin clients and IP-based surveillance cameras are connected to the main network subnet 10.190.1.0:

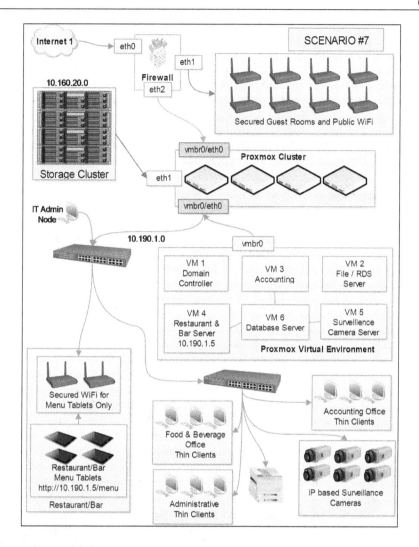

# Scenario 8 – virtual infrastructure for a geological survey organization

**Key requirements**:

- Field surveyors should submit their work orders from their mobile devices through VPN connection
- There must be a failover infrastructure in multi-site network topology

In this scenario, a geographical survey company has a main office and branch office connected with 1+gpbs hardlink network connectivity. Each office has an identical infrastructure setup. All surveyors use mobile devices such as tablets for their survey work. The survey software auto detects which office IP is live and sends data to the infrastructure of that office. All data is replicated at block level in real time between two offices.

If the infrastructure of one office becomes unavailable, staff can simply continue to work out of the infrastructure from another office:

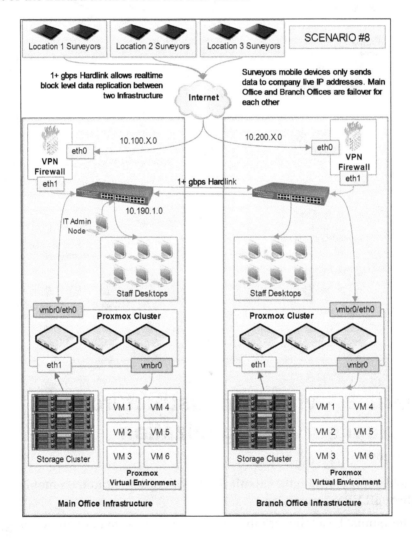

# Summary

Virtual environments are very flexible, so there is no one-network-fits-all configuration. Each network will be unique. The components and requirements described in this chapter are mere guidelines for how to take the correct approach to plan for a production-level Proxmox setup. We saw some of the requirements of a production-level setup, and we covered how to allocate CPU and memory resources properly for both Proxmox host node and virtual machine itself. We also discussed how to give Ceph storage the best chance of providing redundancy along with performance. Finally, we saw how to cool equipment efficiently by leveraging liquid cooling, thus increasing Proxmox computing node density per rack while saving energy.

We also saw some real-world scenarios of Proxmox in action in different industries. We hope this will aid you in your quest to find that perfect balance between performance and budget that all network administrators crave.

In the next chapter, we are going to see some real incident-based issues and how to troubleshoot a Proxmox cluster environment. These issues have been taken from day-to-day clusters running in production enviornments.

# 14
# Proxmox Troubleshooting

In this chapter, we are going to learn about the common Proxmox issues found in a production environment and the solutions to those issues. Once a Proxmox cluster is set up, it usually runs without issues. However, when issues arise, a system administrator's knowledge is tested. Learning how to properly troubleshoot can be easier by learning about other people's resolutions. Throughout this chapter, we will gain some insight into Proxmox troubleshooting and hope that when these issues arise in our own Proxmox clusters, we will be able to identify and resolve the problems quickly and with ease.

All the issues explained in this chapter are those that may be commonly faced by others. It is just not possible to explain all the error possibilities, mainly owing to all the components that work together to make up a stable system. As you run your own cluster, you may face other issues that we have not documented here.

The issues are divided into the following sections:

- The main cluster
- Storage
- Network connectivity
- The KVM virtual machine
- LXC containers
- Backup/restore
- The VNC/SPICE console
- A firewall

# Proxmox node issues

This section contains issues related to the Proxmox node itself.

## Issue – Fresh Proxmox install stuck with /dev to be fully populated error during node reboot

**Solution**: This issue occurs when the OS tries to boot with a non standard VGA driver. To prevent this issue, we need to add and modify some grub options. Restart the node, and then press 'e', without the quotation marks from the Proxmox boot menu. At the end of the Kernel boot line, add the following nomodeset, as shown in the following screenshot:

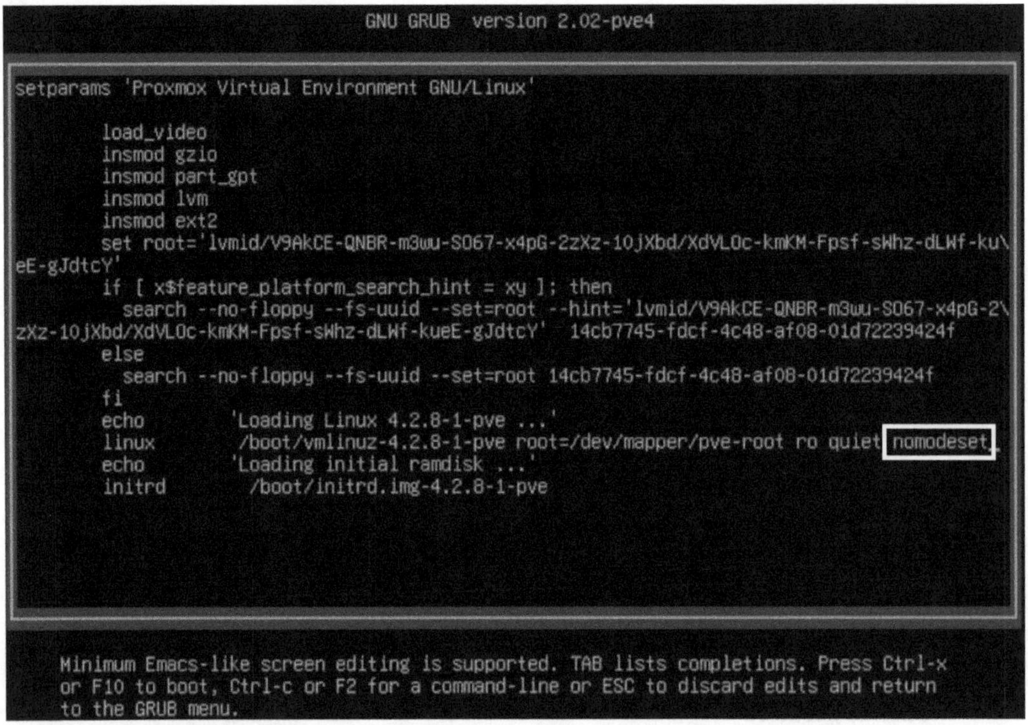

```
                        GNU GRUB  version 2.02-pve4

setparams 'Proxmox Virtual Environment GNU/Linux'

        load_video
        insmod gzio
        insmod part_gpt
        insmod lvm
        insmod ext2
        set root='lvmid/V9AkCE-QNBR-m3wu-SO67-x4pG-2zXz-10jXbd/XdVLOc-kmKM-Fpsf-sWhz-dLWf-ku\
eE-gJdtcY'
        if [ x$feature_platform_search_hint = xy ]; then
          search --no-floppy --fs-uuid --set=root  --hint='lvmid/V9AkCE-QNBR-m3wu-SO67-x4pG-2\
zXz-10jXbd/XdVLOc-kmKM-Fpsf-sWhz-dLWf-kueE-gJdtcY'  14cb7745-fdcf-4c48-af08-01d72239424f
        else
          search --no-floppy --fs-uuid --set=root 14cb7745-fdcf-4c48-af08-01d72239424f
        fi
        echo            'Loading Linux 4.2.8-1-pve ...'
        linux           /boot/vmlinuz-4.2.8-1-pve root=/dev/mapper/pve-root ro quiet nomodeset
        echo            'Loading initial ramdisk ...'
        initrd          /boot/initrd.img-4.2.8-1-pve


   Minimum Emacs-like screen editing is supported. TAB lists completions. Press Ctrl-x
   or F10 to boot, Ctrl-c or F2 for a command-line or ESC to discard edits and return
   to the GRUB menu.
```

Press *Ctrl+X* or *F10* to boot the node normally. To make this option permanent, make the following modifications in /etc/default/grub:

Uncomment GRUB_TERMINAL=console

Comment out GRUB_GFXMODE=some_X,some_Y

# Issue – Rejoining a node to a Proxmox node with the same old IP address

**Solution**: If you are rejoining a Proxmox node back to the cluster with the same IP address, then the joining command must run with the `--force` option. Run the following command from the node that is being rejoined:

```
# pvecm add <any_proxmox_node_ip) -force
```

Without the additional `-force` option, the node will not be joined and an error message will be displayed informing the existence of a certificate.

# Issue – Booting with a USB stick fails in Proxmox

**Solution**: When Proxmox is installed on a USB flash drive, a boot error will occur during the Proxmox boot time. The recommended storage to install Proxmox is SSD or HDD. The only way to install it on a USB stick is to install Debian Linux first, and then install Proxmox on top of it.

 A USB thumb drive or flash drive should never be used as the primary Proxmox OS installation storage in a production environment.

# Issue – Proxmox installation completed but GRUB is in an endless loop after reboot

**Solution:** This is a common occurrence when Proxmox is installed on a newer desktop class with UEFI Bios. Simply disabling the UEFI mode will allow the system to boot. If this does not work, Proxmox should be installed manually over Debian Jessie. To get information on instructions of how to install Proxmox when the ISO installer does not work, refer to: `http://pve.proxmox.com/wiki/Install_Proxmox_VE_on_Debian_Jessie`.

# Issue – LSI MegaRAID 9240-8i/9240-4i causes an error during booting on the Proxmox node

**Solution**: This issue can be prominent in the Supermicro motherboard with the LSI chipset for hot swap bays. There are two ways in which we can use the cards in the Proxmox mode:

## Downloading and updating the LSI driver

We can download and install the latest LSI drivers in Proxmox to activate the LSI cards by performing the following steps:

1.  Run the following command to install the necessary program for compiling:

    ```
    apt-get install build-essential
    ```

2.  Run the following command to install header files for the currently installed kernel:

    ```
    apt-get install pve-headers-<version>-pve
    ```

3.  Download the LSI drivers from: http://www.avagotech.com/support/download-search.

4.  Extract the downloaded driver in /usr/local/src.

5.  After extracting the driver, the directory may appear as follows:

    ```
    /usr/local/src/megaraid_sas-v00.00.05.30
    ```

6.  Enter the driver directory and rename makefile to makefile.orig. Then, copy makefile.standalone to makefile.

7.  Compile the source using the following command:

    ```
    make -C /usr/src/linux-headers-2.6.32-7-pve/ M=$PWD modules
    ```

    It will show some text output and warnings. But it is safe to ignore these. The driver will end up here in the following directory:

    ```
    /usr/local/src/megaraid_sas-v00.00.05.30/megaraid_sas.ko
    ```

8.  Remove or rename the existing driver file in the following directory:

    ```
    /lib/modules/<version>-pve/kernel/drivers/scsi/megaraid/megaraid_sas.ko
    ```

9.  Copy the new compiled driver to the previous directory, as follows:

    ```
    cp /usr/local/src/megaraid_sas-v00.00.05.30/megaraid_sas.ko /lib/modules/<version>-pve/kernel/drivers/scsi/megaraid/megaraid_sas.ko
    ```

10. Back up the initial RAM disk by renaming it, as follows:

```
mv /boot/initrd.img-2.6.32-7-pve /boot/initrd.img-<version>-pve.
bak
```

11. Run the following command to update `initramfs`:

```
update-initramfs -c -k 2.6.32-7-pve
```

12. Run the following command to update grub, and then reboot it:

```
update-grub
```

## Updating the Supermicro BIOS

We can also update the Supermicro BIOS to the latest firmware to use the LSI cards. Always check whether you have the latest firmware before updating it. For instructions on how to update the Supermicro BIOS firmware, refer to: `http://wahlnetwork.com/2013/06/03/the-easy-button-for-supermicro-bios-upgrades/`.

# Main cluster issues

This section contains issues related to the main Proxmox's cluster operations.

# Issue – Proxmox virtual machines are running, but the Proxmox GUI shows that everything is offline

**Solution**: This is usually caused when one of the three services, such as `pvedaemon`, `pvestatd`, or `pveproxy` crashes or stops working for any number of reasons. Simply restarting them through SSH will fix this issue. Run the following commands in the following order:

```
# service pvedaemon restart
# service pveproxy restart
# service pvestatd restart
```

# Issue – Kernel panic when disconnecting USB devices, such as a keyboard, mouse, or UPS

**Solution**: There is no real solution to this issue yet as the issue is not reproducible all the time. This issue has been seen on a variety of hardware with both standard and nonstandard Proxmox installations. However, almost all the time, the issue does not cause the server to freeze permanently. In almost all cases, the panic can just be ignored and you can go on as usual.

Kernel panic seems to mostly occur with kernel 2.6.32-26, 2.6.32-27 and 2.6.32-28. It is nonexistent on kernel 3.2 or 3.10. For regular day-to-day operations of a cluster, this issue can be safely ignored unless it causes the node to freeze on rare occasions.

# Issue – Virtual machines on Proxmox will not shut down if shutdown is initiated from the Proxmox GUI

**Solution**: This issue is not consistent and is not directly related to Proxmox. The Shutdown button on Proxmox's GUI only sends an ACPI signal to a virtual machine to initiate the shutdown process.

Once the VM receives an ACPI signal, it starts the shutdown process. However, if the VM has a number of running processes in the memory, it might take a while to end processes before the shutdown. The ending of processes may take longer, which causes Proxmox to issue a timeout error. The issue may occur for both Windows and Linux. The workaround for this is to access the VM through a console or SPICE and then manually shut down the VM.

# Issue – Kernel panic with HP NC360T (Intel 82571EB Chipset) only in Proxmox VE 3.2

**Solution**: An immediate workaround is to use broadcom for the network interface card. The permanent fix is to download E1000 drivers from the Intel website and compile a module from those sources. The E1000 driver can be downloaded from `http://www.intel.com/support/network/sb/cs-006120.htm`.

# Issue – The Proxmox cluster is out of Quorum and cluster filesystem is in read-only mode

**Solution**: This occurs when a node falls out of Quorum. To prevent any error occurrence in the cluster configuration files, Proxmox puts the cluster filesystem in the read-only mode for the node in question. Run the following commands from the node with this issue. We have to stop the cluster service, start it in local mode, delete or move the existing corosync.conf file, and then restart the cluster. A new corosync.conf file will be synced with the node with a read-only issue. Perform the following steps to overcome this issue:

1. Stop the cluster in the node using the following command:

   ```
   # /etc/init.d/pve-cluster stop
   ```

2. Start the cluster filesystem in local mode using the following command:

   ```
   # /usr/bin/pmxcfs -l
   ```

3. Remove or back up the cluster.conf file using this command:

   ```
   # mv /etc/pve/corosync.conf /home/backup
   ```

4. Stop and start the cluster normally using the following commands:

   ```
   # /etc/init.d/pve-cluster stop
   # /etc/init.d/pve-cluster start
   ```

# Issue – Proxmox cannot start due to the getpwnam error

**Solution**: Boot the Proxmox node in recovery mode using the Proxmox installation disk, or select the recovery option from Proxmox's boot menu at the beginning of the boot process. After the recovery shell is loaded, run the following command from the command prompt and then reboot:

```
# apt-get update && apt-get dist-upgrade
```

# Issue – Cannot log in to the GUI as root after reinstalling Proxmox on the same node

**Solution**: In order to log in as `root` into the Proxmox GUI, local loopback must be enabled in the network interface file. Look for the following two lines to make sure they are not commented out in `/etc/network/interfaces`:

```
auto lo
iface lo inet loopback
```

# Issue – The Upgrade button is disabled on the Proxmox GUI, which prevents the node upgrade

**Solution**: There are three most common reasons why the Upgrade button could be disabled on the Proxmox GUI. Check the following alternatives to fix this issue:

1. If the node does not have a valid subscription, ensure that the pve-no-subscription repository is added. For Proxmox repository information, visit `https://pve.proxmox.com/wiki/Package_repositories`.

2. Refresh the browser cache to reload the graphic interface.

3. Make sure that the root user is logged in to facilitate the upgrade; it's a basic mistake, but it's not unheard of.. The Upgrade button is only visible when you log in with the root privilege.

# Issue – VM will not respond to shutdown, restart

**Solution**: First check whether High Availability of HA is enabled for the VM or not. HA will prevent any manual action such as the VM shutdown, stop, restart, or start because the main purpose of HA is that actions can be taken without user interaction. In order to manually perform any task for a VM, we need to disable HA for the VM, perform a task, and then re-enable HA.

# Issue – The Proxmox GUI not showing RRD graphs

**Solution**: If a node or VM is running fine, but there are no RRD graphs on the Status page, it might be owing to the stuck `pvestatd` service or corrupted RRD cache. Run the following commands to restart the `pvestatd` service and clear the RRD cache:

```
# rrdcache -P FLUSHALL
# service pvestatd restart
```

# Storage issues

This section contains issues related to storage systems supported by Proxmox, such as local, NFS, Ceph, GlusterFS, and so on.

# Issue – Deleting a damaged LVM from Proxmox with the error read failed from 0 to 4096

**Solution**: Run the following command from the CLI:

```
# dmsetup remove /dev/<volume_group>/<lvm_name>
```

# Issue – Proxmox cannot mount NFS Share due to the timing out error

**Solution**: Some NFS servers such as FreeNAS do a reverse lookup for hostnames. We need to add Proxmox hostnames to the host files of the NFS server:

```
# nano /etc/hosts
```

# Issue: How to delete leftover NFS shares in Proxmox or what to do when the NFS stale file handles error occurs?

**Solution**: When NFS shares are deleted from the Proxmox storage; in some cases, it still remains mounted, which causes the NFS Stale File Handle error. Simply manually unmounting the share and removing the NFS mount point folder from the Proxmox directory fixes this issue. Run the following commands from the Proxmox node:

```
# umount -f /mnt/<nfs_share>
# rmdir <nfs_share>
```

# Issue – Proxmox issues—mode session exit code 21 errors while trying to access the iSCSI target

**Solution**: Run the following command from the Proxmox node to fix the error:

```
# iscsiadm -m node -l ALL
```

# Issue – Cannot read an iSCSI target even after it has been deleted from Proxmox storage

**Solution**: When trying to read the same iSCSI target after it had been deleted from Proxmox storage, an error occurs mentioning the target that has already has been added to Proxmox. In these cases, the iSCSI daemon has to be restarted to clear this issue. Run the following command from all the Proxmox nodes:

```
# /etc/init.d/open-iscsi restart
```

# Issue – A Ceph node is removed from the Proxmox cluster, but OSDs still show up in PVE

**Solution**: This is a common occurrence when a Ceph node is taken offline without removing all the Ceph-related processes first. The OSDs in the node must be removed or moved to another node before taking the node offline. Run the following commands to remove OSDs:

```
# ceph osd out <osd.id>
# ceph osd crush remove osd <osd.id>
# ceph auth del osd.<id>
# ceph osd rm <osd.id>
```

# Issue – The 'No Such Block Device' error during creation of an OSD through the Proxmox GUI

**Solution**: When creating an OSD through the Proxmox GUI, sometimes this error occurs. This is not a common occurrence and is not reproducible at all times. Although there are no permanent fixes for this issue, it can be ignored. So just retry to create an OSD.

# Issue – The fstrim command does not trim unused blocks for the Ceph storage

**Solution**: To properly trim unused blocks for virtual disks stored on the Ceph storage, perform the following steps:

1. Use a `virtio` disk type for a virtual disk.
2. Enable the discard option through `<vm_id>.conf`. Add `discard=on` to the drive properties of `virtio0`, as follows:

   ```
   <rbd_storage>:<virtual_disk>,cache=writethrough,size=50G,discard=on
   ```

# Issue – The RBD Couldn't Connect To Cluster (500) error when connecting Ceph with Proxmox

**Solution**: Authentication failure is the most common cause for this error when Ceph RBD storage cannot connect to Proxmox. Proxmox requires a copy of the Ceph admin keyring to authenticate. The name of the keyring must match with the storage ID assigned through the Proxmox GUI. Refer to *Chapter 4*, *Storage Systems*, for information on how to set up the Ceph cluster to be used as storage backend.

# Issue – Changing the storage type from ide to virtio after the VM has been set up and the OS has been installed

**Solution**: If **ide** was used during the initial VM setup, and if it needs to be changed to virtio later, it can be done through the Proxmox GUI without reinstalling the OS. The VM will need to be powered off first, and then the virtual disk needs to be removed through the Proxmox GUI. After clicking on **Remove**, the virtual disk will become unused, as shown in the following screenshot:

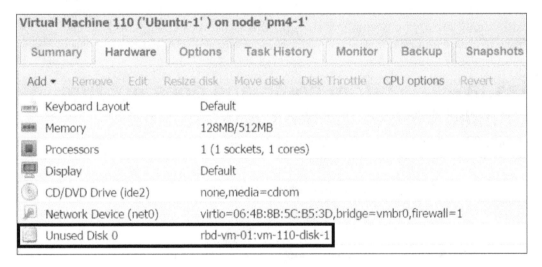

Double-click on the unused virtual disk or navigate to **Add** | **Hard disk** to add it back to the VM. Select virtio as Bus/Device from the dialog box.

# Issue – The pveceph configuration not initialized (500) error when you click on the Ceph tab in the Proxmox GUI

**Solution**: This error occurs when you click on the Ceph tab in the Proxmox GUI without initializing the Ceph storage. If Ceph is not going to be used along with Proxmox on the same cluster, then this error should simply be ignored.

# Issue – The CephFS storage disappears after a Proxmox node reboots

**Solution**: CephFS needs to be mounted in order to make it available for storage service. If the mount point is not set in /etc/fstab, it will need to be remounted after each reboot. The following format is used to enter the Ceph filesystem in /etc/fstab:

```
id={user-ID}[,conf={path/to/conf.conf}] /mount/path  fuse.ceph
defaults 0 0
id=admin,conf=/etc/ceph/conf.conf /mnt/<path>  fuse.ceph defaults 0 0
```

# Issue – VM Cloning does not parse in the Ceph storage

**Solution**: When full cloning is performed on a virtual machine stored on Ceph storage, it loses sparse on the virtual disk. For cloning, Proxmox uses the qemu-img method instead of rbd flattening. Until it is implemented in later versions of Proxmox, VM clones will lose parsing on Ceph storage.

# Network connectivity issues

This section contains issues related to virtual or physical network connectivity within Proxmox.

# Issue – No connectivity on Realtek RTL8111/8411 Rev. 06 network interfaces

**Solution**: Some newer Realtek chipsets don't get compiled with the right drivers. This causes the interface to be up without any network traffic. In order to fix this issue, the older driver needs to be downloaded from the Realtek site and compiled manually. The driver can be downloaded from `http://www.realtek.com.tw/Downloads/`.

Since this driver is manually installed, during a kernel update it will get updated automatically. To prevent this and ensure that the driver builds itself automatically when a new kernel is installed, run the following commands and then reboot the node:

```
# apt-get install dkms build-essentials pve-headers-2.6.32-25-pve
# cat <<EOF > /usr/src/r8168-8.037.00/dkms.conf
PACKAGE_NAME=r8168
PACKAGE_VERSION=8.037.00
MAKE[0]="'make'"
BUILT_MODULE_NAME[0]=r8168
BUILT_MODULE_LOCATION[0]="src/"
DEST_MODULE_LOCATION[0]="/kernel/updates/dkms"
AUTOINSTALL="YES"
EOF
```

# Issue – Network performance is slower with the e1000 virtual network interface

Solution: The performance of e1000 virtual network interfaces is about 30-35% less than vitrio virtual network interfaces. Changing vNICs to virtio will increase the overall network bandwidth of a virtual machine. The virtio drivers are included in all major Linux flavors. For Windows machines, an ISO file with virtio drivers can be downloaded from: `http://www.linux-kvm.org/page/WindowsGuestDrivers/Download_Drivers`.

# Issue – Patch port for Openvswitch in Proxmox not working

**Solution**: Currently, there are three Openvswitch options that are fully supported through Proxmox, such as OVSBridge, OVSIntPort, and OVSBond. The OVSPatchPort option that is required for the patch port cannot be configured through the Proxmox GUI. Thus, even if we manually create a configuration in the network interface file, it still seems to be out of reach. An alternate solution, where the patch port is required, is to use an Openvswitch fake bridge. Fake bridges look and act like full Openvswitch bridges but are tied to a particular `vlan`. A fake bridge depends on an already configured main Openvswitch bridge. Assuming that the main bridge is `vmbr0`, the content of the `/etc/network/interfaces` will look, as follows, for a fake bridge named 11 for `vlan ID #11`:

```
auto vmbr11
allow-vmbr0 vmbr11
iface vmbr11 inet manual
  ovs_bridge vmbr0
  ovs_type OVSBridge
  ovs_options vmbr0 11
```

The entry option for a fake bridge is as follows:

```
ovs_options <main_bridge> <vlan_id>
```

We can now connect a VM to this bridge without assigning any vlan ID to the virtual network interface.

# Issue – Trying to add a node to a newly created Proxmox cluster when nodes do not form quorum

**Solution**: From Proxmox 4.0 and later, we now require the Multicast feature. Without this, nodes will be unable to form quorum. So, when we add a new node to a cluster, if the process gets stuck at **Waiting for Quorum...**, we need to ensure that multicast is enabled in the switch. As soon as multicast is available, nodes will form quorum without any issues.

# Issue – Implemented IPv6 but firewall rules do not get applied

**Solution**: All firewall rules are primarily applied to IPv4 traffic. In order to also apply these rules for IPv6, we need to ensure that the following entry is present in `/etc/network/interfaces`:

```
iface lo inet6 loopback
```

# KVM virtual machine issues

This section contains issues related to KVM virtual machines only.

**Solution**: The Windows operating system can be unforgiving when you convert or migrate from one type of hardware to another. It is certainly possible to convert/migrate just about any Windows OS as long as a proper procedure is followed. For in-depth information on the proper procedure to migrate Windows machines to a virtual machine, refer to `http://pve.proxmox.com/wiki/Migration_of_servers_to_Proxmox_VE#mergeide`.

# Issue – Windows 7 VM does not reboot, instead it shuts down requiring manual boot from Proxmox

**Solution**: This issue causes a Windows 7 virtual machine to shut down when a reboot is initiated from within the OS. A manual power on through the Proxmox GUI is required to power up the VM. This is an issue caused by the installation of Windows itself, especially a VM that is configured with a standard video. Changing the display to SPICE solves the issue for this type of Windows 7 virtual machine. This is not a common occurrence and causes an issue in some Windows 7 VMs, while others just run fine.

# Issue – The qemu-img command does not convert the .vmdk image files created with the .ova template in Proxmox VE 4.1

**Solution**: The .vmdk image files created with VMware's .ova template may present the following error messages during conversion with the qemu-img command:

```
# qemu-img convert -f vmdk disk1.vmdk -O qcow2 vm-101-disk-1.qcow2

qemu-img: 'image' uses a vmdk feature which is not supported by this qemu
version: VMDK version 3

qemu-img: Could not open 'disk1.vmdk': Could not open 'disk1.vmdk': Wrong
medium type

qemu-img: Could not open 'disk1.vmdk'
```

The .vmdk3 format is only supported in pve-qemu-kvm 2.0 and later. Enter the following command to check the version installed in the Proxmox node:

```
# pveversion -v
```

Look for the version number of pve-qemu-kvm. A .vmdk3 file can still be converted by following the instructions given at: http://carlos-spitzer.com/2013/12/26/how-to-convert-vmdk-3-images-to-qcow2-even-when-qemu-img-fails-o/.

# Issue – Online migration of a virtual machine fails with a 'Failed to sync data' error

**Solution**: In order to migrate virtual machines online without powering them off, the virtual disk of the VM must be on a shared storage system. Any VM with a virtual disk on local storage cannot be migrated live. The error will look as follows:

```
Feb 12 19:54:37 starting migration of VM 134 to node 'pm4-2'
(172.17.0.172)
Feb 12 19:54:37 copying disk images
Feb 12 19:54:37 ERROR: Failed to sync data - can't do online migration
- VM uses local disks
Feb 12 19:54:37 aborting phase 1 - cleanup resources
Feb 12 19:54:37 ERROR: migration aborted (duration 00:00:00): Failed
to sync data - can't do online migration - VM uses local disks
TASK ERROR: migration aborted
```

# Issue – Adjusting RAM through the GUI and rebooting the VM does not change allocated memory

**Solution**: A virtual machine must be powered off to make changes to the memory, video, or virtual network interface. No changes will take effect if a VM is simply restarted.

# Issue – No audio in Windows KVM

**Solution**: Sound devices must be added manually by adding the following line in a KVM virtual machine configuration file located in `/etc/pve/qemu-server/<vm_id>.conf`:

```
args: -device intel-hda,id=sound5,bus=pci.0,addr=0x18 -device
hda-micro,id=sound5-codec0,bus=sound5.0,cad=0 -device hda-
duplex,id=sound5-codec1,bus=sound5.0,cad=1
```

After saving the configuration file, the VM will need to be powered off and then powered on. Windows 7 and later will automatically install the necessary driver for the sound device.

# Issue – The virtio virtual disk is not available during the Windows Server installation

**Solution:** The virtio drivers are not included in the Windows Server installation. During the installation, the Windows setup will not see any virtio virtual disks attached with the virtual machine. A virtio driver must be downloaded and loaded during the installation in order to activate the virtio virtual disk with the Windows operating system. The ISO image of virtio drivers can be downloaded from: `http://www.linux-kvm.org/page/WindowsGuestDrivers/Download_Drivers`.

# LXC container issues

This section contains issues related to LXC containers only.

# Issue – A Proxmox node hangs when trying to stop or restart an LXC container

**Solution**: This has been an issue since the initial release of Proxmox VE 4.0. Owing to a bug when shutdown, stop or restart was initiated for LXC container from GUI, the node itself became unusable and all network connectivity was lost. The only way to come out of it was to reboot the entire node. In consecutive later releases, this issue has been addressed and patched by Proxmox developers. If you are in Proxmox 4.0, an immediate upgrade to 4.1 or later is highly recommended.

# Issue – The noVNC console only shows a cursor for LXC containers

**Solution**: Owing to unknown reasons, the noVNC console may only show a cursor, as shown in the following screenshot, when trying to access an LXC container:

This does not mean that the container is frozen. Simply hit **Enter** to get to the login prompt.

# Backup/restore issues

This section contains issues related to backing up and restoring Proxmox.

## Issue – A Proxmox VM is locked after backup crashes unexpectedly

**Solution:** This is commonly caused after a VM backup is interrupted or crashed. Simply unlocking the VM through SSH using the following command will fix this issue:

```
# qm unlock <vm_id>
```

## Issue – How can Proxmox backup only the primary OS virtual disk instead of all the virtual disks for a VM?

**Solution**: By default, Proxmox backup will back up all the virtual disks assigned to a VM. If we want to exclude certain virtual disks from the backup process, we only need to add the backup=no option at the end of a virtual disk line item in <vm_id>.conf, as follows:

```
virtio0:  rbd-hdd-01:vm-101-disk1,size=80G
virtio0:  rbd-hdd-01:vm-101-disk2,size=200G,backup=no
```

In the previous example, the virtual machine has two virtual disks. Disk 1 is for the primary OS and disk 2 is for the secondary. By adding backup=no, Proxmox will skip this disk during the backup process and only back up the primary disk.

## Issue – Backup of virtual machines stops prematurely with an Operation Not Permitted error

**Solution**: This error usually looks like this from Syslog of the Proxmox node:

```
ERROR: job failed with err -1 - Operation not permitted
INFO: aborting backup job
INFO: stopping kvm after backup task
ERROR: Backup of VM 101 failed - job failed with err -1 - Operation
not permitted
```

The primary cause of this issue is that when the backup storage has less space than the total storage required for an assigned backup task. Verify the total storage space that is required for backing up the selected virtual machines.

# Issue – A backup task takes a very long time to complete, or it crashes when multiple nodes are backing up to the same backup storage

**Solution**: When multiple Proxmox nodes are backing up to the same backup storage simultaneously, it tends to take a very long time or the backup is crashed. This is a common occurrence when backup traffic coexists with the main cluster traffic on a gigabit network and the backup node only has one network interface. By separating backups into multiple subnets, we can prevent this issue.

# Issue – Backup of virtual machines aborts a backup task prematurely

**Solution**: During a VM backup, the following error message appears in the backup log after it aborts a running backup task:

```
101: INFO: status: 1% (129309081/4294967296), sparse 0% (886784),
duration 91, 33/33 MB/s
[...]
107: INFO: status: 80% (2706263244/4294967296), sparse 16%
(698703462), duration 1950, 5/4 MB/s
107: ERROR: interrupted by signal
107: INFO: aborting backup job
```

This error usually occurs when there is a version mismatch for the pve-qemu-kvm package in Proxmox. At the time of writing, the available pve-qemu--kvm package version is 2.5-5. Check for the version that is installed when you get this error during a backup. If you're using an older version, then upgrade to the latest version using the following command to fix the issue.

# Issue – Backup storage has a lot of .dat files and .tmp folders using the storage space

**Solution:** Due to a backup crash or unfinished backups, there may be backup leftover files in the backup storages such as the .dat files and .tmp folders. These files and folders can easily be deleted to reclaim storage space.

# VNC/SPICE console issues

This section contains issues related to the VNC and SPICE consoles in Proxmox.

## Issue – The mouse pointer is not shared with SPICE-VIEWER on Windows 8 VM

**Solution**: In order to have a seamless mouse point between the VM and host machine, SPICE Guest Tools must be installed inside the VM. The Guest Tools package contains full driver support for Windows 7 and Windows 2008 R2. However, the support for Windows 8 or 8.1 is close to nonexistent.

## Issue – The SPICE console is unstable or nonfunctioning after updating to Proxmox VE 4.1

**Solution**: After clicking on the SPICE button for a SPICE-enabled VM, the browser gives an empty ticket error. This is a common occurrence if the browser cache is not updated after a Proxmox upgrade. Just refreshing the browser will fix this issue.

## Issue – Remote Viewer is unable to connect to a SPICE-enabled virtual machine on the Windows OS

**Solution**: This issue is caused by a firewall that blocks the SPICE port, which prevents SPICE-enabled virtual machines to be connected to SPICE. Open port 3128 from Windows firewall to allow Remote Viewer to connect to a SPICE virtual machine.

# Firewall issues

This section shows issues regarding the Proxmox firewall feature.

# Issue – Rules are created and a firewall is enabled for vNIC, but rules do not get applied

**Solution:** On rare occasions, owing to changes in the network interface, or other reasons, the firewall service may get stuck. In such cases, we can restart the service using the following command:

```
# service pve-firewall restart
```

If the previous command does not help, then check the syslog of the node to see if there are any clues. If nothing helps, then a reboot will clear any firewall issues. As with Proxmox VE 4.1, if a firewall becomes inactive, it does not fall back on a predefined set of protection. A firewall simply becomes nonexistent.

# Issue – A firewall is enabled for a VM and the necessary rules are created, but nothing is being filtered for that VM. All other VM firewall rules in the same node work properly

**Solution**: This issue may occur when the firewall is not enabled in the virtual network interface of the VM. For each VM, a firewall needs to be enabled in two different places. The first one is under the Firewall tab menu, as shown in the following screenshot:

| Virtual Machine 110 ('Ubuntu-1' ) on node 'pm4-1' | | | |
|---|---|---|---|
| Summary | Hardware | Options | Task History |
| Edit | | | |
| Enable Firewall | Yes | | |
| Enable DHCP | No | | |
| MAC filter | Yes | | |
| log_level_in | nolog | | |
| log_level_out | nolog | | |
| Input Policy | DROP | | |
| Output Policy | ACCEPT | | |

Another place where the firewall needs to be enabled is in the vNIC of the VM, as shown in the following screenshot:

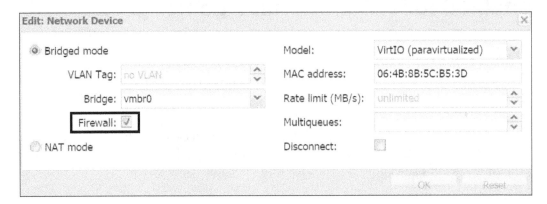

# Summary

We hope this troubleshooting chapter has provided you with some insight into some of the common issues that are most likely to surface in a Proxmox cluster. As mentioned earlier in this chapter, this is by no means a complete list of all the possible issues. If at all possible, always hold off major Proxmox upgrades for a production cluster. Give it some time to work out the bugs. This way, your cluster will have a very little chance of going down owing to any unforeseen bugs.

Purchasing a Proxmox subscription is the best way to ensure that there are fewer bugs in the repositories, since Proxmox Enterprise repositories go through an additional layer of scrutiny and testing. For information on Proxmox subscriptions, refer to https://www.proxmox.com/proxmox-ve/pricing.

The Proxmox forum is also a great place to ask for help or share issues with the community. There are many forum users who are ready to provide their expertise. Visit the forum at: http://forum.proxmox.com.

No amount of reading or studying can equal hands on practice with Proxmox. You may already be a professional in the virtualization field or maybe you are just starting out and looking for a way to stand out among the crowd; hopefully, this book will push you in the right direction. Besides the official Proxmox site and forum, you can also reach out to the author directly to ask questions or to have a discussion through a forum by visiting: http://www.masteringproxmox.com/.

# Index

# G

# H

# I

Intel e1000 driver 176
internal network virtualization
  about 172
  reference 172
IPSet, Proxmox VE firewall 219, 220
iSCSI
  about 93
  reference 93

# K

Kernel-based virtual machine (KVM)
  about 119
  advanced configuration options 137
  creating 120
  creating, by cloning 133, 134
  creating, from scratch 120
  creating, from Template 135, 136
  Full Clone mode 135
  Linked Clone mode 135
  migrating 142
  nested virtual cluster 143-146
  reference 120
key components, production level
  about 324
  budget 327
  current load, versus future growth 327
  hardware inventory, tracking 328
  hardware selection 328
  redundancy 325
  scalable hardware 324, 325
  simplicity 328
  stable hardware 324, 325
Kraken Dash
  URL 319
KVM issues
  troubleshooting 366-368
KVM VM menu
  about 31
  Backup 35
  Console 36
  Firewall 37
  Hardware 32
  Monitor 34, 35
  Options 32

Permissions 38
Snapshot 36
Summary 31
Task History 33

# L

layer 2+3 hash policy 193
layer 2 hash policy 192
layer 3+4 hash policy 193-195
Link Aggregation Control Protocol (LACP)
  about 189
  reference 191
Link aggregation (LAG) 189
Linux containers (LXC)
  about 4
  URL 4
liquid cooling
  about 333
  direct contact liquid cooling 334
  total immersion in 3M Novec 334
  total immersion in oil 333
Live backup 264
live migration 76
local storage
  versus shared storage 76, 81, 82
Logical Volume Management (LVM)
  about 94
  reference 94
LXC container issues
  troubleshooting 369
LXC Container menu
  about 38
  Backup 41
  Console 42
  DNS 40
  Firewall 42
  Network 40
  Options 40
  Permissions 42
  Resources 39
  Snapshots 42
  Summary 38
  Task History 41

limitations, in Proxmox  244, 245
reference, for custom rules  244
**Suricata IDS/IPS**
integrating  242, 243
URL  243

# T

**teaming  189**
**Template  133**
**Totem Redundant Ring Protocol (RRP)  56**
**Totem Single Ring Protocol (SRP)  56**
**triggers**
reference  305

# U

**unprivileged containers**
container processes, checking  167, 168
creating, as root  166
reference  167
versus privileged containers  166
**upgrade**
versus dist-upgrade  288
**User Bean Counter (UBC)  148**

# V

**VirtIO interface driver**
references  176
**virtual bridge**
about  177, 178
adding  178-182
**virtual disk image**
about  82
caching  91, 92
managing  86
moving  88
resizing  86, 87

supported image formats  82
throttling  89-91
**virtualization  1**
**Virtual Local Area Network (VLAN)**
about  184
adding  184-187
reference  184
**virtual machine**
restoring  275, 276
**virtual machine creation process**
CD/DVD tab  122
CPU tab  128
General tab  120
Hard Disk tab  122-124
Memory tab  130
Network tab  130
OS tab  121
**virtual network**
about  172-174
exploring  172
**Virtual Network Computing (VNC)  213**
**Virtual Network Interface Card (vNIC)**
about  176
adding  177
**vmbrX  177**
**VM-specific firewall**
Alias, creating  240
configuring  240
configuring, through CLI  242
IPSet, creating  240
options, for VM zone firewall  241
rules, creating  240
**VM zone firewall**
DHCP, enabling  241
MAC filter  241
options  241
**VNC/SPICE console issues**
troubleshooting  372

# Z

**Zabbix**
 as monitoring solution  298
 configuring  301
 data, displaying with graph  306-308
 Disk Health notification, configuring  308
 host, configuring to monitor  301-305
 installing  299-301
 SNMP device, adding  316, 317
 URL  298
**Zabbix 3.0 server**
 reference  299

**Zabbix appliances**
 download link  299
**ZFS**
 about  96-99
 Raid types  96, 97
 reference  96
**zones, Proxmox VE firewall**
 about  218
 datacenter  218
 host  218
 VM  218

www.ingramcontent.com/pod-product-compliance
Lightning Source LLC
Chambersburg PA
CBHW081503050326
40690CB00015B/2911